DON'T THINK FOR YOURSELF

MEDIEVAL
INSTITUTE
UNIVERSITY OF NOTRE DAME

The Conway Lectures in Medieval Studies 2019

The Medieval Institute gratefully acknowledges the generosity of Robert M. Conway and his support for the lecture series and the publications resulting from it.

PREVIOUS TITLES PUBLISHED IN THIS SERIES:

Jonathan Riley-Smith
Templars and Hospitallers as Professed Religious in the Holy Land (2010)

A. C. Spearing
Medieval Autographies: The "I" of the Text (2012)

Barbara Newman
Medieval Crossover: Reading the Secular against the Sacred (2013)

John Marenbon
Abelard in Four Dimensions: A Twelfth-Century Philosopher in His Context and Ours (2013)

Sylvia Huot
Outsiders: The Humanity and Inhumanity of Giants in Medieval French Prose Romance (2016)

William J. Courtenay
Rituals for the Dead: Religion and Community in the Medieval University of Paris (2019)

Alice-Mary Talbot
Varieties of Monastic Experince in Byzantium, 800–1453 (2019)

Anne D. Hedeman
Visual Translation: Illuminated Manuscripts and the First French Humanists (2022)

Roberta Frank
The Etiquette of Early Northern Verse (2022)

DON'T THINK FOR YOURSELF

Authority and Belief in Medieval Philosophy

PETER ADAMSON

University of Notre Dame Press

Notre Dame, Indiana

Notre Dame, Indiana 46556
www.undpress.nd.edu

Published in the United States of America

Paperback published in 2024

Library of Congress Control Number: 2022935749

ISBN: 978-0-268-20339-9 (Hardback)
ISBN: 978-0-268-20340-5 (Paperback)
ISBN: 978-0-268-20341-2 (WebPDF)
ISBN: 978-0-268-20338-2 (Epub)

When wee believe any saying whatsoever it be, to be true, from arguments taken, not from the thing it selfe, or from the principles of naturall Reason, but from the Authority, and good opinion wee have, of him that hath sayd it; then is the speaker, or person we believe in, or trust in, and whose word we take, the object of our Faith; and the Honour done in Believing, is done to him onely.

—Thomas Hobbes, *Leviathan*

Nine hundred and ninety-nine men in every thousand allow others to do their thinking for them. They take their ideas ready-made from others.

—W. H. Ferris, *The African Abroad*

CONTENTS

	Acknowledgments	ix
	Introduction	xi
CHAPTER 1	*Taqlīd*: Authority and the Intellectual Elite in the Islamic World	1
CHAPTER 2	Too High a Standard: Knowledge and Skepticism in Medieval Philosophy	21
CHAPTER 3	Testing the Prophets: Reason and the Choice of Faiths	41
CHAPTER 4	Using the Pagans: Reason in Interreligious Debate	61
CHAPTER 5	Some Pagans Are Better than Others: The Merits of Plato and Aristotle	81
CHAPTER 6	Finding Their Voices: Women in Byzantine and Latin Christian Philosophy	101
CHAPTER 7	The Rule of Reason: Human and Animal Nature	119
	Further Reading	139
	Notes	147
	Index	173

ACKNOWLEDGMENTS

The chapters of this book were written to be delivered as the 2019 Conway Lectures at the University of Notre Dame and the 2020 Carlyle Lectures at Oxford University. I would first therefore like to thank both institutions for the honor of being invited to give these lectures, and in particular Thomas Burman at Notre Dame and George Garnett at Oxford for issuing the invitations and offering splendid hospitality. I would also like to thank Megan Hall and Graham Lockey for their work in organizing these events and Stephen Little at the University of Notre Dame Press for his enthusiasm for the book project.

I had extensive discussions with students and staff at both Notre Dame and Oxford, and it would take pages to name everyone who gave me useful references, ideas, suggestions, and possible objections. But I would like to thank at least James Allen, Maria Rosa Antognazza, Robert Audi, Teresa Bejan, Suzanne Bobzien, Lesley Brown, David Burrell, Ursula Coope, Therese Cory, Stephen Gersh, Danielle Layne, Fiona Leigh, Anna Marmadoro, Christopher Melchert, Ebrahim Moosa, David O'Connor, Jose Andres Porras, Jenny Rallens, Gretchen Reydams-Schils, Denia Robichaud, Lydia Schuhmacher, Richard Sorabji, Wiebke Marie Stock, Cecilia Trifogli, Jan Westerhoff, Abigail Whalen, Jack Woodworth, and Johannes Zachhuber, all of whom helped make these two lecture series highlights of my academic career.

My work on the themes of the book has profited from reading seminars at the LMU in Munich devoted to some of the authors discussed here, like Plethon and al-Dawwānī, and from conversations with colleagues there, including Hanif Amin Beidokhkti, Fedor Benevich, Matteo Di Giovanni, Rotraud Hansberger, Mareike Hauer, Andreas Lammer, Abdurrahman Mihirig, Michael Noble, and Alexander Reutlinger, all of whom discussed with me topics and texts tackled in the pages of this book. Bethany Somma went further still and made very useful, detailed notes on the whole manuscript. I also received generous and helpful feedback on a previous draft from Deborah Black and John Marenbon. Other colleagues with whom I had useful exchanges that influenced discussions in the book include George Boys-Stones, Charles Brittain, Susan Brower-Toland, Börje Bydén, Amin Ehtashami, Frank Griffel, Dimitri Gutas, Dag N. Hasse, Katerina Ierodiakonou, Jill Kraye, Scott MacDonald, Cecilia Muratori, Robert Pasnau, Martin Pickavé, Peter E. Pormann, Sajjad Rizvi, Sarah Stroumsa, Richard C. Taylor, and Michele Trizio. I would also like to thank Oliver Primavesi and Christof Rapp for making the Munich School of Ancient Philosophy, which I run with them, such a congenial and stimulating center for the study of classical thought and its medieval reception. My gratitude also to Hani Mohseni for his work on the index to the volume.

For support of the research that lies behind chapter 7, I gratefully acknowledge the European Research Council (ERC), which has funded a project at the LMU under the European Union's Horizon 2020 research and innovation program (grant agreement No. 786762). My work on thinkers of the Islamic world has also been supported by the DFG under the aegis of the project "Heirs of Avicenna: Philosophy in the Islamic East from the 12th to the 13th Century."

Finally, as always my greatest debt is to the members of my family: my brother, Glenn, who discussed this book project with me when it was only a gleam in my eye, my parents, and of course my wife, Ursula, and my daughters, Sophia and Johanna.

INTRODUCTION

This is that rare thing, a book on medieval philosophy that is in danger of being overtaken by events. It was written over about a year, from spring 2019 until early 2020. Then in early spring 2020, as I was finalizing the manuscript, came the COVID-19 pandemic, whose wider repercussions will no doubt still be unfolding as the book goes to press. As I explain in chapter 1, I wrote the book in part as a response to a seeming crisis of authority that has come to dominate the political scene over the past years. It's impossible to say now what implications this most recent, and far more concrete, crisis will have for my theme. Perhaps our reliance on the expertise of health professionals and epidemiologists will lead to a renewed respect for expertise more generally. Or perhaps there will be a backlash provoked by the economic consequences of lockdown and social distancing. However things turn out, it seems even clearer now than it was when I started writing the book that a well-considered relationship to epistemic authority, an ability to make intelligent use of knowledge that lies beyond our own competence, is vitally important. Indeed it is a matter of life and death.

As it happens the pandemic has also given me an additional reason to reflect on one of my favorite texts from medieval culture, a text I was already planning to use to introduce the theme of the book as a whole. For it is a text set in a situation of radical social isolation and is in my view also centrally concerned with questions of authority and belief. Called *Ḥayy ibn Yaqẓān*, it was written in the twelfth century by the Andalusian doctor and philosopher Ibn Ṭufayl.[1] It is an unusual, though as we'll see in chapter 3 not unique, work of medieval philosophy in that it is written as a narrative tale rather than a discursive treatise. The title character, Ḥayy, finds himself on a lush island, having arrived there in one of two alternative ways: after being set adrift in a chest by his mother or having been spontaneously generated from the earth. He grows to adulthood without ever encountering another human being. Yet through native wit and observation of his island home and the heavens above, he becomes an accomplished scientist and philosopher, and ultimately a mystic. We see him work out the principles of medicine and natural philosophy, prove the existence of God, and discover the means by which divine providence is exercised. Finally another human arrives, named Absāl. He has come from another island in search of solitude. Once the two learn to communicate, Absāl is thrilled by Ḥayy's wisdom and resolves to bring him home so that Ḥayy can share his learning with the inhabitants of the other island. But the people there fail to appreciate what he tells them, and he and Absāl in the end return to a shared isolation on the island where Ḥayy has spent his life.

While Ḥayy's philosophical discoveries are clearly based on the tradition of Hellenizing philosophy (*falsafa*) in the Islamic world, it is less clear what the purpose of the narrative frame might be. I read it as, among other things, a rejection of the need for authority in belief formation. On this reading, Ibn Ṭufayl's point in having Ḥayy start with a "blank slate" is to show that it would indeed be possible, in sufficiently ideal conditions and with sufficient talent, for a single human being to become an accomplished intellectual with no help apart from the resources of the natural environment. Those of us who did not grow up alone on a remote island depend on teachers and routinely take authorities at their word. But there is no absolute need to turn to other humans to achieve enlightenment. You can, quite literally, do it yourself. In fact, the ending sequence with the second island may suggest that you even might be better off on your own than in human society, at least if the society is in thrall to ignorant beliefs and incorrect values.[2]

This part of the work was potentially provocative, if it was taken to suggest that the second island was meant to stand in for Muslim Spain or Islamic societies in general. One author who was in fact provoked was Ibn al-Nafīs, another doctor with philosophical interests. He wrote an answer to *Ḥayy ibn Yaqẓān* in which the main character is instead called Fāḍil ibn Nāṭiq.[3] Again the hero progresses philosophically while living alone on an island, but then a ship arrives and Fāḍil learns valuable truths of religion from its passengers. Lacking religious revelation and a community that could impart the teachings of the faith, Fāḍil could go only so far. These two works, then, represent antithetically opposed views on the need for what we might call "epistemic dependence." For Ibn Ṭufayl and, as we'll see, other medieval philosophers with Aristotelian leanings, the resources of reason given to each of us at birth make it possible for us to arrive at comprehensive and certain knowledge about the universe and the God who created it. For others, like Ibn al-Nafīs, independent reason needs to be supplemented by some further resource. There is no shame in depending on others for one's beliefs. To the contrary, this is just an inevitable feature of life as a religious believer and, indeed, as a human.

This book, then, is an exploration of how medieval philosophers dealt with the problem of epistemic dependence. In chapter 1, I look at a useful contrast that emerged in Islamic law and theology before being taken up by philosophers. The contrast is between what in Arabic was called *ijtihād*, judgment based on independent effort, and *taqlīd*, acceptance of authority. The question whether *taqlīd* is a bad thing admits of no simple answer. It will depend on, among other things, the status of the believer. On one view, trained scholars should not indulge in *taqlīd*, whereas untrained peasants certainly should. But as we'll see, this straightforwardly elitist account was not unanimously adopted. In chapter 2, I look at the consequences of refusing to engage in *taqlīd*. The Aristotelian tradition brought with it ambitious promises of freeing its adherents from false belief and even from "belief" in general, if this is taken as a contrast to knowledge. In a scientific context, at least, the philosopher could and should achieve the certainty and comprehensiveness of understanding enjoyed by Ḥayy on his island. The problem, I argue, is that the philosophers' aims were so ambitious, their promises so grand, that their project came to seem unfeasible. And this provoked skeptical worries. If knowledge as Aristotle and the other philosophers understood it cannot be attained, then do we really know anything?

Chapter 3 offers a way out of this problem, by suggesting that a lowering of expectations should give us a more plausible, and achievable, set of epistemic goals. Drawing on the Muslim theologian al-Ghazālī, I develop the notion of "justified *taqlīd*," in which one does follow authority rather than try to attain unassailable proof for everything, yet takes care not to follow authority uncritically. I then look at several texts that depict a choice between different belief systems. These model for us the idea of being critical and intelligently selective in religion and, by extension, in other epistemic contexts. From here, we move in chapter 4 to a different sort of confrontation between religions. Now, instead of imagining an impartial judge who needs to decide which belief system to adopt, we have partisans of one faith attacking its rivals. My particular focus is the question whether members of Abrahamic religions felt able to depend on pagan authorities in the context of interconfessional debate. So there is an intimate connection between this chapter and the next, chapter 5. There, I look at texts addressing the relative merits of the two leading pagan authorities, Plato and Aristotle. Again, we have here a concrete instance in which medievals were highly self-conscious about giving credence to a putatively authoritative teacher.

Finally, in chapters 6 and 7 we move away from the "epistemic elite" of philosophers, theologians, and jurists. First, I look at a class of humans that was routinely excluded from the intellectual milieu in medieval culture, namely, women. Women authors nonetheless found ways to take part in intellectual discourse and even to establish a kind of authority for themselves. I then end the book by looking at the contrast between humans and animals. This completes a story that runs throughout the book, in which I show how an epistemic elite of educated men defined itself in opposition to the unlearned, to women, and to nonhuman animals. In each case, we'll see that the line between favored and disfavored group was constantly in danger of being blurred, so as to undermine the elite's self-satisfied self-conception.[4]

That self-conception is eloquently expressed in another parable, one just as populated as Ibn Ṭufayl's is unpopulated. It is found in *The Guide of the Perplexed* by the great Jewish philosopher Maimonides.[5] He asks us to imagine a palace and a king within, representing God. Wandering far from the palace are those who lack religion entirely. Maimonides says that these people are not fully human, since their irrationality places them between monkeys and humans in their mental attainment. These include far-flung peoples like the Kushites but also, says Maimonides, some in his own society. The second-worst group are those whose backs are turned to the palace, because through their own speculation or being misled by others, they have false doctrines. Then there are those who wish to enter the palace but have not managed to reach it; this is the situation of the common run of people. Circling the palace and closest to it without getting inside are people with true beliefs that they cannot prove to be true. Under this heading Maimonides mentions jurists of the Jewish tradition, but, as we'll see, the Muslim philosophers (*falāsifa*) had similar assessments of the theologians (*mutakallimūn*) who were their rivals for intellectual dominance in the Islamic world. Finally there are those who do attain proof and have knowledge of God to the greatest extent possible; they are represented in the allegory by those who are in attendance upon the king himself.

Tellingly, Maimonides's image draws a parallel between scholarly expertise and proximity to political power. Of course, medieval scholars were often farther from the halls of power than they would have liked. Still, quite a few of them consorted with princes (al-Kindī tutored the caliph's son), enjoyed patronage from various potentates (such patronage plays a significant role in Avicenna's biography), or had significant political responsibility in their own right (Bonaventure was head of the Franciscan order). More generally, there is no doubting that the epistemic elite in this period, as in ours, was also a social and economic elite. So one could usefully extend the studies in this book to grapple more fully with the political implications of medieval epistemology. I do touch on political questions in what follows, especially concerning the predicament of oppressed groups like Jews, women, and the inhabitants of the "New World" once they were contacted by Europeans. But for the most part, when I speak of "authority" I mean by this being recognized as a reliable source of belief, not wielding economic or coercive power: think of Aristotle, not Alexander the Great.

And one final note before I begin. Aristotle and Alexander the Great are of course familiar names, but already in this introduction there may have been at least one name that is not familiar, Ibn Ṭufayl. And there are probably many more to come. As I explain in chapter 1, this book ranges widely in chronological and cultural terms. This was a conscious decision on my part. Of course my primary goal is to discuss medieval ideas about authority and belief, showing their surprising nuance and fruitfulness. But a secondary goal is to demonstrate the richness and diversity of medieval philosophy, using this one theme as an example. It may be rather surprising (or even annoying) that I have deemphasized the Latin scholastic tradition that usually occupies center stage in treatments of any theme in medieval thought. The most famous thinker of the medieval era, the scholastic Thomas Aquinas, appears as a significant voice only in chapter 7. This is not to issue any value judgment about Aquinas or scholasticism in general; I am fascinated by both. But I do hope that this book will convince you that medieval philosophy is a far broader phenomenon than just the output of Latin schoolmen. It included Christians working in the Byzantine and Islamic empires; it included Jews and Muslims; it included intellectuals of Africa and central Asia; it included women.

The downside of this approach is that the book involves a cast of many characters, some of whom get starring roles, with many others making cameo appearances. Since it would have been distracting and needed much additional space to introduce each thinker properly, I have made no effort to do this here. I would instead take the liberty of referring readers to my podcast and book series, *A History of Philosophy Without Any Gaps*. It provides detailed overviews of all the philosophers mentioned here, and many more besides. At the end of this book, I offer some guidance for further reading on individual thinkers and movements, but readers are also referred to the chapters' notes for a more detailed bibliography.

CHAPTER 1

Taqlīd

Authority and the Intellectual Elite in the Islamic World

I live in Europe, where people actually ride bicycles, and recently I was riding with my wife through Munich. We came to an intersection. Ahead of me, my wife slowed down, checking for oncoming cars, then went across. It suddenly struck me that it would be perfectly reasonable for me to follow her across the intersection, without bothering to look whether it was safe. After all my wife is reliable and has good judgment, both in general and when it comes to the rules of the road. Indeed, whereas I am a frequently distracted philosopher, she's a normal person, so when it comes to this kind of thing I tend to trust her more than I trust myself. And she would hardly be crossing if a car was coming. So why not ride straight across, trusting her implicitly as I do? I would quite literally be staking my life on the assumption that she made the right decision, but this was a bet that, I realized, I would quite happily make.

Then I looked for traffic anyway, just to be on the safe side. But it got me thinking about how we make decisions and form beliefs, and the fact that we often do so simply by accepting the judgment of other people whom we take to be authoritative. I had been thinking about this for a while anyway, because this very issue lies at the heart of many of our current political controversies. We are increasingly warned against taking our beliefs from sources that were previously considered authoritative: yesterday's "paper of record" is today deemed "fake news";

well-credentialed scientists with expertise in vaccinations or climate change are greeted with distrust. Michael Gove, responding to economists' gloomy predictions of Britain leaving the EU, ventured that "people in this country have had enough of experts."[1] Part of the problem is that many political issues are so vast in their complexity and scope that they defy the ability of individual people to form beliefs in a way that seems responsible. How many of us understand enough about the atmosphere to have a reasonably informed personal opinion about climate change, never mind being in a position to critically evaluate what climatologists might say? On this and many other issues, we are apparently in the politically and epistemologically uncomfortable position of choosing whose opinions we should blindly accept.

What I want to show in this book is that we can learn something about blind acceptance, and how to avoid it, from a surprising source: medieval philosophy. Surprising, because medieval philosophers have a reputation for forming their beliefs in the most uncritical of ways, bound as they were by authority, locked into inflexible worldviews by their theological commitments, and threatened with institutional sanction (or worse) if they dared to step out of line. I will implicitly challenge such assumptions, but that is not so novel. No expert in the field would today accept this description of the medieval mind-set as slavish and merely imitative. My main point will be a different one, namely, that medieval philosophers engaged in explicit and productive reflection on this very question of when, and how, one might responsibly form one's beliefs based on authority.

I am going to cover quite a lot of territory, both chronologically and geographically. I will highlight authors and texts from the end of late antiquity, in the fifth century or so, down to the European Renaissance, in the fifteenth and sixteenth centuries, with occasional forays even later than that. The scope of the book will thus cover what one leading scholar of the field, John Marenbon, likes to call the "long middle ages." Furthermore, I'm going to look at three distinct, yet closely interconnected, medieval cultures. Some of what I will say concerns Latin Christendom, which is the more familiar terrain for many readers. But I will also talk about intellectuals in the Greek-speaking Byzantine empire and in the culture to which most of my own research has been directed, the Islamic world. There will be Christians there too, as well as Jews. But in this first chapter I want to focus on a concept that has its original home within Islam itself, and more specifically in methodological debates that raged between Muslim scholars of law and theology. These scholars did us the favor of finding a single word to describe the phenomenon I am interested in: *taqlīd*.

This word is often translated as "imitation," "uncritical acceptance of authority," or "blind following." It comes from a verb (*qallada*) meaning "to gird" or "to hang something upon the neck," for instance, a necklace placed on a sacrificial animal. Fairly early in the Islamic legal tradition—perhaps in Iraq around the end of the eighth century[2]—it came to be used for reaching judgments on the basis of someone else's authority. Someone who practices *taqlīd*, in Arabic a *muqallid*, has not personally reflected as to whether the judgment in question can be grounded in the sources of Islamic law, namely, the Quran and the *ḥadīth*, or collected reports of the sayings and deeds of the prophet. Such reflection is called *ijtihād*, meaning "effortful exertion"—it relates to the well-known Arabic word *jihād*—and someone who performs *ijtihād* is a *mujtahid*. This terminology was, as I say, first used in legal contexts. But it quickly became important for theologians too, who began to debate the very question I have just been raising. Is it all right to form one's beliefs, notably, one's religious beliefs, just by following apparently reliable authority, hence by engaging in *taqlīd*? Or do we have a responsibility to perform *ijtihād*? As we might put it, should we really try to think for ourselves?

In addition to suggesting that medieval Muslim thinkers had useful insights about this question, I want to suggest an even more surprising historical thesis. Some readers may already have been thinking, when I mentioned the typical prejudices about medieval thinkers, that these prejudices would not apply to at least a handful of philosophers from the Islamic world. These were figures I like to think of as the Aristotelian avant-garde, men like al-Fārābī (d. 950), Avicenna (Ibn Sīnā, d. 1037), and Averroes (Ibn Rushd, d. 1198) who thought that all important beliefs could be established by pure reason.[3] They accepted the religious teachings of Islam but emphasized that these teachings were ratified and ultimately explained by Aristotelian philosophy. For them religion was really just a less technical presentation of fundamental philosophical truths, in a form that could be appreciated by non-philosophers.

With this, the Aristotelian avant-garde espoused a rationalism more radical than we find in practically any thinker of medieval Christendom, in either the Latin or Greek sphere. In Arabic these Aristotelians were often referred to as *falāsifa*, from *falsafa*, which is of course just a loan-word from Greek, based on *philosophia*. Some have exalted the *falāsifa* as the only true philosophers in the Islamic world, and perhaps in any medieval culture, precisely on the grounds of their unabashed rationalism.[4] But ironically, the elitist rationalism of the *falāsifa* was itself an inheritance from the Islamic legal and theological tradition, or so I shall argue. It was by transposing the legal and theological concepts of *ijtihād* and *taqlīd* to the context of Aristotelian philosophy that the *falāsifa* were able to articulate their own self-conception as independent thinkers who followed reason wherever it might lead.

Let us return, then, to the debate over *taqlīd* within Islamic law and theology. Perhaps the most important figure in the beginning of this debate is al-Shāfiʿī (d. 820), the founding figure of one of the four major "schools" (sing. *madhhab*) of Islamic law. Al-Shāfiʿī is well known for his endorsement of rational method in law, which would allow for standardization of legal practice across the enormous Islamic empire. With this, he ushered in a new phase of jurisprudence, in which the judgment of a class of trained experts would replace more informal legal customs, which might differ from one place to another.[5] A well-known example of the methods he proposed is analogy, where the ruling in a clear case is transferred to an unclear case because the second case is relevantly similar to the first. For instance, if wine is explicitly forbidden, by analogy whiskey is also forbidden because it is intoxicating just like wine.

Ijtihād could include the use of analogical reasoning but should not be identified with this or any other *particular* rational method. It is the use of any such method to arrive at an independently derived legal opinion rather than uncritically accepting the judgment of others, which of course is *taqlīd*. Al-Shāfiʿī himself does not always use the term *taqlīd* in a pejorative sense: it is good and proper to be a *muqallid* when it comes to following the Prophet and his companions.[6] But he thought that any jurist worthy of the name should be willing and able to perform *ijtihād*, which he deemed necessary because earlier legal scholars had often disagreed or simply offered decisions without any accompanying basis. As Ahmed El Shamsy has written, whatever reasoning prompted such earlier opinions was a "black box" and could not be a basis for further jurisprudence.[7]

Al-Shāfiʿī's followers were even more forthright in their critique of *taqlīd*, which for them came to have an exclusively negative connotation. This forced them to explain how they could indeed be followers of al-Shāfiʿī himself, a rather ironic project that calls to mind the scene in Monty Python's *Life of Brian* in which Brian instructs his deluded followers, "You've got to think for yourselves! You're all individuals!," at which point they all shout, "Yes, we are all individuals!" The Shāfiʿīs dealt with the problem by either restating, and hence in effect personally endorsing, their master's own legal reasoning to get around the "black box" problem or improving on that reasoning by offering corrections to what al-Shāfiʿī had said or further evidence to support his findings. This set a rationalist standard for jurisprudential reasoning: a qualified jurist is one who can supply an evidential argument or proof (*ḥujja*) for each decision. In contrast to this, *taqlīd* was defined already in the early tenth century as *qubūl qawl bi-lā ḥujja*, "accepting a position without proof."

There is a famous debate among scholars of Islamic law as to how widely, and for how long, independent reasoning, or *ijtihād*, was practiced by jurists. It used to be a commonplace to say that relatively soon after the time of al-Shāfiʿī and other school founders, jurists simply stopped bothering with *ijtihād* and contented themselves with good old uncritical *taqlīd*. But a now-classic article by Wael Hallaq argued that the so-called gate of *ijtihād* was never closed, if this means that legal scholars at some point entirely withdrew from personal reflection. To the contrary, we find even later jurists saying for instance that "it is not possible for an age to be devoid of a *mujtahid*."[8] Simply as a practical matter, independent reflection was needed to deal with new questions, such as the permissibility of using coffee and tobacco, much discussed by jurists of the Ottoman empire. It has, however, been argued that *ijtihād* was applied in exceptional cases by exceptional figures and that most jurists since the Middle Ages restricted themselves to studying and following the tradition. The *mujtahid* would be a bold and even iconoclastic figure, one who effectively sought to play the role of a new founder like al-Shāfiʿī. In light of this, Sherman Jackson has suggested that we simply think of *taqlīd* as a form of legal "precedent," dropping more pejorative translations that have to do with blind obedience.[9]

We don't need to wade into the historical debate over the frequency and historical life span of *ijtihād*. For our purposes it is enough to note that in the Sunnī traditions, it was common to recognize a hierarchy of more and less advanced legal scholars.[10] At the top was the pure *mujtahid*, who worked out a legal reasoning for his decision based directly on revealed sources. At the bottom was the pure *muqallid*. This was the jurist who simply memorized previous decisions and reapplied them. The same status was occupied by ordinary people, often called *al-ʿawāmm*, literally, "the common people," and similar in force to the ancient Greek phrase "hoi polloi" (the Arabic term *al-jumhūr* has the same meaning). As that implies, we are dealing here with a straightforward epistemic elitism: the legal scholar who performs *ijtihād* has real knowledge (*ʿilm*), whereas the ordinary person or *taqlīd*-bound judge is doomed to ignorance (*jahl*) or, more optimistically, mere opinion (*ẓann*). The elitism stands even when we take into account that jurists recognized other levels between the pure *mujtahid* and the *muqallid*. For instance one might perform what was called "*ijtihād* within a school" (*ijtihād fī l-madhhab*) or "affiliated *ijtihād*" (*ijtihād muntasib*), that is, reasoning within the dictates and principles of one's legal tradition. Another way that common believers might avoid slavish passivity was through a minimal form of *ijtihād*, called following (*ittibāʿ*). This did not involve requesting a full rationale for a judgment but simply meant pressing jurists to confirm that they were indeed basing their judgments in valid sources of religious law and not personal opinion.[11]

The Shīʿī legal tradition, meanwhile, attacked the epistemic elitism of the mainstream Sunnī schools for being, in a sense, not elitist enough. For the Shīʿa, Islamic law cannot be properly applied without the guidance of the inspired Imāms who descend from the family of the Prophet through his cousin and son-in-law ʿAlī. What was for them unconstrained legal reasoning, as practiced by al-Shāfiʿī and other Sunnī jurists, resulted in mere opinion, not knowledge.[12] Yet as Shīʿī legal thought developed, it also made a place for *ijtihād*, of course within the guidelines laid down by the *imāms*. So we find Shīʿī scholars too contrasting the knowledgeable scholar with the typical believer who may, and indeed should, engage in *taqlīd*. As one such scholar put it, "It is incumbent on the ordinary person (*ʿāmmī*) to act by *taqlīd* if he is incapable of *ijtihād*."[13]

Intellectuals who engaged in rational Islamic theology (*kalām*) were concerned with, and often formally trained in, Islamic law. So it is no surprise that these debates concerning the permissibility of *taqlīd* found their way into theological discussions. I don't have space here to tell this whole story, any more than I have told the whole story of *taqlīd* in Islamic jurisprudence. But it can at least be mentioned that the early thinkers we usually group under the heading of Muʿtazilism generally took themselves to be carrying out a religious obligation to engage in speculative inquiry (*naẓar*). This was the view of the leading thinkers of the Baṣra school among the Muʿtazilites, like Abū ʿAlī l-Jubbāʾī (d. 915) and his son, Abū Hāshim al-Jubbāʾī (d. 933). It is reported of them that they held the following:

> Whoever is capable of knowledge of God becomes an unbeliever if he does not apply knowledge to know God, regardless of whether he abandons knowledge to pursue imitation (*taqlīd*), doubt, conjecture (*ẓann*), or ignorance.[14]

We know of a dispute between Abū Hāshim and another Muʿtazilite, Abū l-Qāsim al-Balkhī, known as al-Kaʿbī (d. 931). Unusually within this tradition, al-Kaʿbī held that ordinary believers who engaged in *taqlīd* were doing just what they should. He distinguished between, on the one hand, an elite of theologians who had the capacity, and therefore the obligation, to pursue knowledge of God through speculative inquiry and, on the other hand, those who "are morally obligated to apply *taqlīd* and conjecture: these are the laypeople (*al-ʿawāmm*), the slaves, and many women." This of course is simply the familiar elitism of the jurists, applied to the subject matter of theology.

The more demanding attitude of the Muʿtazilites, who wanted all believers to engage in what we might call an *ijtihād* of theological reflection, was taken up by the most famous critic of Muʿtazilism, al-Ashʿarī (d. 935). He and his followers, the Ashʿarites, are sometimes thought of as being less rationalist than the Muʿtazilites. There is some reason for that, because of such teachings as their divine command theory of ethics, which they opposed to the Muʿtazilite view that humans can work out their moral obligations through pure rational reflection. But on the subject of *taqlīd*, the Ashʿarites are remarkably rationalist too. Already in al-Ashʿarī himself we have the idea that the Quran contains clear proofs (*ḥujaj*) and arguments (*adilla*) that establish God's existence and his omnipotence over all created things and that prove the genuineness of Muḥammad's prophecy and the obligation to follow his example. As Richard Frank has written, al-Ashʿarī assumes that "the reasoned arguments are probative and complete on the grounds of theoretical reason alone, for if they are not so, then the Prophet's claim to authority cannot be reasonably accepted."[15]

Taking up this approach, later Ashʿarites cite the Quranic verse, "most of them do not know the truth, so they turn away" (21:24), as a command to avoid *taqlīd*. One theologian said that the verse "shows that to accept *taqlīd* is wrong and that one must carry out the proofs and demonstrations," so that those who practice *taqlīd* "lack knowledge because they turn away from reasoning."[16] Frank has argued that in their strictures against *taqlīd*, the main concern of the Ashʿarites was that believers should be free of uncertainty. A *muqallid* might not be an unbeliever but is a believer in only a qualified sense, because their convictions might be overturned by doubts that occur to them or are put to them by skeptics. In the absence of secure proofs, they will inevitably be vulnerable to this eventuality.

Frank is clearly right about this. For instance, he cites a report concerning the Ashʿarite theologian al-Isfarāʾīnī (d. 1027), who said that commoners (*ʿawāmm*) are of two types.

> One consists of people who are not wholly lacking in a kind of reasoning, even if it is imperfect in its expression and its grounding. Such people are truly believers and in the proper sense, know (*ʿārif*). The second consists of people who are completely unenlightened in this respect and have no real knowledge, rather, since they believe through *taqlīd*, their belief lacks integrity and not one of them is free of uncertainty and doubt.[17]

However, I suspect that the Ashʿarites also had a further concern, which is a specific case of what philosophers now call "epistemic luck."[18] Believers whose convictions are formed by *taqlīd* will only be right if they happen to follow reliable authority, and this will be the case only if they happen to follow authority that is in fact reliable. Thus a report on another theologian, Abū l-Qāsim al-Anṣārī (d. 1072), has him saying that those who lack knowledge have only "belief founded on conjecture and opinion; if they are right in what they believe, they believe by an unreflected acquiescence to the truth, and if they fail to grasp the truth, they are in error and deviate from the truth."[19]

We saw that the jurists qualified their legal elitism by distinguishing between levels of *taqlīd*, with one or more middle positions between outright *taqlīd* and fully independent *ijtihād*. The Ashʿarites did much the same in the theological context. One of their foremost theologians, al-Juwaynī (d. 1085), said that ordinary believers have "knowledge" in an extended sense if they have a sufficiently strong feeling of certainty in their faith. He worried that demanding full-blown rational inquiry from them is "imposing an obligation that cannot be fulfilled," so that "they are required only to have correct belief that is free from doubt and uncertainty, and they are not required to know."[20] Not required to know, that is, in the strict and proper sense of the knowledge attained by an expert theologian, such as al-Juwaynī himself. Another qualification that, again as in the legal case, leaves the elitism standing is that the community as a whole must include select individuals who perform inquiry. In effect the theologian is doing the epistemic work for everyone else, just as there need to be some *mujtahids* in law without every Muslim having to perform *ijtihād*.

The ideas I have just surveyed appear early in the history of Islamic theology and are echoed in the following centuries. Here my discussion is necessarily even sketchier, but allow me to refer to just three later theologians who took strikingly critical positions toward *taqlīd*. I first want to mention the Persian thinker al-Dawwānī (d. 1501), who talked about his own journey from *taqlīd* to *ijtihād*.

> I said to myself: "oh soul which has these beliefs, do you take them to be true and accurate on the basis of intellect or pure *taqlīd*?" The soul replied: "even though they are *taqlīd*, still they arise from something true and from the discernment of intellect." By way of proof, the soul added, "when it comes to my beliefs I am the *muqallid* of someone who is my *mujahhid*, and all his beliefs are true, since they arose through the discernment of intellect. Therefore my beliefs are all true." Even though this proof has been constructed in a perfect arrangement, still when I placed the argument on the scales of intellect it had no weight. So I debated with myself anew and asked my soul, "what do you believe about the truth of the *mujahhid*? Could

> it be that there is an error among his beliefs, or not?" My soul chose the first option. So I said to it, "on that assumption, the major [premise] of the proof, which you built to prove your beliefs, is false. For whoever errs cannot be given confidence such that all his beliefs are certain to be true and accurate. And this argument has as its conclusion that not all the beliefs of the *muqallid* are true. Furthermore, if the aforementioned assumption of the proof were true, then it would follow that the beliefs of the *muqallid* of every religion and creed would be true, by the same reasoning." And then the soul could not respond.[21]

Note that he here invokes the consideration I just mentioned, that *taqlīd* exposes believers to epistemic luck. If you are not yourself engaging in *ijtihād*, you just have to hope that the sources of your *taqlīd* beliefs knew what they were doing. This is vividly supplemented by the final point that adherents of religions other than Islam could happily retain their (false) beliefs by depending on *taqlīd*, with no less justification than the Muslim *muqallid*.

Around the same time in the Islamic West, or Maghreb, we find the Moroccan scholar Muḥammad ibn Yūsuf al-Sanūsī (d. 1490) taking an even stronger line against *taqlīd*. He lays down a blanket ban against it, even for ordinary believers. This "universalist" view has been discussed in a recent book by Khaled El-Rouyaheb, who explains that for al-Sanūsī every Muslim must master the basics of Ashʿarite theology.[22] Everyone has the responsibility to engage in inquiry so as to reach certainty (*yaqīn*), and those who don't do this are unbelievers. When al-Sanūsī demands certainty, he is asking for more than the subjective feeling of confidence that al-Juwaynī had in mind, which could give the ordinary believer "knowledge" in an extended sense. As I've pointed out elsewhere, theologians who allowed *taqlīd* to the non-expert were depending not only on that feeling of certainty, but also on the tacit assumption that the non-expert Muslim has indeed gotten epistemically lucky.[23] The sources of belief he happens to follow are indeed reliable, so his beliefs wind up being true. As al-Dawwānī observed, had this ordinary Muslim been born a Christian or Jew, he or she would have had false beliefs instead. You can see why that would not be enough for al-Sanūsī. He wants believers to do more than feel confident in believing something that is, fortunately for them, in fact true. Believers must go through arguments that *establish* the truth of their beliefs. Their feeling of certainty must be earned and well justified.

Al-Sanūsī was an extremely influential figure, whose works were received (among other places) in sub-Saharan Africa.[24] One short work of his is still taught in modern-day Nigeria, and in the centuries after his death there were commentaries written on his works in Fulfide. The esteem in which he was held is exemplified in one story circulating about him: a member of his circle found himself unable to cook meat, because mere acquaintance with al-Sanūsī made fire ineffective—the point being that his associates were guaranteed to avoid burning in hell. His intellectual legacy included teachings on *taqlīd* by African scholars, such as the seventeenth-century Fulani theologian Muḥammad al-Wālī al-Mālikī (fl. 1688), based in what is now the country of Chad. Like al-Sanūsī he held that there is a universal responsibility laid upon all Muslims to avoid *taqlīd* and become acquainted with argumentative proofs (*adilla*) for their beliefs about God. As Dorrit van Dalen has pointed out, this general demand was in a way an attempt to assert the standing and importance of the scholarly elite. Scholars should provide guidance to common believers by showing them, for instance, that the Quran contains proofs of God's existence and omnipotence. Van Dalen tells the story of a West African town called Sijilmasa, where ordinary citizens were quizzed to see whether they could answer "philosophical questions" about the oneness of God! In that sort of context, theologians would have as reliable a function in society as the driving instructors without whose help you aren't going to get your license.

This is an important point. As was noted by early followers of al-Shāfiʿī, avoiding *taqlīd* does not imply that you actually do everything on your own, with no help. It is consistent with taking advice, what was in a legal context called "consultation" (*mushāwara*), so long as the person who receives the advice understands the reasoning according to which the decision has been reached.[25] In this sense, even theologians who took the "universalist" view that all Muslims should ground their belief in rational understanding typically had a very elitist position. When the early Muʿtazilites, al-Ashʿarī and his followers, al-Sanūsī or Muḥammad al-Wālī, said that every believer should do a bit of theology, that is all they meant: *a bit* of theology, enough to give them a secure, well-justified confidence in the fundamentals of their religion. As expert theologians, these same figures would have seen themselves as occupying a much higher level of rational understanding. And that goes double for theologians who, in a more condescending fashion, advised that ordinary believers avoid independent inquiry entirely.

One theologian who had this sort of view was the great Ashʿarite theologian, philosopher, and mystic al-Ghazālī (d. 1111). He was a student of al-Juwaynī, who to quote Richard Frank again, held that "'real knowledge' is the property of a small elite who are capable, on the basis of their own insight and ability, of independently working out the rational demonstrations of the truth of their belief against any conceivable difficulty or counter-argument."[26] Along the same lines, al-Ghazālī reserved inquiry for the few and prescribed pure *taqlīd* for the many.[27] In yet another version of that hierarchy we saw in the context of Islamic jurisprudence, he distinguished between true scholars who have knowledge and genuine certainty, theologians who attain some rational understanding but still accept many things in religion on the basis of authority, and ordinary people who never get past *taqlīd*. He did concede that some few might rationally grasp the basic principles of Islam on the strength of convincing arguments found in the Quran, as already proposed by al-Ashʿarī. But generally al-Ghazālī thought it was not a good idea for most people to indulge in speculation. In fact he wrote an entire work that, as its title says (*Iljām al-ʿawāmm ʿan ʿilm al-kalām*), was dedicated to discouraging common folk from engaging in theology (*kalām*). Its pursuit would as likely lead them astray as bring them to better understanding. As Frank Griffel has written, for al-Ghazālī "in the case of the ordinary people, *taqlīd* is not only tolerated but welcomed, since an acquaintance with independent thinking would run the risk of having this group of people fall into unbelief."[28]

In al-Ghazālī's most famous work, *The Incoherence of the Philosophers* (*Tahāfut al-falāsifa*), he aims the weapons of the *taqlīd* debate on an unexpected target: the *falāsifa*. These self-styled "philosophers" claimed to be outdoing the theologians in the use of reason, as we'll see in a moment. But for al-Ghazālī they were just engaging in *taqlīd* with different sources. Instead of blindly following a legal scholar, theologian, or even a prophet, they chose to follow Aristotle. Here we have an example of being epistemically *unlucky*. Just as ordinary Muslims have epistemic luck, insofar as their *taqlīd* leads them to embrace genuine truths unreflectively, so philosophers accept whatever the Aristotelians say on the basis of their authority and wind up embracing falsehoods instead. In particular, they come to hold three beliefs that qualify as outright unbelief: that the universe is eternal, that God knows universals and not particulars, and that the afterlife is purely immaterial with no resurrection of the body.[29] This is the charge sheet laid against the *falāsifa* in the *Incoherence*.

Actually only the first of these three teachings, the eternity of the universe, is explicitly present in Aristotle. The second one about God's knowledge is distinctive of Avicenna, though based on Aristotelian premises.[30] The third can also be ascribed to Avicenna but is really a more general Platonic commitment pervasive in philosophy starting with late antiquity. But no matter. Al-Ghazālī's point, and his accusation, is that the *falāsifa* cannot prove these things. How could they, since they are false? So they have been led to believe them through *taqlīd* rather than a reliable reasoning process. Anticipating al-Dawwānī's point that *taqlīd* can explain the religious beliefs of non-Muslims, al-Ghazālī even compares the philosophers' convictions to the way that Jews and Christians accept the religious faith of their parents.

If al-Ghazālī is the most famous critic of the *falāsifa*, then Averroes would be the most famous critic of al-Ghazālī. In several works, including his pointedly titled *Incoherence of the Incoherence* (*Tahāfut al-tahāfut*) as well as his *Decisive Treatise* (*Faṣl al-maqāl*), he rebuts al-Ghazālī and along the way asserts an epistemic hierarchy that mirrors, and seeks to replace, the hierarchies we've seen in Muslim jurists and theologians. In doing so, he is taking up an earlier rationalist theory of philosophical supremacy, offered a couple of centuries earlier by al-Fārābī. As explained in a recent study by Feriel Bouhafa, al-Fārābī's *Book of Religion* (*Kitāb al-Milla*) argues that Islamic law is subordinated to philosophy, in particular, ethics.[31] As Bouhafa puts it, al-Fārābī "requires merely that the jurist hold correct *beliefs* and possess the virtues of his religion" (my emphasis). The jurist's role is to accept the judgments laid down by the religion's founder and his successors, if any—in the case of Islam these would be the Prophet Muḥammad and the four "rightly guided caliphs"—and to apply these judgments to new or unclear cases, thus dealing with particulars rather than reaching universal determinations about human conduct. Similarly the theologian is someone who deals with theoretical issues at the level of mere beliefs (*arāʾ*), without having true understanding. In both the practical and theoretical spheres, such understanding is reserved for philosophy, which provides knowledge at the level of necessary and universal proof, which is dignified with the title "demonstration" (*burhān*). Al-Fārābī thus states that "all the excellent laws fall under the universals of practical philosophy, while the theoretical beliefs (*al-arāʾ al-naẓariyya*) in the religion have their demonstrations in theoretical philosophy (*falsafa*)."[32]

Al-Fārābī assumes that very few people will be in a position to understand these issues at a "philosophical," that is, demonstrative, level. So most adherents to a religion will have to embrace it at the level of mere belief, just like the jurists and theologians. Al-Fārābī introduces an influential way of thinking about this contrast, derived from the Aristotelian logical tradition. Whereas philosophers grasp things at the level of demonstration, everyone else grasps them at the level of "dialectic" and "rhetoric." To put it in another way, philosophers are in possession of proofs constructed in accordance with the strictures laid down in Aristotle's *Posterior Analytics*, and normal people hold their religious convictions having been persuaded by the sort of discourse analyzed in Aristotle's *Topics* and *Rhetoric*. As al-Fārābī puts it:

> Dialectic provides strongly held opinion (*ẓann*) concerning the things for which demonstration provides certainty, or most of them. Rhetoric persuades about most of the things that are not such as to be demonstrated or the subject of dialectical inquiry. The excellent religion does not, then, belong only to philosophers, or to those who are in a position to understand things that are only discussed in a philosophical way. Rather, most of those who are taught and instructed in the beliefs of the religion, and accept its [prescribed] actions, are not in that position, whether this is by nature or because they are too busy for it. These people are not unable to understand commonly accepted or [merely] persuasive things.[33]

Here, "commonly accepted" (*mashhūr*) is a technical term corresponding to the Greek *endoxon*.[34] "Endoxic" propositions are those that are acceptable for use in dialectical arguments, as explained in Aristotle's *Topics*. They are acceptable because they are held by just about everyone, or by those reputed for wisdom. Only when we seek demonstration do we insist on premises that are in fact and without doubt true.

So for al-Fārābī ordinary believers do not have certain knowledge, but this is all right so long as they have epistemic luck. If the beliefs they accept through persuasion or acceptance of commonly held views are those of an "excellent" religion they will have good opinions and will perform good actions. The label "ignorance" is thus reserved for those unlucky enough to adhere to a false religion. The same idea is expressed in the title of one of al-Fārābī's better-known works, which sets out a philosophical cosmology, anthropology, and political philosophy under the heading *Principles of the Beliefs of the Inhabitants of the Excellent City* (*Mabādi arā' ahl al-madīna al-fāḍila*).[35] In other words, philosophy offers the true demonstrative basis for things that members of a successful religious and political community believe without proof.

It should be obvious how close this whole line of thought is to the ideas about *taqlīd* and *ijtihād* held among jurists and theologians. For al-Fārābī the equivalent of the *mujtahid*, who thinks for himself and can give good reasons for his judgments, is the philosopher who has grasped true conclusions by means of demonstrative arguments. Everyone else is engaged in some form of *taqlīd*, following "commonly accepted" ideas or, at best, engaging in some kind of merely dialectical inquiry on the grounds of religious beliefs that are taken for granted. This would be the status of theologians, for instance. The only distinctively religious figures not subject to *taqlīd* are the original lawgiver or prophet and his successors. But they are the exception that proves the rule, because these figures possess understanding at a philosophical level, in addition to the religious function they play. In the case of the prophet, perfect intellectual understanding is fused with a capacity to represent philosophical truths in a rhetorically persuasive way that will successfully induce *taqlīd* in his religious followers, this being the function of revelation.[36] Al-Fārābī thus accepts wholesale the epistemic hierarchy of the elite Islamic scholars, albeit with new labels drawn from the Aristotelian tradition. But he denies that the scholars of Islamic law and theology are the true elite who are capable of engaging in independent reasoning. That status is reserved for the *falāsifa*.

For a more elaborate statement of this philosophical version of epistemic elitism, we can turn to Averroes. As a practicing Muslim jurist, he was certainly well acquainted with ideas about *ijtihād* and *taqlīd*. In fact his own grandfather, also named Ibn Rushd, explicitly set down a hierarchy of scholars within the Mālikī school, in three groups (*tawāʾif*). First are those who practice *taqlīd* of Mālik and his followers by just memorizing and repeating their opinions. Second are those who accept Mālik's authority and can determine what is consistent with the school's teachings but still cannot issue rulings on novel cases; this corresponds to what we already saw under the heading "*ijtihād* within a school." Third are the elite who understand legal methods and can issue novel opinions.[37] In a legal treatise of his own, the famous *Decisive Treatise*, Averroes takes up the question of the status of philosophy in Islam. He boldly argues that philosophy is not just permitted, but actually *obligatory* for those who are in a position to pursue it—those who are not, in al-Fārābī's words, prevented "by nature or because they are too busy for it." With equal boldness Averroes goes on to contend that it is philosophers who are in the best position to understand the true meaning of the Quranic revelation. They alone have independent access to the truth through demonstrative reasoning. Since the Quran is true, and "truth does not contradict truth,"[38] their demonstrated conclusions can be used as a kind of check or constraint on possible interpretations of scripture.

These aspects of the *Decisive Treatise* are well known. Less commonly discussed is the parallel Averroes draws between law and philosophy.[39] He is here a jurist writing for other jurists, so it makes sense for him to argue along the following lines: if the study of jurisprudence is licit or even encouraged within Islam, then philosophy is as well. For example, one cannot argue against philosophical activity on the grounds that it is an innovation (*bidʿa*), because the Prophet's immediate followers did not pursue it. After all, those early followers did not do jurisprudence either and no one infers from this that jurists are doing anything un-Islamic. Indeed the scriptural support for studying the law would provide even stronger support for studying philosophy.

> When the jurist deduces from [God's] statement, may He be exalted, "reflect, you who have vision" (Quran 59:2), the obligation to know juridical argument, how much more worthy and appropriate is it for someone who understands God to deduce from this [verse] the obligation to know intellectual argument![40]

Among these parallels between law and philosophy, the most important for our purposes is that the philosopher is, like the independently minded jurist, entitled to engage in independent reflection. He cites a famous *ḥadīth*, often brandished by defenders of legal *ijtihād*, to the effect that the jurist who engages in *ijtihād* and reaches an independent judgment is rewarded twice if the judgment is correct and once if he gets it wrong. Averroes then adds, "But which judge (*ḥākim*) is greater than the one who makes judgments about being (*wujūd*)?" This judge is, of course, the philosopher.[41]

Following the lead of al-Fārābī, Averroes sets up an Aristotelian version of the legal hierarchy recognized by his own grandfather and other jurists. At the top are those who engage in demonstration, then those of the "dialectical" class who work with nondemonstrative arguments, and finally ordinary people who just believe by being persuaded through a combination of rhetoric and dialectic. These people simply believe what they are told, either because it has been put to them in a powerfully convincing way—Averroes has in mind the power of rhetoric—or because it is "commonly accepted (*mashhūr*)." Again, a commonly accepted proposition is one that everyone espouses or one taught by reputable scholars. As Averroes explains in his paraphrase commentary of Aristotle's *Topics*:

> The dialectical premise is an accepted statement (*qawl mashhūr*). . . . [I]t may be accepted by all, for instance the statement that God exists; or accepted by most people without being rejected by the rest; or accepted by the scholars (*ʿulamāʾ*) and the philosophers (*falāsifa*) without being rejected by the masses.[42]

What of the "dialectical" middle class, the class between ordinary folk who simply accept things by *taqlīd* and the philosophers who engage in *ijtihād* and are satisfied only by demonstrations? Standardly one is told that for Averroes the dialecticians are the *mutakallimūn*, practicioners of theology (*kalām*). He does say in a closely related work, the *Exposition of the Methods Used in Arguments Concerning Religious Doctrines* (*al-Kashf ʿan manāhij al-adilla fī ʿaqāʾid al-milla*), that "the most adequate rank of the art of *kalām* is dialectical, not demonstrative, wisdom (*ḥikma*)."[43]

But in fact he tends to think that the theologians of his own culture, like al-Ghazālī and other Ashʿarites, are *failed* dialecticians. This is because they do not argue as they should from commonly accepted premises but instead proceed on the basis of highly controversial and abstruse assumptions when they do things like proving the existence of God. As a result, their arguments are, as Averroes says, "fitting neither for the scholars nor for the many."[44] There should in principle be theologians who carry out useful tasks like defending the faith using nondemonstrative arguments. But Averroes sees his own society as unfortunately including only two kinds of people who behave as they should: the ordinary person who takes everything on trust and the philosopher who is a kind of Aristotelian *mujtahid.*

There is a lot we can learn from these debates, apart from the need to situate the teachings of the *falāsifa* within wider Islamic culture. For one thing we can now see how ambitious, even unrealistic, it would be to have a blanket ban on *taqlīd.* Averroes's unvarnished elitism is of course rather unattractive. He envisions a tiny handful of knowledgeable experts surrounded by a huge mass of blind believers, a conception typical among the *falāsifa* and also finding many adherents among theologians and jurists. It may have seemed more plausible in a time when most people were not even literate and when half the population—the female half—was in any case typically assumed to be incapable of serious scholarly reflection, even if women did belong to the social and economic elite.[45] Still, unattractive or not, the elitist position was not put forward without good reason. If the alternative to *taqlīd* is to figure everything out for yourself, then how many people will be in a position to avoid *taqlīd*? You might be an expert in particle physics, economics, the plays of Shakespeare, or the history of philosophy, but you're unlikely to have expertise in all four. Even if you were, there would still be plenty of other fields where you would lack even rudimentary understanding.

We might therefore propose that *ijtihād* should be limited to only the most important issues or that as a community we should engage in division of labor. Again the Islamic juridical tradition anticipated both moves. The universalists, who spoke out against *taqlīd*, wanted all believers to understand just a few central religious topics, not particle physics or Shakespeare. When it came to more advanced legal reasoning, it was also admitted that a jurist might be an expert *mujtahid* in one area of the law but an obedient *muqallid* in another, just as today divorce lawyers are not usually criminal attorneys as well.[46] But there are aspects of the Islamic legal tradition that should make us wary of even localized *ijtihād*. A point forcefully put by defenders of legal precedent was that individual judgment, even when practiced by trained experts, is liable to go astray. A much-discussed example was the case of arriving in a city and wanting to know which direction to pray, so as to face Mecca. Would it really make sense to work this out for oneself rather than just adopting the local practice followed by thousands of people? As one jurist put it, "It is extremely unlikely . . . that they could have made a mistake that could be rectified by the reasoning of a single person."[47]

And indeed the perils of *ijtihād* are plain to see. In the Islamic tradition it has often been fundamentalists who adopted a universalist posture and polemicized against *taqlīd*.[48] Proceeding from the plausible assumption that individual believers are responsible for their own piety, these fundamentalists have rejected the edifice of legal and religious learning in favor of returning to a direct engagement with the revelation and evidence about the Prophet and the earliest generations of Muslims. Epistemically speaking, this is the equivalent of political movements in the United States or Europe that encourage their followers to abandon traditional news sources, academic opinion, and the like. The more sweeping the rejection of *taqlīd*, the worse the results: it's what Sandy Hook conspiracy theorists like Alex Jones have in common with Salafi Islamists.

A more refined approach to the problem of *taqlīd* would not require being a *mujtahid* for each and every topic we care about, or if this is too difficult, instead blindly following the nearest authority at hand, thus surrendering to the vagaries of epistemic luck. What we need is a better account of how to form one's own views while realizing that one is dependent on the expertise and authority of other people. As the historian Mary Beard recently observed, "The recognition of complexity and difficulty is not an admission of defeat; it is treating a complex problem with the respect it deserves." Doing this well means depending on authority in an intelligent and discerning way, which is a big part of being a responsible believer and responsible citizen.

CHAPTER 2

Too High a Standard

Knowledge and Skepticism in Medieval Philosophy

The philosopher Laurence Bonjour has written that "if skeptics did not exist, one might reasonably say, the serious epistemologist would have to invent them."[1] One might just as reasonably say that if serious epistemologists did not exist, they would have to be invented by skeptics. Skeptics are in the business of denying that we have knowledge, or even that we could ever have knowledge. So they need to have some conception, whether implicit or explicit, of what knowledge would be if we did have it. This is rather awkward. A thoroughgoing and consistent skeptic will hardly want to defend a theory of knowledge, at least not if this would mean claiming to know what knowledge is. Fortunately, skeptics throughout history have had "serious epistemologists" as their opponents. They have engaged dialectically with these opponents, arguing not simply that knowledge is unattainable, but that *if knowledge is what their opponents say it is*, then it is unattainable.

A case in point would be the ancient philosophers who gave skepticism its name and made it a central force in Hellenistic philosophy. They were aware of theories of knowledge defended by non-skeptical, or as they would say, "dogmatic," philosophers like Plato and Aristotle. But their main interlocutors were the Stoics, who did them the favor of offering a maximally demanding epistemology. For the Stoics, the perfect wise person or "sage" is immune to error. The sage may not know absolutely everything but does have a systematic grasp of all areas of philosophy and in light of this comprehensive understanding is able to refrain from assenting to anything that is uncertain. This means withholding belief in all cases where a so-called cognitive impression is lacking, this being an impression that could not possibly misrepresent the way things are.[2] A famous anecdote illustrates the idea. The Stoic philosopher Sphaerus was presented with wax fruit and tried to bite into it, apparently mistaking it for real fruit. His excuse was that he had not formed the belief that it was real, only the belief that it would be reasonable to suppose that it was real.[3] The Skeptics helped themselves to this strategy, arguing that the complete certainty demanded by the Stoics is never in fact available, since there are no cognitive impressions. Thus, by the Stoics' own policy, we should withhold judgment about absolutely everything.

In fact it would, as Sphaerus might put it, be reasonable to suppose that highly demanding theories of knowledge actually provoke philosophers into turning to skepticism. The more daunting the requirements proposed for knowledge, the more natural it is to worry that the requirements are never met. In what follows, I argue that this hypothesis is borne out by the history of medieval philosophy. This was not due to the impact of Hellenistic skepticism, which was little known in the medieval period. It was almost totally absent in the texts translated into Arabic, so it received no attention in the Islamic world. In the Christian realms some information was available through Cicero and Augustine. But apart from rare exceptions like John of Salisbury (d. 1180), we have to wait until the Renaissance to see profound engagement with the ancient Skeptics. Nonetheless, quite a few "serious epistemologists" raised skeptical worries. This was almost never because they wanted to endorse skepticism but because they were reacting to an epistemology that, in its way, set just as high a standard as the Stoics. This was the theory of Aristotle.

If you know just one thing about Aristotelian epistemology, it's probably that he was an empiricist. You may also have in mind that he was therefore unlike his teacher Plato, who thought that we cannot get knowledge properly speaking through sensation. For Plato, when we seem to learn things for the first time, we are recalling previously acquired knowledge from direct acquaintance with objects that are not sensible but intelligible, the famous Platonic Forms. None of this is wrong, exactly, but it leaves out a deeper agreement between Plato and Aristotle. For both of them, knowledge is to be distinguished sharply from true opinion or belief, in part on the grounds that knowledge must be completely reliable. It must concern eternal verities, not individual, sensible things that change and pass away. That may sound like something only Plato would say, since it fits so well with the claim that knowledge concerns unchanging intelligible objects. But it also holds for Aristotle, whose vaunted empiricism does not prevent him from making remarks like this:

> It is clear that if the premises from which the syllogistic argument is made are universal, then necessarily the conclusion of such a demonstration, one called demonstration in the strict sense (καὶ τῆς ἁπλῶς εἰπεῖν ἀποδείξεως), is eternal. Thus there is no demonstration of things subject to corruption, nor is there knowledge of them in the strict sense (ἐπιστήμη ἁπλῶς).[4]

As he explains at the end of the *Posterior Analytics*, we do glean the principles of scientific demonstration from sensation.[5] But these principles and all the conclusions derived from them, whether immediately or through longer chains of inferences, must be unchangingly true. This means that they are universal, necessary, essential, eternal truths. Knowledge in the strict sense concerns all and only such truths.[6]

All this could be explored at further length, of course, but from the little I have said we may better understand several developments characteristic of medieval philosophy. One obvious example is the elitist account of expertise discussed in chapter 1. If knowledge is as Aristotle described it, clearly it will be attained by very few people, and such figures as Averroes were persuaded that knowledge is indeed as Aristotle described it. Another example is the long-running debate over the eternity of the world that raged between Muslim, Jewish, and Christian philosophers.[7] One reason this topic attracted so much controversy is that the temporal creation of the world, which seemed to be demanded by the Abrahamic faiths, would seem to render Aristotelian science null and void. For if scientific knowledge concerns eternal truths and if nothing apart from God is eternal, then there is no scientific knowledge about anything other than God. (And by the way there is no scientific knowledge about God either, since Aristotle says that we understand things through their causes, and God has no cause.) There are ways of escaping this conclusion. Perhaps our knowledge actually concerns eternal exemplars in God's mind, on the basis of which he creates the world. Or perhaps knowledge has a conditional form: though it would not eternally be the case that there are giraffes with long necks, it could be true that *if and when* giraffes exist they have long necks. But it was still clear that creationism fit poorly with Aristotle's epistemology.

What I want to focus on now, though, is the way that this same epistemology provoked skeptical worries, and also accommodated solutions to these worries. Aristotelian science is both difficult to achieve and leaves out most of what we would say we "know" in everyday contexts. This led many medievals to recognize less demanding forms of knowledge alongside Aristotelian scientific understanding. And it led some medievals to admit that knowledge in the narrowest and most demanding sense is inaccessible to humans through natural means.

The Aristotelian epistemology, especially once it was fused with the Platonist idea that intelligible objects are the appropriate objects of knowledge, seemed to imply that individual, sensible things are unknowable. This would leave us with a kind of limited skepticism, according to which a vast number of things we seem to "know" are actually not known. For instance you cannot "know" in the strict sense that you are reading this book right now, because you and the book are both particulars. While this seems highly counterintuitive, it was a conclusion accepted by most medieval thinkers of the Aristotelian tradition. The conclusion was frequently qualified with an acknowledgment that sense perception gives us knowledge of a sort, which lacks the certainty and reliability of knowledge in the strict and proper sense.

This can already be found in al-Kindī (d. after 870), the first philosopher to write in Arabic using Greek sources as his main inspiration. He invoked the changeability of sensible things to rule them out as objects of the best sort of knowledge.

> Stable, true, complete knowledge within the science of philosophy is knowledge of substance. The knowledge of secondary substance is unceasing, because the object of knowledge is stable, and not susceptible to change or flux. But one only has access to it [sc. the

> knowledge of secondary substance] through the knowledge of primary substance. Sensory knowledge is the knowledge of primary substance, and is in flux owing to the uninterrupted flux of what is known; this ends only when the [object of knowledge] itself ends.[8]

He was also aware of the Platonic theory of recollection and, in another text reporting on this theory, accepted that sensation can contribute to intellectual knowledge only by prompting recall of such knowledge that has been temporarily lost. Note, however, that in the passage just quoted, he does use the phrase "sensory knowledge" (*al-ʿilm al-ḥissī*), perhaps because he worries that if sense perception does not count as knowledge at all, it cannot provide a suitable instrument leading to the best sort of knowledge. Thus he goes on to say that if someone lacks knowledge of both primary and secondary substances (i.e., sensible and intelligible things), then "he will have no hope of knowing any of the human sciences (*ʿulūm*)."[9]

A couple of generations after al-Kindī, we have the most important early Jewish philosopher of the Islamic world, Saadia Gaon (d. 942). His thought is comparable to that of al-Kindī in numerous respects. Though Saadia was not as directly involved in the Greek-Arabic translation movement, he did draw on the fruits of that effort. John Philoponus's arguments against the eternity of the world, for instance, were used by both al-Kindī and Saadia.[10] Furthermore, both of them engaged closely with the ideas of the early Muslim theologians grouped under the heading "Muʿtazilism." Given these commonalities, it is not too surprising to see Saadia expressing ideas in epistemology similar to those of al-Kindī. He likewise sees sensation as a means of knowledge, which is, however, inferior to intellectual knowledge.

But the wider context of Saadia's epistemology is more reminiscent of the later Jewish philosopher Maimonides (d. 1204) than anything we find in al-Kindī. Like Maimonides's *Guide of the Perplexed*, Saadia's *Book of Beliefs and Opinions* is addressed to coreligionists who have fallen into uncertainty (*shubha*).[11] Saadia explicitly rejects skepticism and says that we may put our trust in three sources of knowledge.

> We must mention the roots of truth and providers of certainty (*yaqīn*), which are the source for everything that is known and wellspring

> of all understanding (*maʿrifa*). . . . We say that there are three roots. First, the knowledge that comes through direct witnessing (*ʿilm al-shāhid*); second, the knowledge that comes from the intellect (*ʿilm al-ʿaql*); third, the knowledge of what necessity implies.[12]

Thus we have sensation and intellect providing foundational principles, with a third kind of knowledge consisting in inferences derived from these principles. Shortly thereafter, Saadia adds that scriptural tradition is a fourth source of knowledge. Its reliability is secured through empirical evidence and reasoning. Conversely, biblical texts confirm the validity of the three natural sources of knowledge. Thus religious authority and empirically based rational investigation ratify one another.

At first, the three nonscriptural sources seem to be placed on a par with one another. But later in the work, when introducing his discussion of God, Saadia makes it clear that the work of intellect is superior to that of sensation. True, all "types of knowledge (*ʿulūm*) begin from sensible things," but sensation is shared in common with nonhuman animals.[13] The inquirer's task, therefore, is to use the intellect to move from sensible things to more "subtle" (*laṭīf*) notions like accidental properties, place, and time.

> In this way one reaches the utmost of what one may comprehend. This ultimate thing is the subtlest [thing] one obtains, just as that initial thing [from which one started] was the crudest thing one obtains. On this basis I passed the verdict that the utmost object of knowledge is the one that is the most subtle.[14]

An unusual feature of Saadia's treatment of knowledge is that he tries to explain why this process needs to be so laborious. Why, he asks, did God not simply bestow knowledge upon us, so that we would not be obligated to work upward from the crude to the subtle, from sensation to intellection? Part of the answer is simply that all created things are subject to time and must develop toward their perfection.[15] But Saadia offers a deeper rationale, which is that God alone is without a cause, both in general and in respect of his own knowledge. So, to avoid our being placed on God's level, our knowledge needs to have some cause. This cause consists in "inquiry and investigation, which need temporal duration."[16]

Doubt and ignorance are not arbitrarily inflicted on us by God, then, but are the inevitable initial condition for creatures like us, who depend on a causal process for our perfection.

Another philosopher comparable to al-Kindī, indeed, one who made explicit use of al-Kindī's writings, was Miskawayh (d. 1030). Like al-Kindī he was a harmonizer, whose writings on ethics, cosmology, and metaphysics fuse Aristotelianism with ideas from the Platonist tradition. One of these is a response to an unnamed materialist opponent who has raised questions about knowledge and the soul.[17] In the first question, the opponent states that intellect is dependent on sensation. The intellect grasps universals only on the basis of sense experience, so we can have no trust in affirmations about anything that is not sensible. The opponent's point is, then, that we should be skeptical about such things as an immaterial soul or God. Miskawayh's reply develops the idea we have already seen in al-Kindī and Saadia, that sensation may contribute to knowledge but in a lesser way than intellection. In fact, Miskawayh thinks, the opponent has things wrong. Intellection does not always depend on sensation, but sensation always depends on the intellect. For sensation often falls prey to error, as through visual illusions, and needs to be corrected or confirmed by a higher faculty, namely, the intellect. By contrast, the intellect "has an activity which is particular to itself," when it grasps the "universals and essences of things" by abstracting them from sensation, and knows that this does in fact constitute knowledge. "Were this not the case, it would always grasp knowledge through some other knowledge, and this would go to infinity, which is absurd."[18] Here the superiority of intellection to sensation is explained not only in terms of its different objects, as in al-Kindī and Saadia, but also in light of its reflexivity. Unlike sensation, which needs external validation, the intellect can guarantee its own reliability.

The claim that the best sort of knowledge is self-certifying in this way can also be found in a more famous thinker who comes chronologically between al-Kindī and Miskawayh, being a rough contemporary of Saadia. This is al-Fārābī (d. 950). A short treatise of his called *On the Conditions of Certainty* is a key text for the idea I have been teasing out from these early philosophers who wrote in Arabic.[19] Still more explicitly than the aforementioned thinkers, al-Fārābī asserts that knowledge and even "certainty (*al-yaqīn*)" come in *degrees*. In a sense, this simply draws out an implication of Aristotle's original discussion. He specified that the rigorous constraints he places on knowledge actually concern only knowledge in the strict or proper sense (ἁπλῶς), and al-Fārābī uses a corresponding phrase in Arabic (*ʿalā l-iṭlāq*) to designate the highest form of certainty.

He spells out a cumulative list of six criteria that need to be satisfied before this sort of certainty is obtained, a list clearly inspired by Aristotle's *Posterior Analytics.*

> Absolute certainty is (1) that one believes that a thing is such-and-such or not; (2) that one agrees that [the belief] is in accord with, rather than opposed to, the existence of something external [to the mind]; (3) that one knows that it is in accord with it; (4) that it cannot fail to be in accord [with what is external to the mind], and cannot be opposed [to that thing]; (5) also that it is not opposed [to that thing] at any moment; and (6) that this occurs not accidentally, but essentially.[20]

The third item on al-Fārābī's checklist makes the same point as Miskawayh, that certain knowledge should include knowing that one's belief is reliable. Al-Fārābī introduces this requirement to exclude cases where one holds a true belief but without certainty. Suppose, for instance, that you see me and believe Peter Adamson is standing before you, but knowing that I have an identical twin, you are open to the possibility that this belief may be false. Al-Fārābī's criteria thus range over both first-order and second-order beliefs.[21] At the first order I may believe, for instance, that giraffes are tall; at the second order, that my belief about giraffes being tall is definitely true.

Still more interesting is al-Fārābī's willingness to describe cognitive states that satisfy only *some* of these criteria as "certain," but in a lesser or "qualified" sense.[22] These would be cases where error is impossible, yet no *necessary* truth is involved, like knowing that Zayd is sitting because I see him sit right before me. Or they may be cases involving things that are necessary, yet not eternal, as when we know about a necessarily occurring but transient eclipse. These two categories of true belief fail to satisfy respectively the fourth and the fifth criteria for absolute certainty. A modern-day epistemologist would probably see such beliefs as excellent candidates for knowledge in the full sense, but al-Fārābī does not, because he adheres to Aristotle's demanding criteria for knowledge in the strict sense. It is only *absolute* certainty, he says, that is "used and discovered in philosophy."[23]

Al-Fārābī also excludes from scientific understanding or absolute certainty beliefs that are acquired through testimony, whether it is the testimony of everyone or an expert. Even if one comes to accept something that is necessarily and eternally true on the basis of authority, the belief will be "accidental" and not "essential."[24] Here al-Fārābī shifts Aristotle's essentiality requirement from the first to the second order. For me to be absolutely certain that giraffes are tall, it must not only be the case that giraffes are essentially tall, but that my belief is essentially, not accidentally, related to this state of affairs. This is just a technical, Aristotelian version of a point seen above, namely, that believing something on the basis of authority—especially doing so uncritically, by *taqlīd*—means opening oneself up to epistemic luck. In fact al-Fārābī even says that one may wind up with necessarily true beliefs "by chance" rather than through the causes that should properly give rise to such beliefs.

Deborah Black, author of an excellent study on the treatise just discussed, has also pointed out that al-Fārābī's great successor in the *falsafa* tradition, Avicenna, was somewhat more tolerant of beliefs acquired by testimony.[25] In a discussion of the starting points or principles for syllogistic arguments, Avicenna gives pride of place to propositions that are necessarily true. These include self-evident or "primary" propositions and also propositions based on sensation (*maḥsūsāt*). However, Avicenna also admits the use of propositions that have a lesser status. These include beliefs that, as Black puts it, rely "on communal and social factors."[26] One may achieve certainty through reliable testimony, as in the case of facts for which there is overwhelming historical evidence. In other cases, testimony may fall short of inducing certitude. This would happen where the testimony is not of sufficient quality to rule out the possibility of error, so that accepting the relevant beliefs would count as *taqlīd*.

It is remarkable that Avicenna ascribes certainty to the deliverances of sensation and some cases of testimonial belief. To quote Black one more time, these cases concern "facts of which I can be certain, even though they are not necessary or universal in their own right, and so they provide one of the key motivations for Avicenna's desire to extend the realm of certitude to include the possible."[27] Yet Avicenna remains wedded to the Aristotelian conception of knowledge in the strict sense as dealing with universal, necessary, essential truths. Sensation of individual things is excluded from the realm of scientific demonstration.

> Sensation is not a demonstration, nor is sensation as such a principle of demonstration. For demonstrations and their principles are universal, not particularized by time, individual, or place. Sensation supplies a judgment about a particular, at a time and place proper to it. Therefore . . . nothing from [sensation] is universal knowledge (*ʿilm kullī*).[28]

To mark this difference, Avicenna at one point draws a rather artificial contrast between two Arabic words that may both be translated as "knowledge," namely, *maʿrifa* and *ʿilm*.[29] Whereas *ʿilm* designates the universal knowledge that satisifies Aristotle's criteria from the *Posterior Analytics*, the word *maʿrifa* refers to our knowledge that a given particular falls under a universal. Thus if I have *ʿilm* that humans are rational, I could combine this with my *maʿrifa* that Zayd is a human to get to the insight that Zayd is rational.

One implication of Avicenna's epistemology is that a completely perfect and necessary being should lack the lower forms of cognition, certitude, and "knowledge" that have to do with contingent facts and individual things. Hence his notorious teaching that God has no knowledge of particulars "as such." Avicenna is driven to this conclusion simply by the Aristotelian account of knowledge in the strict and proper, or "unqualified," sense and the realization that a God free of sensation, change, and contingency could only have knowledge in this strict sense.[30] To put it in the terms of the terminological distinction just mentioned, it's clear that God has *ʿilm* and less clear whether God can have *maʿrifa*, and if so how. Interpreters of Avicenna still argue over his answer to these questions.

Less widely discussed is the fact that, like al-Fārābī and Miskawayh, Avicenna thinks that first-order certainty should involve second-order certainty. Even in "lesser" types of certain belief, like those derived from overwhelming testimony or one-off sensory experiences, one may be certain that one's belief is certainly true. So even as Avicenna lowered the bar for "certainty" and "knowledge" by accepting that cognition below the rank of full-blown intellection may be dignified with these terms—and thus answered the skeptical worry that most types of apparent "knowledge" are not knowledge after all—he left open a route to a more general skeptical attack. The skeptic can try to show that *second-order* certainty is unattainable, in other words, that I cannot know for any putative bit of knowledge that it really is knowledge. This would mean that we cannot have the sort of knowledge Avicenna would say we can have through our grasp of first principles, through demonstrations, and even through testimony and sensation.

Here it would be helpful to look again at Miskawayh. He made intellect superior to sensation on the grounds that sensation needs to be ratified by intellect, as shown by various kinds of mistakes that befall sense perception when it is left to its own devices. Intellect, by contrast, is self-ratifying. In his intellectual autobiography, *Deliverer from Error* (*al-Munqidh min al-dalāl*),[31] al-Ghazālī shows the vulnerability of this maneuver. Early on in this work he recounts a skeptical crisis he endured as a young man. Tellingly, the crisis was brought on when the younger al-Ghazālī formulated to himself the following high standard for genuine knowledge: "the object of knowledge should be revealed in such a way that there remains no uncertainty, and excludes all possibility of error or [false] supposition."[32]

He went on to consider possible sources of such certainty, beginning with sensation. This source is ruled out by adducing standard cases of sensory illusion, for instance, the apparently small size of the visible sun (an example already mentioned by Aristotle). Al-Ghazālī agrees with Miskawayh that such mistakes can be corrected by the intellect. He describes his younger self being instructed by his own faculty of sensation.

> Don't you realize that your trust in intellectual things is like your trust in sensible things? Previously you trusted in me [i.e., sensation], but then the judge (*ḥākim*) of the intellect came along and falsified me. Had it not been for the judge of the intellect, you would still deem me true. So it may be that beyond the perception of the intellect there is some further judge, and once it appears, it will falsify intellect with its adjudication, just as the judge of the intellect did in falsifying sensation with its adjudication.[33]

This famous passage gestures toward a potential regress of validation, in which every type of cognition needs a further type to provide second-order certainty. In al-Ghazālī's own experience, such certainty came from God, who "cast a light into his breast."[34]

We might be tempted to read this as a retreat from the rationality of the philosophical tradition into some form of mysticism, a temptation that could be further encouraged by al-Ghazālī's positive treatment of Sufism later in the work. But this would be inaccurate. Admittedly, he does not believe that the deliverances of reason are self-evident in such a way that they stand in no need of further ratification. But God's light here is invoked precisely to reassure al-Ghazālī that the intellect is indeed reliable. So he is far from rejecting the use of intellectual first principles, such as "ten is greater than three" or the principle of non-contradiction, examples given by al-Ghazālī himself. It is just that he needs God to reassure him of their reliability.[35] With this confirmation in hand, al-Ghazālī has "certainty" in such principles and in the further conclusions inferred from them. This fits with his impatient dismissal, later in the same work, of skepticism concerning logic and mathematics. For al-Ghazālī these are absolutely certain fields of knowledge, and it is foolish to question them.

For another thing, what the younger al-Ghazālī wanted is also what the philosophers always demanded: knowledge that is certain in the sense that it excludes all error by grasping necessary truths. His *Incoherence of the Philosophers* displays this same expectation. There al-Ghazālī repeatedly complains that the arguments of the "philosophers," by which he means Avicenna, fail to rise to the requisite standard of proof. Echoing a point also made in the *Deliverer from Error*, al-Ghazālī says that the philosophers claimed to have achieved in theology and metaphysics the degree of rigor and demonstration we find in mathematics. But in fact they fell far short of this standard.[36] The most notorious example of this is that the "philosophers" thought that natural causal relations are necessary. Thus, if nothing prevents, when fire touches cotton it necessarily burns the cotton. But for al-Ghazālī, these causal relations are not in fact necessary. This is either because the relations are real but subject to being overturned by a miracle or because in fact God is the only cause, who directly brings about such things as the cotton's burning, with created causes like fire exerting no causal influence.[37] If we have "knowledge (*'ilm*)" that things will go as we habitually expect, then this must be implanted in us by God.[38] This is why I "know" that, say, the book in my house will not turn into a horse and urinate all over the rest of my library while I am out (his example, not mine).

In his counterattack against this work, the *Incoherence of the Incoherence*, Averroes insisted that al-Ghazālī's position would lead to epistemic disaster.

> Denial of cause implies the denial of knowledge, and denial of knowledge implies that nothing in this world can be really known, and that what is supposed to be known is nothing but opinion, that neither proof nor definition exist, and that the essential attributes which compose definitions are void.[39]

The response is a predictable one. As a faithful Aristotelian, Averroes assumes that if we cannot make necessary generalizations about the essences of things, we will be left with skepticism. On one point, though, al-Ghazālī and Averroes agree. Both think that knowledge in the strict sense—the knowledge that philosophy should provide, if it is able—should be necessary in character. For Averroes, miracles threaten to undermine such knowledge, by making apparent certainty into nothing more than habitual prediction. While he pays lip service to the possibility of miracles, he seems therefore to believe in a God who never alters the course of natural events, so that our scientific generalizations retain their necessary character. For al-Ghazālī, by contrast, God is the only true source of certainty. God's omnipotence and untrammeled freedom render apparent necessities into mere possibilities, possibilities that are realized by God's will and about which we can have real knowledge only if he lets us know his plans.

One way out of this impasse would of course be to deny that God can intervene in ways that would undermine scientific knowledge. But a more popular solution was finally to stop making such ambitious demands in epistemology. As we've seen, a number of philosophers had been willing to admit lesser forms of certainty or knowledge, as when Avicenna granted the possibility of arriving at certainty through testimony. But they still held that some few people, the epistemic elite, attain a gold standard form of understanding, in which the essences of things are known without possibility of error by grasping necessary and universal truths. Increasingly this viewpoint came under fire from the *kalām* tradition, especially members of the Ashʿarite school, who emphasized God's power over his creatures and the contingency of everything on his will. In the face of this pressure, even partisans of Avicenna began to make more modest claims about the status of propositions that are suitable for use in philosophy.

I'll just give one example of this, which comes from the polymath Naṣīr al-Dīn al-Ṭūsī (d. 1274), who was at once an Avicennan philosopher, a Shīʿite theologian, and a scientist with particular expertise in astronomy. In one of his works he confronts a battery of skeptical arguments posed by Fakhr al-Dīn al-Rāzī (d. 1210).[40] Fakhr al-Dīn was both an influential expositor and incisive critic of Avicenna, who wrote commentaries on his works and several massive treatises covering the full range of issues raised in philosophy and theology up to his time. One of these is the question of foundational truths, that is, truths to which we assent without any further justification. This leads Fakhr al-Dīn to discuss skeptical challenges against self-evident propositions, during which he mentions hypothetical scenarios like the one envisioned by al-Ghazālī, concerning the book that turns into a horse. Here, we are asked to imagine a more welcome transformation, in which my dishes turn into scholars of logic and geometry. Such an event could, in theory, take place by "divine will." Faced with this, al-Ṭūsī responds:

> The intellect has no doubt concerning what it has resolved (*jazama*) as a result of what he says. Even if this resolution is not like the one it makes to the effect that "the whole is greater than the part," still the difference between them is not such that one of the two resolutions is mere belief (*ẓann*) [i.e., as opposed to knowledge]. Take for instance judgments based on empirical investigation (*al-qaḍāyā al-tajribiyya*): they are not resolved the way the primary truths (*al-awwaliyyāt*) are, but they come with certainty that is far removed from doubt. According to the philosophers, it is absurd that a scholar should be generated without material causes, preparatory factors, and education.[41]

Which sounds reasonable enough. But in the context of the philosophical background I have been sketching, it is actually a significant concession.

Al-Ṭūsī now allows for degrees of certainty even *within* the propositions used in scientific contexts. Even when we are talking about knowledge in the strict and proper sense, we might be certain or *really* certain, and either sort of certainty suffices.

But what does it mean to be "really" certain? In a study of these passages on skepticism in Fakhr al-Dīn and al-Ṭūsī, Pirooz Fatoorchi has insightfully drawn a parallel between al-Ṭūsī's position and similar ideas found in fourteenth-century scholasticism.[42] This exemplifies a more general phenomenon, namely, that many debates in Latin scholastic philosophy were unwitting replications of earlier debates in post-Avicennan Arabic philosophy. In this instance, the emergence of voluntarism in the late thirteenth and fourteenth century confronted scholastics with the same challenge faced earlier by the Ashʿarites. If God can actualize any possible state of affairs, as insisted by voluntarists like Duns Scotus (d. 1308), then doesn't this undermine all ambitions of having certainty about the created world? God could, for example, cause you to see a simulacrum of Peter Adamson that is not me but is indistinguishable from me. So you could never have certainty that you are seeing me.

This is only one of many hypothetical scenarios discussed in Latin medieval philosophy, especially in the fourteenth century. Could God change the past? Could God make a person exist in two places at the same time, so that a man could cut off his own head and survive the experience?[43] Or, speaking of heads, can we really be sure that the pope has one? Not if our sensory experiences depend for their reliability on the assumption that we are not prey to some supernatural illusion, something of which we can never be certain. This point, with the example of the pope's head, was made by Nicholas of Autrecourt (d. 1369), the late medieval thinker most celebrated for his exploration of skepticism.[44] Like other medieval thinkers who discussed such problems, though, Nicholas was not trying to defend a skeptical position. Rather he sought to draw out skeptical consequences from Aristotelian epistemology.

If Aristotelian science rests on evident first principles, then these principles had better be really evident. And, given the threat of divine intervention, no beliefs derived from sensation would seem to fit this bill. Nor can we rely on our experience of causal connections to make necessary generalizations. Sounding to an astonishing degree like al-Ghazālī before him—and David Hume after him, who turns out to have been reinventing an already reinvented wheel—Nicholas says that we have only a "conjectural habit (*habitus conjecturativus*)" of expecting the similar effects to arise from similar causes. In fact, Nicholas can only think of one principle that has maximal certainty, namely, that two contradictories cannot both be true (e.g., "giraffes are tall" and "it's not the case that giraffes are tall"). We may have other beliefs that are true, but the only ones that constitute certain knowledge are those that are equivalent to this principle. These are roughly the ones that are now called "analytic truths," the ones that follow purely from the meanings of the terms involved, though Nicholas claims that not even mathematical truths, which we would consider analytic, are on a par with the principle of non-contradiction.[45]

A cogent response to this line of argument was offered by John Buridan (d. ca. 1360).[46] Much like al-Ṭūsī admitting that science often deals in truths less certain than the principle that "the whole is greater than the part," Buridan conceded to Nicholas of Autrecourt that contradictions are false with a degree of certainty that is rarely, if ever, attained in natural philosophy. But this is not problematic, because natural philosophy does not pursue that level of certainty. As Aristotle famously said in his *Nicomachean Ethics* (1094b), in each discipline we should aim at the level of exactness appropriate to that discipline. Just as the judge's task is to pass a verdict on the accused in the way indicated by the evidence, which may occasionally mean condemning an innocent man, so the natural philosopher's job is to generalize on the basis of experience. The goal is to inquire into *natural* causes and effects, so the fact that God could *supernaturally* intervene, to prevent fire from burning cotton or allow someone to cut off his own head, is simply irrelevant.

This gives us a better idea of how to fill out al-Ṭūsī's proposal that scientific truths are certain but less certain than evident first principles. In natural philosophy we would attain a lesser but appropriate degree of certainty asserting for instance that "fire burns," even though we realize that God could choose to intervene miraculously to stop fire from burning. Since such miraculous intervention is simply outside the purview of the natural philosopher, it can be ignored. Another way of thinking about this was implicitly suggested by Nicholas of Autrecourt when he set up the skeptical challenge in the first place. We might say that we do have certainty that "fire burns *if* not prevented from doing so by God." Our beliefs would be restored to full certainty by phrasing them in a hypothetical form, much as I suggested earlier regarding the eternity of the world ("if and when giraffes exist, they have long necks"). The difference would simply be that here, we may never know for sure that the hypothetical condition—that God is not supernaturally intervening on this occasion—is satisfied. But phrasing the solution in this way may have seemed less attractive from the scholastics' point of view, since Aristotelian science is meant to consist of predications (e.g., all A's are B's), not hypothetical statements (if X, then Y).

At this point I should admit an ambiguity that has run throughout this whole chapter, one that you may already have spotted. A central term in all these debates has been "certainty," which we have frequently seen explained in terms of the impossibility of error. But something might be true in such a way that it cannot be false, without me, you, or anyone *realizing* that it is true in this way. So we should distinguish between objective and subjective certainty. Something is objectively certain if it must be true, subjectively certain for the person who knows it must be true. Medieval Aristotelians typically wanted both kinds of certainty, at least when it came to the highest kind of knowledge. Al-Fārābī was the earliest thinker I discussed who made this point: for him, absolute certainty requires that one believe in a truth that is in itself, or is objectively, necessary, and *in addition* that one knows it is true. Note that the subjective element here involves a second-order belief. To be absolutely certain that giraffes have long necks, I must know that my first-order belief to this effect is true.

Medieval arguments for skepticism targeted both of these requirements. To deny the eternity of the world, or to admit the possibility of God intervening in an otherwise stable natural system of cause and effect, was to threaten the Aristotelian ambition of grasping eternal, universally invariant features and powers of things. What were meant to be objectively necessary truths were deemed instead to be merely contingent truths, if that. In a sense medieval Aristotelians were well prepared to fend off this threat. They had already allowed for lesser forms of certainty, for instance, regarding the individual, contingently existing things that we grasp through sensation rather than intellection. So the idea that certain beliefs might concern themselves with things that are contingently true, true only "for the most part," or true only when the universe exists, could be accommodated within an Aristotelian framework.

Arguably, the medievals were less well placed to cope with the skeptical attack on second-order, subjective certainty. The radical skeptical hypotheses entertained in both the Islamic world and Latin Christendom seemed to suggest that nothing is certain at all. Each experience could be an illusion, or the whole world could be a radically contingent phenomenon explained from one moment to the next only by God's arbitrary will. These concerns, which of course prefigure similar skeptical worries in early modern philosophy, were typically forestalled simply by trusting that God is no deceiver. Thus al-Ghazālī quotes the line from the Quran, "you will find no change in God's custom (*sunna*)" (48:23). (Averroes quotes it too, though in his case one may doubt whether he truly believes that God can miraculously intervene in the course of nature.) The Latin scholastics took refuge in the distinction between God's absolute and ordained power: absolutely, God can do whatever is intrinsically possible, but he has made a covenant with his creatures that he will abide by certain laws.[47] And in fact the skeptical hypotheses considered by medieval thinkers are not quite as radical as they might be. Al-Ghazālī and Fakhr al-Dīn warn that God might turn a book into a horse or dishes into scholars, and the fourteenth-century scholastics worried about divinely created illusions, but these scenarios always seem to be one-off events, not thought experiments involving systematic deception like Descartes's evil demon hypothesis or the modern-day variant that invokes an immersive virtual reality.[48] This helps explain why Buridan could cheerfully accept the possibility of an occasional, miraculous intervention. So long as this is the rare exception and not the rule, natural science could still be certain within its own terms.

The issue of second-order certainty is closely related to the issues I raised in chapter 1. There we saw that philosophers in the Islamic world, like many jurists and theologians, liked to style themselves as independent thinkers who proved things for themselves rather than forming their beliefs on the basis of authority. In light of what I've just discussed, this ambition becomes a bit clearer. If philosophical knowledge demands second-order certainty, then it can hardly be compatible with following authority. For while an authority might convince you of something that is *objectively* certain, it seems that no authority can give you *subjective* certainty. To have that, you would need to put yourself in a position to understand that the belief in question is indeed certain. But that would apparently require being an expert yourself. How can you be really sure, for instance, that all giraffes have long necks, unless you are thoroughly trained in zoology or at least in that most important part of zoology that concerns giraffes? Well there might be a way, actually, as we'll see next.

CHAPTER 3

Testing the Prophets

Reason and the Choice of Faiths

Don't let anyone tell you that philosophy is useless. True, it has a reputation for being an abstract and chronically inconclusive enterprise. But "applied" forms of philosophy like medical ethics and business ethics have enjoyed a boom in recent times, and in earlier periods philosophy was also applied in eminently practical contexts. Medicine was a good example back then too. Galen, the second-century AD author whose writings were nearly synonymous with medical science for well over a millenium in Europe and the Islamic world, appropriated ideas from ancient natural philosophy in his humoral theory and pharmacology. Another example is the study of the heavens. The cosmological theories of Aristotle provided a theoretical basis for Ptolemy, who lived at about the same time as Galen and whose writings about both astronomy and astrology were widely influential in medieval culture. This sounds less practical at first, but astrology—known through texts from both Greece and India—was one of the main topics pursued in the Arabic translation movement, again for eminently practical reasons. What, after all, could be more useful than using the stars to predict the future?

Many people today think of philosophy and religion as being antithetical, with philosophy devoted solely to reason and religion founded in faith. But in the medieval period, religious thought was frequently just another kind of applied philosophy. Ideas about knowledge, metaphysics, or the soul would be appropriated and used to interpret, expound, and defend revelation. Indeed we've already seen that Averroes, for one, thought that philosophy provided the *only* reliable basis for scriptural exegesis. Obviously this was not a widely held view, and there were certainly some medieval theologians who were frankly hostile to the use of philosophy in religious contexts, going all the way back to the early Christian church father Tertullian, who famously wanted to know what Athens has to do with Jerusalem. Examples from the three medieval cultures examined here might include Ibn Taymiyya (d. 1328), who very unusually went so far as to reject the study of logic, which he deemed more trouble than it was worth (like "camel meat at the top of a mountain"); Bernard of Clairvaux (d. 1153), who justified the intellectual persecution of Peter Abelard by complaining that Abelard was "ready to give reasons for everything, even for those those things which are above reason"; and Symeon the New Theologian (d. 1022), a monk at the Stoudios monastery in Constantinople who acidly remarked that the Holy Spirit is "not sent to philosophers . . . but to the pure in heart and body."[1]

But in this chapter, I look at figures who had a more nuanced view, one that falls between the bold rationalism of Averroes and the invective of these outright critics of philosophy (who, by the way, also left plenty of space for rationality in their own approaches to religion). On the one hand, these middle-ground figures perceived the philosophical tradition as a kind of rival, or at least alternative, to religious faith. On the other hand, they believed that natural reason could be used to support religious faith and even to justify one's religious affiliation. I'll focus on several works written in dialogue form, which explore the choice between religions by putting them in literal debate with one another. Tellingly, "philosophy" tends to appear in these dialogues as another option on a par with Islam, Judaism, and Christianity. The central claim made by such texts is, therefore, that the neutral and fair-minded person who is simply using natural reason should give credence to one of the Abrahamic faiths. By arguing for this conclusion, they suggest that reason points beyond itself, establishing the need for a religious revelation that supplements our natural understanding of the world and of our own obligations.

As context for the discussion of these dialogues it will be useful to return to the dilemma I explored in chapter 1. To recap, I argued that we need a way of forming beliefs that lies between outright *taqlīd*—the blind acceptance of authority—and outright *ijtihād*, where we are only satisfied once we have worked things out for ourselves. The challenge is well articulated by al-Ghazālī.

> Reason does not suffice without revelation nor does revelation suffice without reason. The one who would urge pure *taqlīd* and the total rejection of reason is in error and he who would make do with pure reason apart from the lights of the Quran and the Sunna is deluded.[2]

And as it turns out, he also articulates a compelling answer to our question. This comes in al-Ghazālī's aforementioned intellectual autobiography, *Deliverer from Error*,[3] the context of a discussion about accepting the genuineness of Muḥammad's prophecy. Al-Ghazālī writes:

> If you are in doubt about whether a certain person is a prophet or not, certainty can be had only through knowledge of what he is like (*bi-ma ʿrifa aḥwālihi*), either by personal observation or reports and testimony. If you have an understanding of medicine and jurisprudence, you can recognize jurists and doctors by observing what they are like, and listening to what they had to say, even if you haven't observed them. So you have no difficulty recognizing that al-Shāfiʿī was a jurist or Galen a doctor, this being knowledge of what is in fact the case (*ma ʿrifa bi-l-ḥaqīqa*) and not a matter of *taqlīd* shown to another person. Rather, since you know something of jurisprudence and medicine, and you have perused their books and treatises, you have arrived at necessary knowledge about what they are like. Likewise, once you grasp the meaning of prophecy and then investigate the Quran and [*ḥadīth*] reports extensively, you arrive at necessary knowledge that [Muḥammad] is at the highest degree of prophecy.[4]

Here, while encouraging us to rise above *taqlīd*, al-Ghazālī sets the epistemic bar lower than independent *ijtihād*. Rather than telling us to work everything out for ourselves, he instructs us to reach a level of understanding that will allow us to judge whether or not someone counts as an authority worth following.

Though the context concerns prophecy, his examples show that this is a generalizable policy. For example, if you are trying to do medicine, you should acquaint yourself enough with this field that you can affirm Galen's status as an expert doctor. But you don't have to be at Galen's level yourself. You just have to put yourself in a position where you are accepting Galen's teachings on justified grounds. Just a couple of pages later, al-Ghazālī says that we often do not understand the function of medicines for the body and religious prescriptions for the soul (or "heart"). In such cases we must simply follow the recommendations of doctors and prophets; and here he even uses the word *taqlīd* for our obedience to those recommendations.[5]

So we might call this "justified *taqlīd*." It is a kind of epistemic bootstrapping, in which we submit to an authority in some domain but only after understanding the domain well enough to satisfy ourselves that these authority figures have genuine expertise. We should seek independent knowledge that the authority is indeed authoritative, but we do not need to have the same kind of independent knowledge possessed by the authoritative figure. This has an analogue in the realm of Islamic law, as discussed in chapter 1: instead of exerting *ijtihād* by solving each case through independent effort, one might exert *ijtihād* by choosing which legal school to follow. This would not count as full-blown *taqlīd* because going on to do one's jurisprudence "within a school" would itself flow from a well-considered, independent choice.[6]

We are again dealing here with second-order beliefs, that is, belief about other beliefs. In particular, we are trying to decide whether the beliefs expressed by a putative authority rise to the level of knowledge. If so, then by engaging in justified *taqlīd* and taking their beliefs as our own, we will be ensured against error. This would shield us from the problem of epistemic luck. If we have good methods for testing the putative authority, then even without independently derived knowledge we can still be sure that we are avoiding error. Of course, there would be much more to say about how to identify an authority. Al-Ghazālī seems to place most weight on the integrity and character of the candidate prophet, jurist, or doctor: "what he is like." He cites several statements of Muḥammad concerning moral and spiritual affairs, which show him to be reliable in these domains. He considers, but rejects, the idea that prophecy is proven through miracles. His reason for this is that miracles could be tests sent by God or simple fakes, like magic tricks.

Al-Ghazālī also gives us an example in which, according to him, *taqlīd* has gone wrong. He attacks those who follow a supposedly infallible *imām* who is authoritative in interpreting the Islamic revelation. These are Shīʿite Muslims, more specifically, Ismāʿīlīs, who on al-Ghazālī's telling reject all use of *ijtihād* in favor of total submission to the teachings of their *imām*. He has good fun mocking this position, adapting an example we saw earlier by asking what the Ismāʿīlī will do if it is time to pray and does not know which way Mecca lies. Should he travel to the city where his *imām* resides, to ask? No, clearly he should work out the answer for himself before the time of prayer is past. Such examples license the use of *ijtihād* in religious matters. The most important such use, as we just saw, is the identification of which prophet or prophets to follow. This is rather ironic, by the way, because we can find Shīʿite thinkers recommending a policy of justified *taqlīd* too. They argued that a fair assessment shows their *imāms* to be the guides we need. Al-Dawwānī's rejection of *taqlīd* quoted above in chapter 1 came precisely in the context of defense of the Shīʿite view on the *imām*.

As this shows, there were significant disputes within medieval Islam over the nature of authority, and over the question of which authorities should be followed. But a more obvious context for raising that issue was the rivalry between the Abrahamic religious faiths. Al-Dawwānī warned that *taqlīd* could justify the Christian in being Christian and the Jew in being a Jew, just as much as it would justify a Muslim in accepting Islam. This is a classic case of "epistemic luck," where the Muslim's true beliefs would result simply from the happenstance of having Muslim parents. Al-Ghazālī had a similar concern, as we can see from a passage early on in his autobiography where he cites a famous saying of the Prophet Muḥammad.

> Thirst for grasping the true natures of things was a habit and practice of mine from early on in my life, an inborn and innate tendency (*gharīza wa-fiṭra*) given by God in my very nature, not chosen or contrived. So as I neared maturity the bonds of *taqlīd* weakened for me and I was emancipated from inherited beliefs. For I saw that young Christians always grew up to accept Christianity and young Jews to accept Judaism, while young Muslims always grew up to accept Islam. And I heard the *ḥadīth* related of the prophet, "every child is born in the innate condition (*fiṭra*) but his parents make him a Jew, Christian, or Magian."[7]

Here we can see that the problem of *taqlīd* and epistemic luck relates intimately to the problem of religious pluralism. In the medieval period no less than today, there was vivid awareness of other faiths, and the challenge was to explain why one's own faith had the best claim to truth.

This brings us to the aforementioned texts that dramatize the choice of faiths in dialogue form. I'll look at four authors: the Jewish philosophers Judah Hallevi (d. 1141) and Shem Ṭov ben Joseph Falaquera (d. ca. 1295) and the Christian philosophers Peter Abelard (d. 1142) and Ramon Llull (d. 1316). The first of these figures, Hallevi, lived in Islamic Spain but died in the Holy Land. He is the author of the *Kuzari*,[8] based (very) loosely on the historical events that took place in the Caucacus in the eighth century, when a group called the Khazars converted to Judaism. In Hallevi's imaginary reconstruction, the king of the Khazars has a dream in which he is told that his beliefs are pleasing to God, but his actions are not. In an effort to discover where his error lies, the king interrogates a philosopher (*faylasūf*), a Christian, and a Muslim to see which of them can persuade him of their doctrines. Dissatisfied by all three, he turns in desperation to the Jews, whom he previously dismissed because of their low social standing. This last interlocutor persuades him to convert to Judaism. The king appoints the Jewish spokesman as his mentor and the two engage in a wide-ranging dialogue about various philosophical and religious issues, which takes up the bulk of the text.

The rather artificial setting of the dialogue allows Hallevi to explore the question raised by al-Ghazālī, which is likely no coincidence given that Hallevi was apparently familiar with his works.[9] The king is in precisely the situation envisioned by al-Ghazālī: he seeks to test three prophetic, revelatory traditions and decide which one should claim his allegiance. Hallevi's dialogue thus provides us with an implicit account of the grounds on which the choice of faiths may, and (given the happy outcome) presumably should, be made. As mentioned before, philosophy is here treated almost as a fourth religion, an alternative to the Abrahamic faiths rather than a handmaid of theology. For Hallevi, the word *falsafa* (philosophy) does not have quite the meaning we would anticipate but is tied to a very specific set of doctrines, namely, those of Avicenna. This is typical of post-Avicennan philosophy, as shown by the apparently generic title al-Ghazālī chose for his attack on Avicenna: *The Incoherence of the Philosophers.* Averroes's response to al-Ghazālī was an attempt to reassert Aristotelianism, instead of Avicennism, as definitive of "philosophy" in Islamic culture. But this attempt fell on deaf ears and from the twelfth century on, the word *falsafa* and even the word "Peripatetic" were generally synonymous with Avicenna's teachings.

So Hallevi has his "philosopher" present his teachings to the king, with a heavy emphasis on precisely those ideas of Avicenna that had been attacked in al-Ghazālī's *Incoherence*, like the eternity of the world and the impossibility of God's knowing particulars. The king is unimpressed, in part because the philosopher explicitly says that his doctrines have merely to do with intellectual convictions, not concrete practice. (This is one philosopher who is not interested in an "applied" version of his discipline.) Since the king's dream reassured him that his beliefs were acceptable, but his practices were displeasing to God, the king quickly concludes that philosophy is not the system of thought he is looking for. He turns to the Christian and rejects his religion as well: "There is no scope for rational argument (*qiyās*) here, in fact rational argument deems what has been said to be absurd. . . . I cannot bring myself to accept these things, having them sprung on me without having grown up with them."[10] This is an interesting rationale for not becoming a Christian. It's not surprising to see a Jewish author suggest that Christianity flies in the face of reason by asserting the incarnation of God and the Trinity. Yet Hallevi has the king imply that had he been raised believing these apparent absurdities, he might have an easier time believing them. As al-Ghazālī said, young Christians grow up to accept Christianity, even though this religion diverges from our natural, inborn conceptions (our *fiṭra*).

The king's rejection of Islam is similar but even less hostile. He explains that since the Quran is in Arabic, a language he does not speak, he cannot really judge it as a miraculous, revelatory text. Here Hallevi alludes to the doctrine of *i ʿjāz*, which states that the Quran is "inimitable" by humankind and thus must have a divine source. Muslims had by this time adopted the doctrine that the Quran was Muḥammad's sole miracle, one amply sufficient to prove that he was a genuine prophet. Since the king is not in a position to evaluate this particular supposed miracle, he thus has no reason to adopt Islam for himself. Note that, unlike al-Ghazālī, the king would be willing to accept miracles as proof of prophecy. But he says that, to be really persuaded, he would want to see a different kind of miracle: one that overturns the normal course of natural events and is securely confirmed by a large number of witnesses.[11]

This, according to Hallevi, is what Judaism alone can offer. The miracles recorded in the Hebrew Bible, such as those that accompanied the flight from Egypt, were witnessed by many people and have been transmitted across many centuries with an astonishing degree of unanimity.[12] And these miracles did violate the usual laws of nature, which turns out to mean God's customary actions in the world.[13] Not that Hallevi is an occasionalist. He thinks that there are natural causes to which we can appeal to explain some phenomena. For instance, fire heats, and water cools. But such brute natural forces have no wisdom and are thus insufficient to explain the providential ordering of the universe.[14] Even such routine events as the generation of an animal require God's guidance, using brute physical causes as "instruments" in a way that lies beyond our full understanding.

> Natural, generated things are all determined, balanced and proportioned in their mixtures from the four natures, and by the slightest adjustment they become perfect and well-shaped, and take on the animal or plant form to which they lay claim. Yet the slightest thing can corrupt the mixture of the form that shapes it. Haven't you seen an egg being corrupted by the least accident of excessive heat, cold, or movement, so that it fails to receive the form of a chicken? . . . So to whom is it given to determine the actions as far as the divine produces them, other than God alone?[15]

When a miracle occurs, this is not merely God working his will in the world but God working his will in an *unusual* fashion.

> Nature speaks through custom, the Law through the breach of custom. The two may be reconciled: those customs that are breached were only natural [in the first place] because they were within the eternal will, conditional upon it and instituted according to it, since the six days of creation.[16]

It is on such divinely willed "breaches of custom" that belief in Judaism should rest. But this is not quite where the epistemic buck stops, because, as we saw, the miracles themselves are proven by extensive and reliable testimony. So the king's conversion, and more generally the case for choosing Judaism over its rivals, in fact comes down fundamentally to that testimony, which in chronological age and number of witnesses trumps anything that philosophers, Christians, or Muslims can say in favor of their own belief systems.[17]

Is this *taqlīd*? Perhaps Hallevi would admit that it is, given that at one point he mentions that Aristotle's errors can be explained by his being left to his own devices, without any reliable tradition he might "trust through *taqlīd*."[18] But Hallevi would want to insist that the Jew believes by what I have called justified *taqlīd*. We are to believe in the miracles of the Hebrew Bible not simply because we were born into Jewish families, say, but because we recognize that the evidence for those miracles is overwhelming. Some medieval Jewish thinkers gave still greater scope to reason in arguing for their faith. None more than Falaquera. His dialogue *The Epistle of the Debate* features fewer characters than Hallevi's *Kuzari*, pitting a rationalist against a traditionalist Jewish scholar. Whereas the other dialogues under discussion here feature a philosopher who is outside the Abrahamic faiths, in this one the spokesman for reason is a convinced Jew. His goal in the debate is to persuade his coreligionist scholar, who is deeply suspicious of philosophy, that rational argumentation is compatible with Judaism and indeed provides its firmest support.

Just as it is more convincing to see something with your own eyes than to have it reported by a witness, so religious belief will be firmer when grounded in rational argument than in *taqlīd*. Thus Falaquera's philosopher promises his interlocutor, "Your faith will be stronger if you attain it through your intellect than it is [when you attain it] through tradition."[19] In fact even biblical patriarchs like Abraham must have grasped God through "demonstrative proofs." This is simply obvious, since it is the only way they could have had genuine knowledge.[20] Anyone who fails to engage in rational justification of the faith is in the same position as a "child" or "ignoramus," who simply affirms Jewish belief without having any real conception of it in their souls. For this reason the philosopher says to the traditionalist, "You are imperfect in this faith of yours; the way by which its truth and its reason may be made manifest to you is science."[21] The traditionalist's failure to rise above *taqlīd* is shown even in his rejection of philosophy, since as he admits he has not studied philosophical books and opposes them merely on hearsay.

None of which is to say that *every* Jew should be aiming at "perfection" in the faith. The rationalist admits that "demonstrative instruction is only suitable for the few, for the scholars perfect in their opinions, and not for the multitude of people whose conception is not intellectual but rather by way of the imagination."[22] Falaquera's elitist rejection of *taqlīd* for the scholarly class, the relegation of other believers to the level of non-intellectual belief, and the daring claim that philosophical reasoning provides the basis for interpretating revelation may all remind us of Averroes, whose *Decisive Treatise* made parallel claims about the role of philosophy in Islam. There's a good reason for this resonance, which is that Falaquera knew Averroes's works and was powerfully influenced by them.

But he qualifies his Averroist rationalism by having his spokesman emphasize that Aristotelian philosophy is to be used selectively. As he puts it, we take the fruit and throw away the peel.[23] This allows Falaquera to criticize the "philosophers" more openly than Averroes would have done, for instance, because they wrongly denied the possibility of miracles and the temporal creation of the world. There are also practical requirements placed upon Jews that go beyond the demands of philosophy: while philosophers would endorse the Ten Commandments, they say nothing about observing the Sabbath. Though Falaquera does not dwell at length on the incompleteness of philosophy, this is a significant admission. It recalls Hallevi's much more emphatic discussion of the supra-rational aspects of Jewish law, "supra-rational" simply in the sense that religion lays obligations upon us that reason would not. This was important for the king in the *Kuzari*, who wanted to know why his actions were not pleasing to God. Without converting to Judaism he would never have adopted the rituals, dietary laws, and so on demanded by God.

Now, Hallevi believes that these prescriptions are *in harmony* with reason. In fact, at one point he has the Jewish scholar character insist that all his teachings are in accordance with reason.[24] But this does not mean the legal prescriptions are *derivable* from reason. It actually lies beyond human capacity to determine all the norms that should govern our lives, at least as perfectly as the divine law has done. For example, we might realize that we occasionally need to rest from our labors, but it is only divine will that lays down the Sabbath as the ideal form of rest.[25] The obligations placed on Jews by the law are much like God's customary, non-miraculous interventions within nature. In both cases God fine-tunes what is natural so as to ensure the realization of his providential order.

We might wonder whether something similar happens on the epistemic front. Are there true *beliefs* that reason cannot supply, the way it cannot supply an account of our practical *obligations*? Falaquera for one seems to think not, and in that respect he is a faithful follower of Averroes. But this was by no means a universally, or even widely, held view in medieval Jewish thought.[26] One might think here of Ḥasdai Crescas (d. 1410). In his *Light of the Lord* (*Or Hashem*) he took exception to the attempt of his illustrious predecessor, Maimonides, to identify "principles" of the faith that all Jews should accept. For Maimonides, the most fundamental of these principles, which were thirteen in number, could be established by philosophical argument. These included the claims that God exists, is one, and has no body. But Crescas found weaknesses in the proofs given for these claims. His student Joseph Albo (d. 1444) tended to agree. Of these three propositions he thought that only the first, God's existence, can be rationally demonstrated. For Albo, Maimonides's project of founding Judaism in rationally provable truths was in any case misconceived. In a fideist version of the bootstrapping strategy, he suggested that there are three roots (*ʿiqqarim*) of Judaism, the existence of God, the revelation of the Torah, and recompense in the afterlife. Once these are accepted by faith, all other religious convictions would follow like corollaries from fundamental theorems.

We might expect medieval Christians to be more tempted by this kind of approach and less tempted by the sort of rationalist project found in Averroes, Falaquera, and Maimonides. All Christians in this period were, after all, committed to at least some doctrines that seem obviously insusceptible to rational proof: that God was incarnated as Christ; that God is a Trinity; that bread becomes Christ's flesh in the sacrament of the Eucharist. Indeed, in an application of the Augustinian formula that the Christian should "believe in order to understand," many Christian intellectuals thought that reason's role in theology was to defend, understand, and build upon doctrines we accept by faith. The most famous example here would of course be Thomas Aquinas (d. 1274), for whom theology as a science is distinguished by its use of certain "principles" that are believed by faith, not demonstrated by reason, as Maimonides wanted. In fact these principles *cannot* be demonstrated by reason, though reason could show that the teachings definitive of Christianity involve no absurdity and then build a rational science of theology using them as a foundation.

This fusion of reason and faith struck many Christian intellectuals as giving too large a role to reason. A good example is provided by a controversy that dominated late Byzantine philosophy.[27] In the fourteenth century the works of Aquinas and other schoolmen were read by Greek scholars and translated into Greek, which helped provoke a series of attacks on Latin scholasticism. In fact, Greek Orthodox intellectuals would for many centuries (well after the fall of Constantinople) be driven by attempts to distance themselves from Latin theology. One of the first such attacks came in 1335, when Barlaam of Calabria (d. 1348) complained of how Western theologians were using syllogistic arguments to talk about God's nature. This is impossible, because Aristotelian demonstrations should provide certain knowledge, and humans cannot have certainty about God. When Barlaam was attacked for this stance by his more famous contemporary, Gregory Palamas (d. 1359), it was not because Palamas thought we can construct theology on the model of an Aristotelian science, as Aquinas had done. He simply wanted to insist that we do have certainty about God but through faith, not reason.

All of this may seem to suggest that the bootstrapping strategy of justified *taqlīd* would be unavailable to Christians. Rather than use reason to establish the reliability of Christian authority, you are supposed simply to submit to authoritative sources first, and only then try to understand what these sources have said. Yet there were exceptions, Christian thinkers who wanted to push the boundaries of what reason could do by way of establishing the faith. One of them was the twelfth-century logician and theologian Peter Abelard (d. 1142). His suspicion of unvarnished appeals to authority arguably motivated his work *Sic et Non*, which cites authoritative texts on both sides of many theological issues, without indicating how the dilemmas should be resolved. There is a nice story about him that makes the point more explicitly. Abelard's rival Alberic of Rheims challenged him to defend one of his more daring views, with the stipulation that he should only cite authorities and not give arguments. When Abelard was able to quote Augustine in support of his position, Alberic said that the Augustine quote needed to be interpreted differently, at which point Abelard said, "That's irrelevant, because you are only looking only for words, not interpretation."[28]

Abelard's high hopes for natural reason were displayed in his comments on the subject of the Trinity. Already before him, scholars associated with the so-called school of Chartres had cautiously suggested that the third of the trinitarian Persons, the Holy Spirit, might have been anticipated by Plato under the guise of the "world soul" described in the dialogue *Timaeus*. This proposal is especially associated with William of Conches (d. after 1154), who wrote in his glosses on the *Timaeus*:

> God wanted to make the world an intelligent animal, but nothing can be intelligent without soul, so he excogitated the soul (*ergo excogitavit animam*). [Plato] did well to say "excogitated" and not "created," insofar as the soul is said to be the Holy Spirit. For the Holy Spirit is not made, created, or generated by God, but it proceeds.[29]

This suggests that William was convinced that Plato had to some extent anticipated the doctrine of the Trinity, using nothing but his natural gifts—even though William says in the same set of glosses that he is willing neither to affirm nor to deny the equivalence of world soul and Holy Spirit.[30]

Abelard took a new approach to the question, by asserting that the doctrine of the world soul is obviously absurd if taken at face value. If the whole universe had a soul, then each of us would be infused with that soul in addition to our own souls, so we would all have two souls. This is just silly, and certainly not the sort of thing we should ascribe to Plato. So, says Abelard, we should take the talk of the "world soul" in Plato to be a veiled or allegorical way of referring to the Holy Spirit.

> What the philosophers said about the World-Soul should be accepted as figurative expression. Otherwise we would have to deplore Plato as not the greatest philosopher but the greatest fool. For what is more absurd than judging the whole world to be a rational animal, unless that is it was put forward as a figurative expression?[31]

This is just one example of Abelard's idea that the pagan philosophers often anticipated the truths of Christianity, something they could manage given their intellectual gifts and also their virtuous and ascetic way of living. The implications of this view for my central question are clear. If the pagans were able at least dimly to perceive such doctrines as the Trinity using reason, then reason gets us pretty far toward ratifying Christianity as the belief system most worthy of our adherence.

A text that explores this idea more fully and explicitly is Abelard's *Dialogue Between a Philosopher, a Jew, and a Christian.*[32] As the title already indicates, this work is comparable to those of Falaquera and, especially, Hallevi. The frame of the dialogue is rather different though. It starts with a rather desultory indication that the work belongs in the grand tradition of medieval dream narratives, which takes inspiration from ancient texts like Macrobius's commentary on Cicero's *Dream of Scipio* and includes more famous and literary examples, like the *Romance of the Rose* and *Piers Plowman.* In Abelard's dream, he is appointed as the judge of a debate between the three main characters, on account of his "preeminence in mental keenness and knowledge of all the Scriptures." Even while asleep, Abelard was rather pleased with himself.

A central theme of this work is what Abelard would, had he spoken Arabic, have called *taqlīd.* What is definitive of the character of the "philosopher" here is not, as in Hallevi, any particular body of doctrines but a method. He has no commitment to any revelatory text and simply follows reason wherever it leads. He says that his role is "to investigate the truth by means of reasons (*rationibus*), and in all things to follow not people's opinion but reason's lead," and later challenges the Christian and Jew to say whether their religious beliefs are based on reason or involve "following mere human opinion and the love of your own kind of people (*an solam hic hominum opinionem ac generis vestri sectemini amorem*)."[33] The implicit charge is of course one we've seen explicitly in texts from the Islamic world: in the latter case, religious belief would be a matter of epistemic luck. And indeed Abelard's "philosopher" immediately goes on to give a variant of the worry about simply following the religion of one's family: in mixed marriages, the child often adopts the belief system of their *favorite* parent.

But the Jew and Christian deny the charge of *taqlīd.* For the Jewish character, it is fine for children to follow their parents' lead in matters of religion, but upon maturity they should think for themselves, for "it is not as fitting to follow opinion as it is to search out the truth."[34] Similarly the Christian accepts that "no discerning person forbids investigating and discussing our faith by means of reason" and agrees with the philosopher that rational argument carries more weight than the citing of authorities.[35] But the most interesting remark about the relation between reason and authority is given to the character of the philosopher:

> If all people used the same authorities, there wouldn't be so many different religious faiths. But just as everyone deliberates with his own reason, individuals pick the authorities they follow. . . . Those who wrote only on the basis of reason, whose views are seen to abound with it, have *earned* their authority, their being worth believing. But even in their judgment, reason is put *before* authority. . . . Authority is regarded as having last place, or none at all, in every philosophical disputation.[36]

Note especially the philosopher's endorsement of justified *taqlīd*. When we follow the authority of, say, Aristotle we have a good reason for doing so, namely, that Aristotle himself showed good use of reason. His skill in argumentation establishes his credentials as someone whose views are worth at least taking seriously, and perhaps taking over for ourselves.

But Abelard's philosopher character and apparently Abelard himself think that it is better to think for oneself. As shown by that anecdote in which he embarrassed Alberic, it is never appropriate to try to settle a dispute simply by citing some authoritative witness, at least not if one belongs to the intellectual elite as do Abelard and the three characters in his *Dialogue*. Unfortunately, this work ends abruptly in the midst of the debate without any judgment being passed down. So, though we can take it for granted that Abelard would have gone on to declare the Christian the victor, we don't know for sure on which grounds he would have done so. Incomplete though it is, the *Dialogue* is clear regarding the weaknesses of the Jew's position. It is not a rabidly anti-Semitic text by medieval standards, as the Jew is allowed to defend his faith at length and with considerable sophistication, but both the philosopher and the Christian criticize Judaism for its supposed concern with bodily instead of spiritual goods. More relevantly for our purposes, one of the Jew's main arguments for his religion is that we may expect God to hand down a law to humankind, and the Jewish law is the best candidate because of its antiquity and high standing according to general human opinion (*ex vetustate et communi hominum opinione nacta est auctoritatem*).[37] Given how similar this is to the rationale Hallevi would later offer in support of Judaism, this is hardly unfair on Abelard's part. But when the Jew appeals to "authority" and common "opinion" we are no doubt meant to realize that this is a weak basis for belief, as Abelard has made clear elsewhere in the dialogue.

More difficult is the choice between philosophy and Christianity. The character of the philosopher openly admires the Christian spokesman for his philosophical acuity,[38] and the Christian is able to persuade him on a number of points, especially concerning the nature of the afterlife. But since this philosopher believes in the afterlife anyway and is a monotheist, the doctrinal difference between the two is not large. In the text as we have it, there is also no exploration of such distinctive Christian ideas as the Trinity or Incarnation. It is emphasized that the Greeks, that most rational of peoples, converted to Christianity on rational grounds. Yet when the philosopher explains why he himself has not converted, his explanation suggests that for Abelard, reason alone does not suffice to establish the truth of the Christian faith.

> We don't yield to their authority in the sense of not discussing their statements rationally before we approve them. Otherwise we would be ceasing to do philosophy, if while disregarding the investigation of reasons we mainly used topics from authority (*si videlicet rationum inquisitione postposita, locis auctoritatis . . . plurimum uteremur*).[39]

One issue here may be that, like Hallevi and Falaquera, Abelard recognizes the gap between rational and religious obligations. He has the philosopher say to the Christian that many biblical commands are in agreement with natural reason, while others impose an additional obligation chosen by God.

> [The Bible] hands down certain natural commandments (*naturalia praecepta*) you call moral, such as loving God and one's neighbor, not committing adultery, not stealing, and not committing murder. But others belong so to speak to positive justice. They are adapted to certain people for a time. For example, circumcision for the Jews, baptism for you.[40]

So perhaps Abelard, despite his rationalism, is after all more comparable to Hallevi than to Falaquera or Averroes. He clearly thinks that reason supports Christianity and would never conflict with it, but there are more truths about life in heaven and on earth than are dreamt of in the philosophy of the pure rationalist.

That would have been a great line to end this chapter, but unfortunately I have one last work to discuss. Well, actually it isn't all that unfortunate, because the author of this work is the endlessly fascinating and idiosyncratic Ramon Llull. Apparently in response to the multireligious culture of his native Majorca, he devised a new way of doing philosophy—his famous "Art"—that he thought would replace scholastic methods, convert Muslims and Jews to Christianity, and establish lasting peace across the world. These ambitions were, to put it mildly, not fully realized. But what he could not achieve in the world, he could bring about in a fictional setting, namely, that of his *Book of the Gentile and Three Wise Men*, written in Catalan and already translated into Latin, French, and Spanish in the Middle Ages.[41] We have a now familiar cast of characters, as the "gentile" is a trained philosopher, shown in discussion with a Jew, a Muslim, and a Christian. The dialogue unfolds with extravagant courtesy as each spokesman shows respect for the others and presents his case for his own religion.

The opening sentence of this work states Llull's motive in writing it, which is that "unbelievers," that is, non-Christians, should be brought to salvation. Yet as apologetic texts go, this one is remarkably restrained. There is not only the polite tone of proceedings but also a kind of twist ending: the three "wise men" representing the Abrahamic faiths tell the gentile they would rather not hear his judgment as to who has made the best argument, because they prefer that "each be free to choose his own religion."[42] As a result the message that comes across most strongly is that it would be good if everyone could agree on some one religion, as this would promote peace. One of the wise men—tellingly, Llull does not say which—explicitly outlines the project that arguably lies behind all the dialogues I have been discussing.

> Think of the harm that comes from men not belonging to a single sect, and of the good that would come from everyone being beneath one faith and one religion. . . . Since we cannot agree by means of authorities, let us try to come to some agreement by means of demonstrative and necessary reasons.[43]

As in the other texts, rational demonstration is presented as the means to escape *taqlīd*, the mere appeal to authority that can never resolve interreligious dispute. One passage identifies a problem we have seen several times already, that believers usually adhere blindly to the faith into which they were born.

> Men are so rooted in the faith in which they found themselves and in which they were raised by their parents and ancestors, that it is impossible to make them break away by preaching, by disputation, or by any other means man could devise.[44]

Llull's philosophical method is the instrument by which the deadlock will be resolved.

Again, he is remarkably evenhanded in the way that this instrument is used. All three spokesmen are experts in the Llullian "Art" and are in substantive agreement on core religious doctrines. They affirm the existence of an afterlife and the existence of a single God, ideas that are completely new to the gentile (which is a stark contrast to the theistic "philosophers" in Hallevi and Abelard). In fact, when it is the Christian's turn to speak, he does not even bother trying to establish monotheism, because the Jewish spokesman has already proven this adequately. Still, it is clear where Llull's own sympathies lie. He has the Jew admit the same supposed weakness in his faith already identified by Abelard, namely, that Judaism is overly concerned with this world and not the next.[45] The cross-examination of the Muslim is also more severe than that directed at the other two spokesmen.

Yet Llull has all three Abrahamic characters embrace and pursue his own ambitious program of grounding faith in reason. As Anthony Bonner has pointed out, Llull wanted to recast biblical prophecy as a systematic philosophy. Whatever one believes by true faith must also be demonstrable by reason.[46] The need for this project is nicely illustrated by a story Llull tells elsewhere, in which a Muslim king is shown by a Christian missionary that Islam is false. When the missionary is unable to follow this up by arguing convincingly for his own religion, and says that it should be accepted by faith instead, the king blames the missionary for leaving him with no religious convictions at all: "You disproved the faith that I had (*legem quam habebam*), but then cannot prove yours to me with rational argument (*cum rationibus*)."[47] In keeping with this, each spokesman in the *Book of the Gentile* begins by setting out a list of principles distinctive of the relevant religion and then works through the list to show that each principle can be proven. Actually there are two remarkably rationalist assumptions here: that a given religion is defined by its doctrinal commitments (and not, say, its ritual practices) and that the commitments of the one true creed can be proven in a way convincing to any fair-minded judge.

Which is not to say that the proofs will be easy. The Christian spokesman warns the gentile:

> The articles of our faith are so sublime and so difficult to believe and understand that you will not be able to comprehend them unless you apply all the strength of your mind and soul to understanding the arguments by which I intend to prove the above-mentioned articles.[48]

But this is not an admission that we need to believe first in order to understand. To the contrary, the Christian emphasizes that if anyone rejects the proofs of his faith, it will be the fault of the skeptic and not the proofs themselves: such a skeptic "thinks that no proof has been given of something that is in fact quite provable."[49] And indeed the Christian goes on to present the Trinity, not—as Aquinas for instance would do—as something we believe by faith, and can explain and defend with reason, but as something that can be proven through pure philosophical argument, on the grounds that God is identical to His own infinite power, knowledge, and love.

Perhaps because Llull is so unsympathetic to Islam, he allows his Muslim spokesman a moment of weakness, in which he settles for something less convincing than demonstration and more like the bootstrapping strategy of al-Ghazālī. Like al-Ghazālī, the spokesman appeals to his Prophet's personal virtues. Muḥammad's "charity and justice" prove that he really was a messenger sent by God. The "gentile" character is not impressed. He observes that, since Christ too is greatly honored, the same argument can be used to confirm the truth of his claim to be the incarnated God.[50] Here Llull has put his finger on a potential weakness of the bootstrapping approach. If I verify that one authority is worthy of my credence, nothing excludes that another potential authority figure will turn up who seems equally reliable. One would then be in the position of, say, a patient who gets a second opinion and is forced to choose between two conflicting pieces of medical advice, without having medical knowledge of her own to guide that choice.[51] If she chooses the better advice it will just be a matter of epistemic luck, precisely what we were trying to avoid by engaging in justified *taqlīd.* The problem is encapsulated in a remark of William Blake's, who said that "the man, either painter or philosopher, who learns or acquires all he knows from others must be full of contradictions."[52]

On my view this is not a fatal weakness of the bootstrapping approach. All it shows is that this approach will, at best, get us to rationally justified *belief* and not *knowledge*, the more ambitious goal pursued by al-Ghazālī. Remember that he spoke of "necessary knowledge" that Muḥammad was a true prophet. The idea is apparently that if I *know* the Prophet's message is true, then whatever I believe by following him through *taqlīd* will itself become knowledge. This would be as if I knew that my doctor had unerring medical knowledge. I could then be confident that any conflicting second opinion would simply be wrong. In fact, though, mere justified *taqlīd* can never put us in such a strong epistemic position, because it is hard to see how I could know *for certain* that the authority has expert knowledge without having such knowledge myself.

But this doesn't mean that justified *taqlīd* is the wrong approach. There is a good reason that the uncompromising rationalism of figures like Averroes, Falaquera, Abelard, and Llull was not a mainstream view in the Middle Ages. The background assumption of their dialogues on choosing faith is that the choice must be an outcome of rational demonstration. They demand proof in place of authority. But that demand may itself be unreasonable. Sometimes we have to make do with authority and be satisfied with justified belief rather than knowledge. Our own limitations in talent and time may make it impossible for us to establish all the truths we need on our own. Or the truths we believe may not be susceptible of proof at all. That could be the case with something as recondite and mysterious as the doctrine of the Trinity or something as banal as past events we did not witness and can access only through the testimony of others. It's unrealistic always to insist on *ijtihād*, and often *taqlīd* will be the right approach. But when we resort to *taqlīd* we should do so in the way recommended by al-Ghazālī: still think for ourselves, by thinking about which authority is worth believing.

CHAPTER 4

Using the Pagans

Reason in Interreligious Debate

Here's an unusual reason to believe in Christianity: it uses a large number of languages. Its two Abrahamic rivals, Judaism and Islam, have scriptures in only one language, respectively, Hebrew and Arabic. And a single linguistic community could conceivably cooperate to fabricate a false religion. But how could the Christian Gospels, whose texts exist in numerous Semitic, European, and African languages, be the product of a conspiracy? This many tongues can't lie, at least not if they are all saying the same thing. Or so goes the argument of a Christian convert from Islam named Enbaqom (d. ca. 1561). It appears in his book *Anqaṣa Amin*, or *The Door of Faith*, which he wrote in 1540, decades after moving to Ethiopia and becoming a monk.[1] The treatise draws on Enbaqom's knowledge of his former faith, as he points to passages in the Quran that are contradictory or support Christian belief. And the argument about languages may also reflect Enbaqom's life experience. He produced translations from Arabic into the Ethiopic language Ge'ez. It might have been Enbaqom who translated his own *Door of Faith* from an original Arabic version in fact. And he also knew Coptic and Portuguese, as well as a bit of Latin and Armenian.

Enbaqom was, in short, a one-man representation of the linguistic and geographic diversity of premodern Christianity. Christian literature and intellectual endeavor existed in virtually every language of the Near East and in realms that fell under both Christian and Islamic political dominion. This is an important fact for the history of philosophy, in part because Near Eastern Christians were avid transmitters and consumers of pagan philosophy. It was they who mostly translated Aristotle and other Greek thinkers into Syriac and then Arabic, for one thing. Once we appreciate their contributions, we will give up on the simplistic idea that medieval philosophy was divided into religiously homogeneous geographic spaces. To the contrary, Christians, Jews, and Muslims lived side by side and debated one another, whether in Islamic lands like Iraq, Christian lands like Ethiopia, or places that changed hands, like Antioch.

Enbaqom makes the point about linguistic diversity concerning the books of the New Testament, but it also holds for philosophy. Consider a work like *The Life of Secundus*, which tells of how a philosopher takes a vow of silence after inadvertently driving his own mother to suicide and then writes down a list of wise sayings for a king.[2] It was originally written in Greek, but there were versions in Syriac, Latin, Armenian, Arabic, and, on the basis of the Arabic, Ge'ez, as well as various European vernacular languages. Or take a more familiar name from Greek philosophy, Aristotle. His works were translated into Latin and Arabic of course and commented on in both languages. But there were also translations and exegetical treatments of Aristotle in Syriac, Armenian, and Georgian. Wherever you could find Christians, there were intellectuals who wanted to learn about Aristotelian philosophy, especially his logic, often for the sake of using Aristotle in theological contexts.

This is the story I want to tell, at least partially, in this chapter: the way that pagan philosophy was pressed into the service of interreligious debate, especially between Christians and Muslims in the Near East. The texts I'll discuss are different in kind from those considered in chapter 3. We saw there how fictional narrative frames were used as a setting for rational consideration of the three Abrahamic faiths, with philosophy itself sometimes thrown in as an additional option. In theory at least, Hallevi, Falaquera, Abelard, and Llull were impartially judging the rival claims of all these belief systems. The works I'll consider now are much more polemical and, it must be said, for the most part less overtly philosophical. Yet they do employ the tools, or perhaps we should say "weapons," of pagan philosophy, especially Aristotelianism.

Exploring this phenomenon provides another perspective on the central theme of this book, medieval approaches to authority. It might, after all, seem rather strange to appeal to pagan authorities in the context of a controversy between Christianity and Islam. We might even suspect that originally pagan material was used in Abrahamic interreligious debates more or less unwittingly, simply because it had pervaded the intellectual culture of the times. When kids today learn about the Cartesian coordinate system in geometry class, they don't consciously think about Descartes as an authority figure. Likewise, at least the basics of Aristotelian logic were drummed into the young men, and very occasionally young women, of the medieval scholarly elite. This was an inheritance from the late antique teaching curriculum, which was passed on with some modifications to all three medieval cultures. Thus referring to, say, genera and species, or universals and particulars, in the context of a dispute over the Trinity needn't have involved any conscious invocation of Aristotle at all, never mind an appeal to his authority.

Still, there is plenty of evidence that Christian theologians thought carefully about the status of pagan ideas and explicitly sought to justify their use. In the Greek Christian tradition this is well illustrated by the Cappadocian fathers Basil of Caesarea (d. 379), Gregory of Nazianzus (d. ca. 390), and Gregory of Nyssa (d. ca. 395). In chapter 5 I touch on a dialogue written by the latter Gregory, in which he models a dialogue between himself and his sister Macrina on Plato's *Phaedo.* His brother Basil of Caesarea tackled the question of pagan wisdom even more directly in his influential work, *To the Youth on How to Make Use of Hellenic Literature.*[3] As the title intimates, it is aimed at those who were made to engage in the study of pagan works. Basil explains why Christian youngsters should be motivated to read such works carefully, using a series of famous analogies for this purpose. Pagan texts are like leaves sheltering the fruit of Christian wisdom; the young student is like an athlete in training preparing for the competition of living virtuously. And most famously, the Christian should imitate bees, taking a selective approach to the intellectual nectar to be found in pagan writings.

> It is exactly on the model of bees that we should partake of this literature (λόγοι). For they do not come to all the flowers indiscriminately (παραπλησίως), nor do they try to carry away whatever they happen upon, rather they take only what is servicable for their work, and leave the rest alone. So do we, if we are wise, gather for ourselves

> whatever is appropriate for us (οἰκεῖον ἡμῖν) and akin to the truth, passing over whatever is left.[4]

Basil thinks that the pagans are especially useful for orientation in ethical matters. He cites such paragons as Pythagoras and Socrates for their outstanding virtue. If we are on our guard, we can emulate these figures without being corrupted by false pagan teachings about the gods. This analogy would be repeated by another theologian who was himself a model for other Christians when it came to the use of pagan philosophy in defending and expounding religious belief: John of Damascus (d. 749).[5]

He is often considered a "Byzantine" figure, even though he in fact lived in cities that belonged to the Umayyad empire; as his name indicates he hailed originally from Damascus, and he lived in Palestine. It's in the prologue to his work *The Philosophical Chapters*, the first of three parts in his massive *Fountain of Knowledge*, that he compares himself to a bee. His role is simply to select and present useful texts by other authors for the edification of his readers. Often these other authors are among those he calls the "outside" philosophers, that is, those not of the Christian faith. While he does at times contrast these "outside" thinkers to church fathers, for the most part he is content to present his audience with their system of logic and views on such matters as the soul and its immortality. This prepares the way for the rest of the *Fountain of Knowledge*, which puts the pagan ideas to work while explaining the subtleties of "orthodox" belief concerning such matters as the Trinity and Incarnation. The final section of the treatise deals with various heresies. Its culminating chapter is an early example of Christian polemic against Islam, which is for John a "harbinger of the Antichrist."

In a kind of backhanded compliment to the Christians' use of philosophy, refutations of their faith written by Muslims and Jews also deploy terminology and concepts that can be traced to Aristotle, a case of, if you will, fighting Greek fire with Greek fire. We can find this already in Abū ʿĪsā al-Warrāq (d. 861), who worked around the middle of the ninth century, even as Greek philosophy was in the process of being translated into Arabic. Abū ʿĪsā's religious affiliations are actually rather unclear. He has been seen as everything from an early Shīʿite Muslim to a Manichean dualist, and his editor and translator, David Thomas, concludes that he was perhaps more an unaffiliated monotheist.[6] One thing that Abū ʿĪsā certainly was *not* is a Christian. He polemicizes in great detail against the doctrines of this religion, showing a solid understanding of the differences between the various Christian confessions and aiming separate refutations at the so-called Nestorians, Jacobites, and Melkites. The result is a kind of guidebook for refuting Christianity, which offers advice on how to respond to likely lines of defense and warns the reader about the tricks to which Christian opponents may resort.[7] Abū ʿĪsā is keen that his own refutation be seen to rise above such tactics. He emphasizes the methodical and complete nature of his own project, even as he accuses Christians of taking positions that defy reason (*ʿaql*) and employing verbal expressions that have no meaning (*lafẓ* without *maʿnā*).

A good example of Abū ʿĪsā's procedure is his attack on the Christian idea that the Persons of the Trinity are three "hypostases" in a single divine "substance."

> Why are His hypostases differentiated so that one is Father, the other Son, and the third Spirit, although the substance, according to you, is one in its substantiality, eternal and undifferentiated in itself, and not composed of various genera? If they claim that the hypostases are actually differentiated as individuals, say: why make them differentiated as individuals rather than making them agree as individuals, since according to you they agree in substantiality, and then there is no cause that differentiates between them?[8]

Note here the use of logical terminology, like "genera" (*ajnās*), which is typical of Abū ʿĪsā. He elsewhere asks whether the Persons are accidents (*aʿrāḍ*) and mocks the Christians for saying that the Persons are one in substance, genus, species, or attribute but not one in number.[9] Similarly, his attack on the Incarnation offers reflections on the problem of universals, as when he asks whether the divine nature united to the universal nature of humanity or only one individual and then draws out absurd consequences from both options.[10] All this terminology will be familiar to readers of Aristotle or even the introduction (*Isagoge*) that Porphyry wrote for Aristotelian logic, which by the way was another text that was translated and commented on in many languages of the Near East. There is even a surviving commentary in Armenian by the splendidly named David the Invincible (sixth century).[11]

But it is not only Abū ʿĪsā's pervasive use of philosophical language that is interesting; it is also the philosophical nature of the refutation itself. Consider again the argument about differentiation just cited. The point is that if there are three Persons that have something in common—here "substantiality" (*jawhariyya*)—there must also be some principle that differentiates them. This is just a theological application of the problem of individuation, which occupied the attention of so many subsequent medieval thinkers. And in fact Abū ʿĪsā's argument is startlingly similar to one mounted by the much later, and much more famous, Muslim philosopher Avicenna. In his metaphysical works, he argues that as a Necessary Existent, God must be absolutely "one." There cannot be more than one Necessary Existent, nor can a Necessary Existent have internal parts or differentiation. Why not? Because, as Abū ʿĪsā had already pointed out a few centuries earlier in this anti-Christian polemic, some *cause* would be needed to explain the distinction between the different instances or aspects of necessary existence. But it belongs to the very meaning of "necessarily existent" that such an existent has no cause.[12]

This example shows how permeable was the membrane between *falsafa* and *kalām*. Avicenna, the most important *faylasūf* of them all, was not above borrowing arguments and concepts from *kalām* sources (though presumably not directly from Abū ʿĪsā himself).[13] To which we might further add that Abū ʿĪsā was, in his own way, a rationalist. He thought that religious beliefs should be not merely internally consistent but also based on convincing evidence or argumentation. We can see this in a passage where he complains about the Christian belief that God was incarnated, and only once. How do we know it happened only that one time and will never happen again? This is something, he says, that the Christians accept only on the basis of "report (*khabar*)," not "proof (*ḥujja*)."[14]

If you wanted to name another text from around the time of Abū ʿĪsā that is reminiscent of his treatise against the Christians, you could do worse than to choose a far briefer work by his contemporary al-Kindī, the earliest of the *falāsifa*. He too wrote a refutation of the doctrine of the Trinity, which is only a page or two long. Actually there is a historical coincidence here, as well as coinciding concerns. The polemic of Abū ʿĪsā and this little work by al-Kindī are preserved today because of the Christian philosopher Yaḥyā Ibn ʿAdī (d. 974), who quoted both authors for the sake of refuting them.[15] But as a leading figure in the

Greek-Arabic translation movement, al-Kindī is unsurprisingly more explicit—and perhaps more conscious—than Abū ʿĪsā had been that Hellenic philosophy is the basis of his refutation. He refers by name to Aristotle's *Topics* and Porphyry's logical *Introduction.* His rationale for using the latter source, which comes at the end of his argument, is worth quoting in full.

> Those are among the things which refute the Christians' statement that the three are everlasting [Persons], even if the falsehood of this is clear in many [other] ways. We wished, however, to refute it by using [Porphyry's] *Introduction* because it is the book with which youths and students begin, in order that this [refutation] can be easily understood even by someone with very little theoretical skill and paltry learning. Moreover, this book we have used in our proof can be found in just about every one of their [the Christians'] homes. So perhaps this will increase their doubts and help them to awake them from their slumber.[16]

It would be hard to find a more direct confirmation of our sense that Aristotelian logical works were common intellectual property, a legacy that was passed on to both Christians and Muslims in the Near East. And note that al-Kindī also confirms the use of pagan writings in the training of young men. That, at least, has not changed since the time of Basil of Caesarea.

But what does he mean by saying that Porphyry's *Introduction* was his main tool in refuting the Trinity? Nothing very subtle. His argument simply goes through the five predicables recognized by Porphyry on the basis of Aristotle's *Topics*, namely, genera, species, specific differences, common accidents, and properties, as well as the notion of an "individual," and asks under which of these six headings the trinitarian Persons might fall. He rules out each possibility and concludes that there is no way to speak of divine Persons at all. Mirroring the reasoning of Abū ʿĪsā, al-Kindī's primary rationale is that if God were subject to a Porphyrian predicable, then he would be "composite," and then he would have some *cause* for his composition. For instance, the Persons cannot be "properties" while agreeing in being "substance" (again, the term is *jawhar*), for the following reason:

> By "Persons" they mean "individuals," and by "single substance" they mean that each one of them exists through a property of its own. Therefore the trait of substance (*ma ʿnā l-jawhar*) exists in each Person, and the Persons agree in this, and each one of them has an everlasting property through which it is differentiated from both of its companions [the other two Persons]. It is thereby necessary that each of them is composed from substance, which is common to [all of] them, and from its own property (*khāṣṣa*), which is proper to it [alone]. But everything composed is caused, and everything caused is not eternal. Therefore the Father is not eternal, nor is the Son eternal, nor is the Holy Spirit eternal.

But Ibn ʿAdī was himself no slouch when it comes to Aristotelian logic. He wrote numerous treatises on the subject (in fact, he was sometimes referred to by other authors as "the logician"). So he was able to rise to the defense of the trinitarian doctrine, affirming that the Persons are indeed "properties," in a sense. He denied that this would imply their being *accidents* of the divine substance. He also denied that the Persons enter into "composition" with the substance, or with one another, at least in the sense of undergoing a temporal *process* by which multiple things are brought together (*al-ḥādith min al-tarkīb*). There is indeed causation within the Trinity, since the Father begets the Son, and begetting is a kind of causation. But the causation in question is eternal and does not imply that the cause precedes the effect. This is nothing strange, since we are familiar with other examples in which the effect occurs simultaneously with the cause, like a light and the illumination it provides.

This response to al-Kindī was not the only time that Ibn ʿAdī used his philosophical training to expound Christian doctrine. He wrote several works on the Trinity and Incarnation, in which he makes moves like comparing the three divine Persons to the Aristotelian doctrine that God is the subject, object, and activity of his own intellectual thinking.[17] But Ibn ʿAdī's main strategy for explaining the Trinity is to identify the Persons with "attributes (*ṣifāt*)" or "traits (*ma ʿānī*)" that all belong to God, without rendering his essence (*māhiyya*) multiple.

> The Christians say that God is three insofar as he is benevolent, wise, and powerful. Thus there is in him the trait (*ma ʿnā*) of benevolence,

> the trait of wisdom, and the trait of power. Each of these traits is distinct from the others, and the statement indicating his quiddity is combined from these three traits, so that [one] substance is said to be generous, wise, and powerful.[18]

And in another treatise called *On Unity*:

> The attributes (*ṣifāt*) that exist in the Creator, great and exalted, as witnessed by his effects made manifest in the things he has created—and which [the created things] require to exist as they do, while not needing any others—are these three we have mentioned, namely benevolence, wisdom, and power.[19]

This sort of maneuver was already known to Abū ʿĪsā al-Warrāq, writing a few generations earlier. He presented an argument given by some Christians, which goes as follows. Things are divided into substances and accidents, and God must be a substance since this is better than being an accident. By similar reasoning God must be living, since this is better than not living, speaking, which is better than not speaking, and generating, which is better than not generating. Thus God is "a substance that is alive, speaking, and generating (*jawhar ḥayy nāṭiq wālid*), one in His substance and three through life, speech, and generation."[20]

Abū ʿĪsā raises various objections to the argument, among which is the problem that the same rationale could be used to establish that God is wise too, and also knowing. Why not say, then, that there are a fourth and fifth "property" (*khāṣṣa*), and hence Person, in this divine substance?[21] Not a bad point, especially when you consider the following two observations. First, in Latin Christendom and about two centuries later, Anselm of Canterbury (d. 1109) would be developing his famous "perfect being theology" in the *Proslogion*, by arguing that any number of attributes must belong to God if he is "that than which nothing greater can be conceived." The most famous part of this theology, his "ontological argument," is only the first application of the reasoning, in which God is said to have the perfection of existence, or necessary existence. But Anselm goes on to spin out a whole range of divine attributes, like goodness, power, and incorporeality, on the basis that the possession of these attributes is better than their lack. So this sort of argument doesn't seem a good way to establish three, and only three, Persons.

Second, it is rather embarrassing from the Christian point of view that when Yaḥyā Ibn ʿAdī later presented his own version of the doctrine, he selected a different selection of "attributes," namely, goodness, wisdom, and power, with one of these, "wisdom (*ḥikma*)," being Abū ʿĪsā's candidate for a fourth "Person." Doesn't this show that any putative list of attributes used to generate a Trinity is being selected ad hoc to yield the requisite number? To his credit, Yaḥyā Ibn ʿAdī was alive to the problem. Right after the passage cited above from his *On Unity*, he goes on to insist that the attributes are neither more than three nor fewer, since the *only* features of God we can derive on the basis of his having created the universe are the three named. His version of the case for the Trinity is arguably stronger than that of the Christian opponent presented by Abū ʿĪsā, because he does not derive the attributes simply from the idea of perfection. There are, after all, any number of attributes we might consider to make a thing more perfect, as we can see from Anselm's discussion. Rather we know about the divine attributes solely from observing God's effects. And the fact that God created a well-designed world licenses *only* the inferences that he is good, wise, and powerful.

A remarkably similar line of thought can be found in a contemporary of Ibn ʿAdī's, the Jewish philosopher Saadia Gaon. As we saw in chapter 2, his *Book of Doctrines and Beliefs* sets out an epistemology of what I called empirically based rational investigation. Using this approach, we can know God only indirectly, arriving at an understanding of his existence and nature only on the basis of his having created the universe. We can also avail ourselves of the additional resource of revelation. Turning to the Bible, we find the prophets informing us that God is "one, living, powerful, knowing, with nothing else like him."[22] This is confirmed by the deliverances of reason, as Saadia goes on to argue in detail. Particularly interesting is his explanation of the three attributes life, power, and knowledge.

> I say that I have found through inquiry (*min ṭarīq al-naẓar*) ways to show that God is living, powerful, and knowing. Namely, we found that he created things, and it is innately obvious to our reason that no one can make without being powerful, and no one is powerful

> without being alive. Nor can anything be made perfectly without someone knowing beforehand how the thing made should be. So we found by our reason that these traits evidently belong to our Maker, all at once (*wāḥidan*). For through what he made, it is established that he is living, powerful, and knowledge, as has been made clear, and reason is unable to arrive at any of these traits before the others. It arrives at them in one fell swoop (*duf'atan*).

In fact, Saadia goes on to explain, it is only the limitation of human language that compels us to speak of God as having three distinct features. Instead, we simply grasp him as a Creator and the three attributes in question are an attempt to express in words what this single idea means in our "reason" or "mind" (*'aql*).

Which brings us to the Christians. In the following chapter, Saadia provides what today's philosophers would call an error theory. That is, he explains how the Christians came falsely to believe that God is a Trinity. Not all Christians, mind you, for the "common run (*'awāmm*)" of these believers really just think of God as a body, so they are far from understanding that he is simple. The "select (*khawāṣṣ*)" among them, though, understand that God is incorporeal and ascribe to him the three traits just mentioned on exactly the same grounds Saadia has presented. This is their reason for saying that God is a Trinity. Note how Saadia here echoes the epistemic elitism of *falsafa* and *kalām*. One almost has the sense that Saadia feels a kind of solidarity with his more sophisticated colleagues among the Christian intellectual class, who share with him (and with contemporary Muslim theologians) the understanding that God is immaterial. But sophisticated or not, these Christians fail to grasp that the three "traits are a single attribute (*ṣifa*); it's just that language cannot put them into words all at once, as the mind can do in knowing."[23] The better Christians also failed to realize that, in ascribing three *distinct* traits to God, they wound up making him a composite substance, which commits them to the implication that God is a body after all, as supposed by the Christian masses.

And this, of course, is the nub of the dispute. If we think of the three divine Persons as representing different traits or attributes of God, is this multiplicity of attributes compatible with a single, incorporeal divine substance? Ibn 'Adī's position was that ascribing three "properties" to God would be unproblematic, precisely because threeness in *property* does not imply threeness in *essence* or *substance*. This looks like a paradigmatically Aristotelian logical distinction, so it is no surprise to see it turn up in the thought of an expert in Aristotelian logic like Ibn ʿAdī. But it appears in the works of other Near Eastern Christian authors too, who are not normally thought of as philosophers at all. We can see this by going back to the time of Abū ʿĪsā or even slightly earlier. The Jacobite Christian Abū Rāʾiṭa (d. ca. 835), from Takrit, wrote several works expounding Christian doctrine.[24]

God, says Abū Rāʾiṭa, is not one in genus or species, since if God were a genus he would have multiple species, and if he were a species he would have many individual members (which, by the way, is exactly the rationale used by al-Kindī to argue that the supposed Persons of the Christian Trinity cannot be genera or species). Instead, for Abū Rāʾiṭa, God has several "properties" but is one in substance (*jawhar*) while being transcendent as a "spiritual and incorporeal" (*rūḥānī ghayr jismānī*) entity.[25] The advantage of thinking about the Persons as "properties" is that two properties can belong to the same substance while being themselves distinct. Thus the Father can be distinct from the Son because begetting is not the same as being begotten, even though the Father and the Son share the same essence.[26] This, says Abū Rāʾiṭa, is like the way that two humans might also be the same in their essence, namely, humanity, even though one is the father of the other. A dangerous comparison, since he of course needs to avoid saying that the divine Persons are distinct in the way that two human individuals would be. The crucial difference is that human individuals are distinguished in time and place, whereas God has no before and after and no place because of his "spiritual" nature.[27]

As accounts of the Trinity go, this one is remarkably rationalist. The relation between the Persons can be understood adequately using the same kind of logical concepts we apply to created things. We just need to correct for God's being outside of time and space. One may suspect that the dialectical context, in which Abū Rāʾiṭa is living among Muslims and trying to justify his beliefs in a dispute with them, has pushed him to accept such a rationalist account. In partial confirmation of this suspicion, we may consider the following passage. Abū Rāʾiṭa imagines his Muslim opponents demanding that he admit the oneness of God and then responds:

> As for your claim that the proof (*ḥujja*) is in your hands, and that correctness and truth lies in what you say: insofar as we testify to you that God is one, along with all his other attributes, the people of truth must not refute what is correct, nor fight against it, whichever hand it may be in. . . . It is incumbent upon us to investigate this [the claim that God is a Trinity] thoroughly and consider it properly, not being led by partiality away from the open path. If what we have mentioned on the topic of the Trinity is true, let it be accepted. If things are otherwise, and our view is found to be false, then let the wind take it; no one is compelled to accept it.

Abū Rāʾiṭa here shows himself willing to accept the outcome of rational disputation between Christianity and Islam, confident of course that his faith will prevail so long as the issues are considered fairly.

Of course, one might take this to be a mere rhetorical posture. But rhetoric matters. Such appeals to proof and rationally acceptable argumentation provide a context for the use of originally pagan methods and concepts. As we saw most explicitly in al-Kindī and his use of Porphyry's *Introduction*, the canons of Aristotelian logic could provide a kind of neutral ground on which representatives of rival faiths might sort out their differences. The result was a polemical literature that featured genuine argumentation rather than mutual abuse. On the Christian side, this seems to be more true of interreligious disputations written within the Islamic world. Unsurprisingly, such works show better understanding of Islam and are also more polite about Muslims, compared to polemics written within the Byzantine empire.[28] Around the time that Abū ʿĪsā al-Warrāq and al-Kindī were refuting Christianity, Niketas of Byzantium (ninth century) wrote a refutation of Islam at the behest of the Byzantine emperor Michael III. In the words of the historian Hugh Goddard, this text presents the Prophet Muḥammad as "an impudent impostor," whose religion is "fundamentally idolatry. Despite the claim that it led the Arabs to worship God, in fact it led them to worship Satan; its so-called revelation comes from the Devil, and those who hear it are led to worship the Devil."[29]

Philosophers in Byzantium found it sufficient to aim invective, rather than rational arguments, against Islam. The Aristotelian commentator Eustratius (d. ca. 1120) paused while commenting on the sixth book of the *Nicomachean Ethics* to rail against Islam.[30] This digression was brought on by Aristotle's mention of the soul's faculties, each of which may develop good dispositions leading to virtuous action. Eustratius takes this chance to rail against the Prophet for his licentiousness and adultery. Muḥammad, he claims, lived a life dominated by the pleasures of sensation and imagination, "and therefore is far from God. Therefore, how can someone who is far from Him and is the cause of such a deception for his followers be a prophet sent by God?"[31] As Michele Trizio has shown in a paper on this digression, the reduction of Islam's meaning to sexual depravity and enthrallment to lower, "irrational" desires carries on the sort of polemic used by Niketas of Byzantium. Niketas likewise presented the contrast between Islam and Christianity in moral terms: "Our faith promises the opposite of yours: the latter promises intemperance, the first temperance; yours promises gluttony, ours self-control; yours promises concupiscence, ours liberality; it is evident that your religion is harmful and not appropriate to God, for it renders its followers more similar to the irrational animals."[32]

Of course, it's not as if disputation in the Islamic world was always marked by ecumenical restraint. John of Damascus was hardly gentle in his account of the Islamic "heresy." On the Muslim side, the literary stylist and theologian al-Jāḥiẓ (d. 869) wondered at the fact that the Greek Christians, despite being "a people of religious philosophers, physicians, astronomers, diplomats, arithmeticians, secretaries and masters of every discipline, could say that a man who . . . ate, drank, urinated, excreted, suffered hunger and thirst, dressed and undressed, gained and lost weight, who later, as they assume, was crucified and killed, is Lord and Creator."[33] In fact Muslims often attributed to Christianity a decline in Greek scholarship. Al-Jāḥiẓ himself pointed to the fact that the Byzantines fell well short of the standard set by figures like Plato, Aristotle, and Euclid. More generally, the great Greek-Arabic translation movement sponsored by the ʿAbbāsids can be seen as a conscious attempt to present Islamic, and not Greek Christian, culture as the true heir of Hellenic science.[34] Occasionally Christians conceded that the Muslims might have a point. The Byzantine philosopher John Italos (d. 1082) complained that the "Assyrians" were outdoing the Greeks in science, and the great thirteenth-century Syriac scholar Bar Hebraeus (d. 1286) lamented, "We, from whom [the Muslims] have acquired wisdom through translators, all of whom were Syrians, find ourselves compelled to ask for wisdom from them." He himself exemplified this state of affairs, since his own writings drew extensively on Avicenna and other Muslim philosophers and theologians.

This mention of Syriac and the translation movement brings us to what is surely the most spectacular example of interreligious polemic from the medieval Near East. It is a dialogue written in Syriac, which describes a confrontation between no less than a patriarch of the East Syrian church and the caliph himself.[35] As if that weren't good enough, this patriarch translated a work of Aristotle, the aforementioned *Topics*, supposedly at the behest of the caliph whom he debated. The protagonists are the patriarch Timothy I (d. 823) and the ʿAbbāsid ruler al-Mahdī. It is Timothy who reports what transpired between the two, giving us a fairly evenhanded and respectful account of a debate between them held over the course of two days while of course making it clear that Christianity has the better case and can respond effectively to the objections put by the caliph. Timothy may have been asked to translate Aristotle's *Topics* because its exploration of dialectic might provide useful tools for, as Dimitri Gutas puts it, "the exigencies of inter-faith discourse."[36] This sounds plausible, and it gets confirmation of a kind from a story told by Timothy himself, in which he was approached at the caliphal court by a Muslim theologian with expertise on Aristotelian philosophy who wanted to discuss Christian belief with him.[37]

Yet it must be said that the debate between Timothy and al-Mahdī is not marked by explicit reference to Aristotelian argumentative *topoi*, or such ideas as "commonly accepted opinions (*endoxa*)," an idea from the *Topics* whose Arabic reception I discussed in chapter 1. The text is however "dialectical" in the looser sense that both interlocutors try to gain an advantage by appealing to the commitments of the other. Particularly striking is the way that the patriarch and the caliph try to justify their religious traditions by appealing to each other's scriptural texts. According to al-Mahdī, the Bible predicts the prophecy of Muḥammad, while Timothy points out that in the Quran God speaks of himself in the first person *plural*, a hint at the truth of the trinitarian doctrine.[38] When the caliph responds that this is just the use of the "royal we," Timothy cleverly turns the tables by saying that a ruler like al-Mahdī refers to himself as "we" precisely because he represents a plurality, namely, those over whom he rules. But there is a difference from the case of God, for the caliph is made up of a soul and a body, which is further constituted from the four Aristotelian elements, whereas God is incorporeal and not composed.

Earlier in the record of the debate, Timothy used metaphors to explain how it is that God can be incorporeal yet also a Trinity. He gives other examples in which three items form a unity: the soul, its thought, and uttered speech; the sun, its light, and its warmth; an apple, its scent, and its taste.[39] At least one, and possibly two, of these analogies go back to the Aristotelian logical texts Timothy knew so well. The "trinity" of soul, thought, and speech is presumably inspired by the famous passage at the start of Aristotle's *On Interpretation* (16a3–7), which teaches that uttered words represent "affections of the soul (παθήματα τῆς ψυχῆς)." As for the apple, I suspect that this may be related to an example that became standard in Aristotelian commentaries, of an accident that is generated from a substance.[40] This might well be compared to the way that the soul generates thoughts or the Father begets the Son.

Admittedly, if this was Timothy's inspiration, it is awkward that the commentators point out the possibility that an apple's scent can linger in the absence of the apple, which obviously should not have a parallel in the case of the Trinity. Later on in the dispute, the caliph even raises an objection, in what Timothy calls a "philosophical manner," as to whether there can be separation between the trinitarian Persons like between parts of the body.[41] Timothy insists that this is impossible: precisely because God is immaterial, the Persons can be in one another while also not being "mixed." Again, this is like the interrelation of sun, light, and warmth; apple, taste, and scent; and soul, thought, and word. When Timothy is challenged by al-Mahdī for using physical examples to illustrate an immaterial plurality-in-unity, he responds that we cannot do otherwise, given the limitations of our language and understanding.[42] This is a larger concession than what we found in Saadia, who thought that human reason can indeed grasp God, albeit indirectly as creator of this world, and that it is language alone that falls short in trying to express this.

Timothy's coreligionists seem to have agreed with him on this point. The sun does a pretty good job of being like God in that it is omnipresent as an analogy in Christian literature of the Near East. Timothy's contemporary Abū Rā'iṭa uses it and also apologizes for having to use imperfect comparisons that draw parallels between God and created things. And, coming full circle by returning to sixteenth-century Ethiopia, it also appears much later in the Christian polemicist with whom I began, Enbaqom. He also deploys other strategies already pioneered in the early phase of Christian-Muslim debate, for example, using the Quran against its adherents. Both he and Patriarch Timothy seize upon the mysterious, individual letters that begin some chapters of the Quran and argue that these obscurely testify to Christian belief: Timothy, for the straightforward reason that three such letters could represent the Trinity; Enbaqom, on the more elaborate grounds that numerology can be used to extract the name of Christ from them.[43]

For our purposes, another group of witnesses invoked by Enbaqom is more significant: the pagan philosophers. In a remarkable passage, albeit one that has precedent in the Arabic tradition, he brings forward a series of sages including Hermes, Plato, and Aristotle who more or less affirm the truth of Christianity.[44] The quotations are, of course, spurious.

> The philosopher Plato said: the first cause is the benevolence moved by pity for all things; the second cause is the idea that is creative of all things; and the third cause is the spirit that makes that life which is the life of all things.

Enbaqom sees here an endorsement, or at least intuition, of the Trinity. But it seems also to be a reminiscence of Neoplatonism, if not Platonism, and is in fact comparable to a sentiment put into the mouth of Socrates by the aforementioned early Muslim philosopher al-Kindī.

> He used to say: Nature is the handmaiden for the soul, soul is the handmaiden for the intellect, and the intellect that of the Creator (*mubdi*ʿ), because the first thing created by the Creator was the form of the intellect.[45]

This sort of thing is far from uncommon in Arabic literature. There are entire compilations of supposed quotations, or "wisdom literature," that foist Neoplatonic ideas on a wide range of ancient philosophers, with Socrates and Plato often figuring centrally.[46]

But it is particularly intriguing to see this practice used in support of Christian theological dogma. This may not seem much like the use of Aristotelian logic to argue for or against the cogency of that same dogma. But in fact the two strategies have something in common. To suggest that a pagan like Plato already intuited the trinitarian structure of the divine, as we just saw Enbaqom doing, was both to borrow his eminent standing as a thinker for the Christian cause and to suggest that human reason is actually led naturally to this truth rather than recoiling from it as the Muslim polemicists argued. This does not render revelation superfluous, of course. But it offers testimony independent of revelation, a kind of confirmation that could impress those who are not (yet) adherents of the revelation and increase the confidence of those who are. Likewise with the frequent use of Aristotelian logic, whose tools were used to establish at least the rational acceptability, if not inevitability, of one or another Abrahamic faith.

The difference, of course, is that Aristotle's logic was used to mount arguments that were meant to be convincing to any fair-minded hearer. Simply quoting Plato or Hermes, by contrast, is not to give an argument. Rather, it is an invitation to engage in *taqlīd*, to believe in the Trinity because a great authority already did so (more or less). The fact that in this case, the great authorities in question are pagans was actually very useful. If you are trying to score points against Muslims, it's better to cite famous pagans than famous fathers of the church. As a cultural legacy available to members of all three Abrahamic faiths, pagan philosophy was thus useful, even if, as John of Damascus and Basil warned, it needed to be used selectively and judiciously. And it was useful in a variety of ways, enlisted both in contexts where an appeal to authority was seen as sufficient and in contexts where the standards were higher, and proof was demanded. Those higher standards would apply when the audience or opponents were intellectuals on the other side, like the relatively sophisticated Christians mentioned by Saadia or the Aristotelian theologian who confronted Timothy at the caliphal court.

I can't resist adding a final thought concerning the cultural context where I began and ended: Ethiopia. If you have ever heard of a philosophical work from Ethiopia, it will probably be a pair of treatises composed in the seventeenth century. These treatises were written by Zera Yacob and his student Walda Heywat, in Ge'ez, the same language used by Enbaqom. If, that is, these documents are authentic. There is an ongoing debate about them, since they may be forgeries produced by Giusto d'Urbino, the scholar who announced their "discovery" in the nineteenth century.[47] This controversy, unsurprisingly, turns on numerous philological and technical issues, but one main reason for suspicion is that the ideas put forward by Yacob and Heywat seem remarkably "modern." In particular, they strongly endorse a critical attitude toward religion. One should not adopt a faith simply because it is that of the family into which one is born but rather withhold belief until one has proof. Heywat makes this point as follows:

> Do not say in your heart: we stand firm in our faith which cannot be false, but hold on to this: men lie in matters of faith, because in no way do they agree and they do not demonstrate to us what we should believe. . . . Which one of these faiths is the true one that we should believe in? Tell me if you know, because I myself do not know. That I may not be misled in my faith, I believe nothing except what God demonstrated to me by the light of my reason.[48]

This might look rather suspicious, because it seems like such an Enlightenment or post-Enlightenment attitude. Like Descartes in his *Meditations*, Heywat encourages us to adopt a skeptical attitude and drop it only once skepticism is defeated. Why not then think that the author is indeed a post-Enlightenment European, namely, d'Urbino, and not an implausibly freethinking and innovative Christian of seventeenth-century Ethiopia?

The answer, as you'll already have guessed, is that this attitude would have been far from implausible or innovative in seventeenth-century Ethiopia. To the contrary, it is a pretty standard expression of animus against *taqlīd*. Al-Ghazālī is as good an example of a pre-Enlightenment thinker as you could want, and we already saw him worrying about the "epistemic luck" of being born a Muslim instead of a Christian or Jew. In fact, the same concern was voiced by an early Christian polemicist against Islam, Theodore Abū Qurra (d. ca. 820).[49] And we've seen other medieval authors, like Hallevi and Abelard, envisioning a rational "choice of faiths" and followed that up by observing the use of rational argumentation and pagan philosophy in interreligious disputation. So I have little trouble believing that the treatises of Yacob and Heywat were indeed written by Ethiopian philosophers a century or so after Enbaqom.

But obviously, you shouldn't take my word for it.

CHAPTER 5

Some Pagans Are Better than Others

The Merits of Plato and Aristotle

Around the turn of the tenth century, two men from the same city got into an argument. They were from the Persian town of Rayy, near modern-day Tehran, for which reason they were both called al-Rāzī. One of them, Abū Ḥātim al-Rāzī (d. 934), was a philosopher and devotee of Ismāʿīlism, the Shīʿite branch of Islam that al-Ghazālī attacked for recommending thoughtless obedience to the teachings of their *imāms*. The other man was also a philosopher, as well as a doctor and, according to Abū Ḥātim, a heretic. His name was Abū Bakr al-Rāzī (d. 925). We know about the dispute between the two men because Abū Ḥātim wrote about it.[1] In a book devoted to refuting Abū Bakr's supposed rejection of prophecy, Abū Ḥātim began by talking about face-to-face meetings between the two where they discussed, among other things, *taqlīd*.

Few scholars would think to compare Abū Bakr al-Rāzī to al-Ghazālī, given that the latter is still considered a leading authority of Islamic theology while the former has a reputation for unorthodox teachings, if not the outright heresy of which Abū Ḥātim accused him. Yet they have remarkably similar things to say about religious belief that is based on *taqlīd*. Here is Abū Bakr:

> The followers of the religious laws (*ahl al-sharāʾiʿ*) have learned their religion (*dīn*) through *taqlīd*. They reject and forbid inquiry (*naẓar*) and investigation (*baḥth*). . . . They transmit traditions in the

> name of their leaders, which oblige them to refrain from speculation on religious matters, and declare that anyone who contradicts the traditions they transmit must be branded an infidel (*kufra*). . . . If the people of this mission (*daʿwā*) are asked about the proof for the soundness of their religion, they flare up, get angry and spill the blood of whoever confronts them with this question. They forbid inquiry, and strive to kill their adversaries.[2]

Abū Ḥātim presents this as if it were a general attack on Islam, or even revealed religion in general. But I have argued elsewhere that the complaint was actually directed specifically at Abū Ḥātim's Ismāʿīlī creed (the word *daʿwā* in the passage just quoted hints at this).[3]

In any case, it elicits a response from Abū Ḥātim that is, in turn, remarkably similar to al-Ghazālī's endorsement of what I have called justified *taqlīd*.

> We say that the people of truth and justice do not allow *taqlīd* regarding the principles, for example, acknowledging [God's] oneness, the topic of prophecy, or the affirmation of the imamate. Accepting these on the basis of *taqlīd* is not allowed. But, once one has affirmed [God's] oneness, agreed on the topic of prophecy, and affirmed the imamate, after this, it is allowed to engage in *taqlīd* to the true, just, knowing *imām*. It is not in the constitution of man to reach the furthest end of knowledge, "since God is knowing above all who have knowledge" (Qurʾān 12:76). If one were to abandon *taqlīd* after acknowledging these principles as indicated, and all people were obligated to pursue the final end [without guidance], then they would be obligated to do something of which they are incapable.[4]

Abū Ḥātim here anticipates the move that will later be made by al-Ghazālī, namely, that one can rationally accept one's beliefs from a superior authority after one has verified that that authority really is reliable. The difference is that he applies this strategy to following the *imām*, as well as the Prophet. (The *imāms* are divinely inspired figures beginning with ʿAlī, cousin and son-in-law of the Prophet, and continuing through a line of his descendants.)[5] Finally Abū Ḥātim argues that this is not just legitimate, but unavoidable: the limitations of human nature mean that we cannot do without (justified) *taqlīd*.

In fact, Abū Ḥātim makes another point that will later turn up in al-Ghazālī, namely, that "philosophers" too engage in *taqlīd* by thoughtlessly following their own authorities, like Aristotle. But Abū Bakr pleads innocent to this charge. He claims that all humans are equally endowed with the power of reason and should use this power to engage in inquiry (*naẓar*). Naturally, one may find oneself agreeing with earlier authorities, and one should even study their works to learn from them. But this should always be done in a critical spirit. The inquirer is, Abū Bakr says, "someone making an effort"; here the Arabic is the loaded, and to us familiar, word *mujtahid*.[6] And it must be said that Abū Bakr al-Rāzī practiced what he preached. While he was certainly interested in philosophy, his main occupation and preoccupation was medicine. One of his most interesting works is a stunningly irreverent critique of the greatest authority in medicine, the second-century AD doctor Galen. Titled *Doubts about Galen* (*Shukūk ʿalā Jālīnūs*), Abū Bakr's work finds fault with passages drawn from a wide range of Galenic treatises.[7] This despite Abū Bakr's great admiration for Galen.

Or perhaps we should say, this *because of* his admiration for Galen. As he points out, Galen was hardly shy in criticizing his own predecessors, and he is simply holding Galen to the same standards upon which Galen himself insisted. These are the high standards I discussed in chapter 2: if one is going to assert something in a scientific context, one had better offer good reasons for the assertion, which should ideally rise to the level of full "demonstration." Galen wrote a whole book about this, called *On Demonstration*, which Abū Bakr calls "the most exalted and most useful of books, after those sent by God."[8] He was no Aristotelian, but his devotion to Galenic medicine and especially Galen's strict methodology meant that, no less than an al-Fārābī or an Averroes, he thought intellectuals should aspire to give absolutely certain proofs.

If Abū Bakr al-Rāzī was not an Aristotelian, then what was he? On some topics at least, he was a Platonist. He says so himself in another part of the debate as reported by Abū Ḥātim al-Rāzī. Here the two are in the midst of debating Abū Bakr's theory of "absolute time," or eternity, a universal duration that is constantly elapsing independently of bodies or motions. When Abū Ḥātim objects that time is known only through the heavenly motions, Abū Bakr concedes that this is Aristotle's view and indeed that Aristotle went so far as to say that time is actually brought about by these motions. But Abū Bakr disagrees with this, instead offering his allegiance to Plato: "What Plato says is hardly different from what I believe concerning time, and this, according to me, is the best thing that has been said about it."[9]

As a staunch critic of *taqlīd*, of course Abū Bakr doesn't assert his theory simply on the basis of Plato's authority. He has arguments for the existence of an absolute, independent, and eternal time; for example, time cannot be generated or created since it would have to be created *at a time*, which will of course not be available if time does not yet exist. In fact even the statement of allegiance just quoted leaves open that he may disagree slightly with Plato, whose view is "hardly different" (*lā yakādu yukhālifu*) from his. Still, Abū Bakr is happy to be seen in Plato's company and to associate his own view with Plato's rather than with Aristotle's.

This may come as a surprise, since philosophy in the Islamic world usually owes far more to Aristotle than to Plato. If Abū Bakr was an exception, it is perhaps because, as already mentioned, he was really more a doctor than a philosopher. So he came to ancient philosophy by an unusual route, having immersed himself in the writings of Galen, who likewise admired Plato as the greatest of philosophical authorities while reserving the right to make up his own mind. In fact, Galen was also the route by which Platonic texts reached Abū Bakr and other readers of Arabic, since his paraphrases of the Platonic dialogues were translated into that language, but the original dialogues were not.

Having said that, Abū Bakr was not the only self-styled Platonist of the Islamic world. In the twelfth century both Suhrawardī and Fakhr al-Dīn al-Rāzī (also from Rayy) claimed to be in some sense followers of Plato. Fakhr al-Dīn actually does this in the same context of discussing time and whether or not it depends on bodies. He prefers the view of "*imām* Plato" to that of "Aristotle the logician."[10] As for Suhrawardī (d. 1191), we find him placing Plato in a pantheon of philosophical authorities, whose legacy he claims to carry on with his own "illuminationist" philosophy.

> For what I have mentioned of the science of lights, all that is built upon it and more besides, I have been helped by all who traveled the path of God, the exalted. It is the "taste" [i.e., mystical insight] of the *imām* and chief of wisdom, Plato, a man of strength and light.

> Likewise those who were before him, from the time of the father of the sages, Hermes, up to [Plato's] time, among the great sages and pillars of wisdom like Empedocles, Pythagoras, and others. The words of the ancients are symbolic, and there is no gainsaying them. Though one may criticize the surface meaning (*ẓāhir*) of their statements, one cannot criticize the import (*maqāṣid*) of what they say, since there is no gainsaying the symbolic.[11]

The reasons for this twelfth-century surge in admiration for Plato remain a topic for speculation. My guess is that these figures were thereby trying to position themselves relative to Avicenna. At this time Avicenna had, in the eyes of both his supporters and his detractors, effectively replaced Aristotle as the central figure of philosophy. Yet Avicenna's philosophy was identified as carrying on the Aristotelian tradition; as already mentioned, in this later period the term "Peripatetic" effectively just meant "Avicennan." So it may have seemed natural for critics of Avicenna to align themselves with Plato, a famous authority who was known to have disagreed with Aristotle on many important issues. It's a classic case of "the enemy of my enemy is my friend."

At which juncture, you may be wondering, were they really known to have disagreed? Wasn't it, to the contrary, a standard assumption beginning in late antiquity that the philosophies of Plato and Aristotle were fundamentally in harmony? And wasn't this assumption passed on to the Islamic world? Well, yes and no, but more no than yes. It is true that the Neoplatonist philosophers who dominated late antique thought from the third century on tended to think that Plato and Aristotle were in harmony on most if not all issues. This tendency can probably be traced to Porphyry, the student and editor of the great Plotinus and the first Platonist to write commentaries on Aristotle.[12] Beginning with him there was a tendency to treat Aristotle as a more introductory philosopher, whose works on logic and then natural philosophy could be used to train students, very few of whom might go on to the study of the Platonic corpus. The idea was more or less "Aristotle for undergraduates, Plato for graduate students." And that approach had a massive impact on the way philosophy was conducted in all three medieval cultures. The proliferation of commentaries, paraphrases, and textbooks like Porphyry's own *Introduction* to logic meant that the philosophical literature available to the medievals was overwhelmingly Aristotelian in content, despite having been written mostly by Platonists.

That's the "yes" part. The "no" part is, first, that the Platonists did not always insist on harmonizing the two great authorities. A notable exception to the rule was Syrianus (d. 437), who wrote a highly critical commentary on Aristotle's *Metaphysics* dealing specifically with the parts that rejected Plato's teachings. And second, that other Platonists did not in fact simply *assume* the harmony of Plato and Aristotle. They realized that there were many apparent disagreements and that serious exegetical work would be needed to show the deeper agreement. A passage often quoted in this context comes from one of the last pagan Platonists, Simplicius (d. 560), who is here describing the task of the commentator on Aristotle.

> He must not convict the philosophers of disharmony (διαφωνία) by looking only at the letter (λέξις) of what [Aristotle] says against Plato; but he must look towards the spirit (εἰς τὸν νοῦν), and track down the harmony (συμφωνία) which reigns between them on the majority of points.[13]

Furthermore, the harmonizer would seem to owe us an explanation of why two such outstanding philosophers would have presented us with the problem in the first place. Why weren't they writing clearly enough to make it obvious that their reasoning coincided? Much ingenuity was devoted to answering this question. Commentators like Simplicius excused the difficult and compressed writing style of Aristotle as an attempt to keep inexperienced and unqualified readers at bay, while Platonic exegetes like Proclus offered elaborate accounts of the allusive, literary, and allegorical strategies of the dialogues.

Which is to say that neither Plato nor Aristotle was in fact thought to have written in a demonstrative mode. Aristotle's *Posterior Analytics*, or for some Galen's *On Demonstration* (tellingly, they had the same title in Arabic: *al-Burhān*), set the ideal standard for scientific discourse, discourse suited to the high standards of knowledge already discussed. But it was actually very useful to admit that neither Aristotle nor Plato wrote works in that register. This opened a space for interpreting admittedly difficult texts, showing how seeming discord obscures a more fundamental accord. We get an early glimpse of this in al-Kindī, who wrote two texts on the soul that juxtapose Plato's and Aristotle's views on this topic as if there were no disagreement between them. In one of these, which is just a note or perhaps a brief fragment from a longer, lost work, al-Kindī quotes remarks on the soul from Plato and Aristotle, then goes on to show that when understood properly these can be shown to agree with one another and with what both philosophers say elsewhere.[14] Al-Kindī's devotion to the harmony thesis is shown even by the translations produced in his circle, for instance, in their Arabic version of the works of the Neoplatonist Plotinus. It "translates" a passage in which Plotinus refutes Aristotle's definition of soul in such a way as to turn it into a warning against a possible misreading of that definition, on which Aristotle's theory would be incompatible with Platonism.[15]

But in the Islamic world, the most famous attempt to establish the harmony of the opinions of these two philosophers is a text called *On the Harmony of the Opinions of the Two Philosophers*.[16] It is ascribed to al-Fārābī, though doubts have been raised about this, partially on the grounds that the real al-Fārābī was in fact happy to admit disagreements between Plato and Aristotle.[17] Without weighing in on that question here, I will simply call the person who wrote it "the harmonizer." He writes:

> These two sages are the sources of philosophy, the ones who set down its beginnings and its roots, and brought to fruition its ends and branches. One depends on them for the great and the small in [philosophy], and has recourse to them for trivial and weighty matters in it. What comes from these two in every department of [philosophy] is a dependable root, free of blemish or muddiness. Tongues have affirmed this and intellects testified to it, or if not all have, then most have done so who had clear minds and pure understanding.[18]

A bit further on, he adds that it is hardly credible that Plato and Aristotle would be so widely esteemed if they were not really philosophers of the first rank.

> We know with certainty that there is no more powerful, persuasive, and decisive proof than when different understandings testify to one and the same thing, and many intellects (*ʿuqūl*) agree upon it. For intellect, as all agree, is a proof (*ḥujja*).[19]

This makes it sound as if the harmonizer is establishing the authority of Plato and Aristotle through a kind of popularity contest.

Yet the stated purpose of the work as a whole is to refute another widespread belief, namely, that the two thinkers disagree on many points. Hence the the treatise begins, "I have seen many people in our time . . . alleging that there is disagreement between the two preeminent and righteous sages Plato and Aristotle," especially concerning the eternity of the world.[20] Thus the harmonizer, immediately after declaring common consent to be a "proof," adds:

> Do not be misled by the existence of many created beings whose opinions are disordered, for a group that engages in *taqlīd* regarding a single opinion and submits to a leader (*imām*) who goes before them and leads them concerning what they agree upon, is tantamount to [only] a single intellect, and a single intellect may err on occasion about a given thing, as we have mentioned, especially if it has not repeatedly considered the opinion it endorses, examined it several times, and looked at it with a scrutinizing and skeptical eye.[21]

How can he get away with invoking commonly held views as proof and then in the next breath dismissing commonly held views as the mere product of *taqlīd*?

It would be nice if he said more about this. But I think we can understand his point with the help of his contrast between the action of many intellects and what is tantamount to a single intellect. In the former, reliable case many individuals have *independently* looked into an issue and come to the same conclusion. In the latter, unreliable case a single person has thought about something and come to a conclusion and then a large group has uncritically followed this one person. It doesn't matter how many uncritical followers you have, whereas it could matter quite a lot how many critically minded people agree with you. This is a helpful distinction and offers a useful supplement to my earlier discussion of *taqlīd*. Effectively, the harmonizer here articulates another reason to trust experts. When many people apply their expertise independently and come to similar conclusions, that is a powerful sign that they are all in the right, though it may fall short of the absolute proof touted by the harmonizer.

Something like the reality of man-made climate change would be an obvious example here.

All the more reason, though, that we should worry about disputes between the two foremost experts, Plato and Aristotle. Why do so many thoughtful people judge them to agree given their apparent disagreements? For the harmonizer, the salient word here is *apparent*. He draws a repeated contrast between the surface meaning and deeper import of a text, the *ẓāhir* and the *bāṭin*. This is terminology that is also used in the quotation given earlier from Suhrawardī, and it is the same idea used by Simplicius in his contrast between "the letter" and the "spirit" (λέξις as opposed to νοῦς). The harmonizer concedes that Plato and Aristotle often *seem* to disagree but insists that closer consideration of their writings reveals inner agreement. This contrast extends even to their ways of life. It is said that Aristotle was politically and practically engaged—he advised Alexander the Great, after all—whereas Plato withdrew from the world. "On the surface (*ẓāhir*)," admits the harmonizer, "this contrast implies belief (*ẓann*) and trust that there is variance between their convictions on the matter of this life and the hereafter (*fī amr al-dārayn*)."[22] But Plato did write about politics, and could have been politically active if he had felt that his talents lay in that direction. He simply wanted to concentrate on leading a good ethical life at the individual level.

When it comes to their writings, the harmonizer argues that the "surface level" misleads readers because of the terminology or expressions used by the two philosophers. Not that this is their fault exactly. Their choice of wording had to do with limitations of the intended audience, or it may simply have been impossible to find unambiguous expressions.[23] He applies this solution to the differing views of the two great thinkers on the topics of vision and cosmology, in the latter case suggesting that the Platonic phrase "world of the intellect" alludes to the connection between celestial intellects and heavenly spheres, a thoroughly Aristotelian teaching.[24]

The strategy reappears when it comes to the notorious question of the world's eternity. Many believe, complains the harmonizer, that Plato believed in a creator God who originates the universe with a beginning in time, whereas Aristotle saw the universe as uncreated and eternal. In fact, though, Aristotle denied a "temporal beginning (*badʿ zamānī*)" of the universe only to convey that God causes it to exist without his action being a process that unfolds over time.

> The meaning of his saying that the world has no temporal beginning is that it is not generated one part after another as, for instance, plants or animals are generated. For when something is generated one part after another, some of its parts precede others in time.[25]

This sounds like an attempt to Platonize Aristotle. But actually, on this topic at least, the harmonizer is assimilating both Plato and the genuine Aristotle to pseudo-Aristotle.[26] The harmonizer assumes that the so-called *Theology*, a collection of Arabic translations of Neoplatonic authors including Plotinus and Proclus, was really written by Aristotle. His discussion of divine causation is designed to show that both the cosmology of Plato's *Timaeus* and Aristotle's remarks in works like *On the Heavens* and the *Metaphysics* can be reconciled with the Neoplatonic idea that the universe timelessly proceeds from divine causes through emanation. The phrase "world of the intellect," which I just mentioned, sounds more Neoplatonic than Platonic and indeed comes from the Arabic versions of Plotinus and Proclus. The harmonizer may even have borrowed his point about the misleading use of temporal vocabulary from the Arabic version of Plotinus in the pseudo-Aristotelian *Theology*. It includes an original discussion that has been inserted in the translation, explaining that Plato talked about the creation of the world as if it involved temporal priority, even though the priority in question is in fact causal.[27]

As the harmonizer says in another context, Plato and Aristotle should only be held to disagree "if they were to form a judgment from one and the same point of view regarding one and the same topic." Disambiguation of terminology can show that this is not the case, as can more generally the observation that both philosophers wrote in a difficult and unclear way.

> [Plato] chose to write in symbols and riddles, intending to set down what he knew and had decided in such a way that no one could get at it except for those who deserved to. . . . Whereas Aristotle's approach is to state things openly and clearly, setting them down and putting them in order, writing informatively, uncovering, and

> clarifying, carrying this out in whatever way he could find. These methods are obviously different. On the other hand, anyone who has persisted in investigating Aristotle's scientific discussions (*ʿulūm*) and the instruction in his books will have noticed that his approach involves various kinds of obscurity, enigma, and complexity, even though he seems to want to make things evident and clear.

It's hard to disagree with that. But the harmonizer is not blaming Aristotle for inadequacy here. Instead he echoes the late antique commentatorial tradition, which insisted that Aristotle wrote in a compressed and obscure manner quite purposefully. This was in part an attempt to shield the great authority from critique, in part a way to underscore the need for the commentator's own labors, as already mentioned. His task was to supply missing premises, make implicit arguments explicit, eliminating apparent inconsistencies, and to "read Aristotle through Aristotle" as commentators on Homer had earlier begun to read Homer, bringing together far-flung passages from the Aristotelian corpus so as to show the unity of the greater whole. The commentator, in other words, sought to establish the harmony of Aristotle with Aristotle, a task still more urgent than showing the harmony of Aristotle with Plato.

These late ancient interpretive techniques were carried on in Arabic commentaries written by al-Fārābī and his Christian colleagues in the Aristotelian school of tenth-century Baghdad. And they were carried on still more directly in Byzantium. A high point in the tradition of Byzantine commentaries came with the circle gathered around the princess and historian Anna Komnene (d. 1153–35) in the twelfth century.[28] They were completists, who undertook exegesis on Aristotelian treatises not yet covered by late ancient commentaries and imitated the approach of those commentaries. This includes the familiar tendency to Platonize, or rather Neoplatonize, Aristotle. A nice example is the commentary of Eustratius on Aristotle's *Nicomachean Ethics*. Michele Trizio has called its treatment of the sixth book of the *Ethics* "an amazing piece of philosophical rhetoric, in which the author deepens the interpretation of the Aristotelian text by a careful line by line reconstruction of the source material offered by Proclus' works."[29] When it came to the famous rejection of Plato's Form of the Good in the first book of the *Ethics*, Eustratius offered a rebuttal on Plato's behalf but tried to stay out of the dispute, concluding, "We do not say this as proponents of the Ideas, since those who wish to abolish the Ideas may have no difficulty refuting these words."[30]

But some Byzantine intellectuals were more willing to take sides. If we look beyond the tradition of commentary on Aristotle, we find a number of authors blaming Aristotle for erroneous teachings on such topics as providence, the eternity of the world, the mortality of the soul, and the significant role of external goods like wealth, health, and family in the good life.[31] Already the Cappadocian father Gregory Nazianzus had inveighed, "Strike against . . . Aristotle's uncharitable providence, his artificiality, his perishable arguments about soul and the humanity of his doctrines!" Even intellectuals who felt drawn to Aristotle might have misgivings about him, like Arethas (d. 932), an avid book collector who compared Aristotle to the Sirens calling Odysseus to his doom in the *Odyssey*.[32] He complained of Aristotle's disloyalty to his teacher and came to prefer Platonic doctrines over those of Aristotle. Some Byzantine thinkers, especially Michael Psellos (d. after 1081), adhered to the late ancient idea that Aristotle was an acceptable introduction to philosophy, with Plato having the wisdom and exalted insight to explore the higher topics of intelligible reality.[33] Nonetheless, Psellos bridled when a contemporary called him a "follower of Plato."[34] He saw this for what it was, a veiled accusation of departing from Orthodox belief, and accordingly rejected the charge of allegiance to pagan philosophy.

But if pagan philosophy was always at least potentially problematic in Byzantine culture, it could still be the case that some pagans are better than others. Plato seemed to be a less problematic thinker than Aristotle, since his *Timaeus* seems to envision a creator God and since he clearly endorsed the immortality of the soul. Especially as we approach the end of Byzantine civilization, we find philosophers admitting the disharmony of Plato and Aristotle and siding with the former against the latter. In the Palaiologan period, when Greek rule was restored after the Crusaders' sack of Constantinople, Theodore Metochites (d. 1332) subjected Aristotle to heavy criticism. Aristotle's famous obscurity was not a cunning strategy chosen for pedagogical purposes, or for fending off unqualified readers. It was just a way for him to hide his own shortcomings in such subjects as mathematics and to hide the extent of his dependence on his teacher, Plato.[35]

A generation later, Metochites's student Nikephoras Gregoras (d. 1361) wrote a work called the *Florentius*, modestly subtitled *On Wisdom*. It is a dialogue pitting against one another representatives of the Eastern Greek and Western Latin intellectual traditions. Gregoras delights in pointing out that "neither astronomy nor most other branches of wisdom that have thrived among the Greeks have citizenship in the Latin countries," which is typical of what Börje Bydén has called the "anti-Latin edge" of the work as a whole.[36] The Westerners have failed to progress past logic, the elementary subject on which Aristotle is a competent guide. He is less competent when it comes to natural philosophy, a field where his expertise had been recognized even by late ancient Neoplatonists. Even Aristotelian epistemology is unconvincing, since it demands necessary and unchanging knowledge of physical things, which are subject to constant change (yet again, the standards of Aristotle's theory of knowledge are deemed too ambitious to be satisfied). As Bydén has pointed out, it is telling that this whole critique comes in the context of a dialogue. Plato is Gregoras's literary model, Aristotle his intellectual whipping boy.

But most intellectual historians would consider these writings of Theodore Metochites and Nikephoras Gregoras a mere warm-up act for the most famous anti-Aristotelian polemic of Byzantine culture, which was written by George Gemistos Plethon (d. 1452 or 1454). It is called *On Aristotle's Departures from Plato*.[37] He lived in the fifteenth century, and died either one year before or one year after the fall of Constantinople. Given the circumstances, it may seem odd that Plethon would still be concerned with upholding the values of Greek intellectual culture over that of Latin Christendom. Wouldn't the Ottomans be a more pressing worry? But the *Departures* begins by complaining of Plethon's many contemporaries who "admire Aristotle above Plato," having been convinced of his superiority by "the Arab Averroes."[38] This seems a clear allusion to Western scholasticism, and perhaps Italian scholasticism in particular, which was indeed powerfully influenced by Averroes's commentaries on Aristotle.

Plethon attended the famous church council of Ferrara and Florence, which tried but failed to achieve union between the Eastern and Western churches. Reportedly he stated that the theological controversy was a matter of life and death.[39] In light of this, we might take the *Departures* to be motivated in part by an attempt to assert the intellectual supremacy of the endangered East over the apparently flourishing West. The achievements of Latin scholastics were nothing to brag about, since they focused all their efforts on understanding Aristotle, instead of his teacher, Plato, who was the greater thinker and far better studied in the Greek-speaking East. At this time, after all, most of Plato's dialogues had yet to be translated into Latin. That project would be carried out by Marsilio Ficino (d. 1499), using a manuscript of Plato's dialogues brought to Italy by none other than Plethon himself.[40]

If this reconstruction of Plethon's motive is accurate, then we can see his *Departures* as carrying on the anti-Latin polemic of Gregoras. We can also draw a parallel between this feature of late Byzantine thought and what we observed in the Islamic world. There, figures like Suhrawardī and Fakhr al-Dīn al-Rāzī styled themselves as followers of Plato, in order to distance themselves from the Aristotelianism of Avicenna, whose thought had come to dominate their intellectual landscape. In much the same way, Plethon attacked Aristotle and endorsed Plato as a way of rejecting the scholastic movement that had come to dominate the intellectual landscape of Christianity.

One difference is that Plethon knew vastly more about Plato than did Suhrawardī and Fakhr al-Dīn. He was thoroughly versed in the whole Platonic tradition, which allowed him to adopt what may seem a rather strange maneuver in his *Departures*. He accuses Aristotle (who quite literally sat in Plato's classes) of misrepresenting Plato's teaching and uses late ancient authors like Proclus (who lived the better part of a millennium after Plato) as a more reliable guide to Platonic thought.[41] But inaccurate reporting of his teacher's doctrines is only one of Aristotle's intellectual sins. He is mocked for his skewed sense of priorities, talking more about shellfish than about God. When he did talk about God, he said a few respectful and pious things but then failed to make good on them in his philosophical theology. He was furthermore thoughtless (ἀπερίσκεπτος), and frequently unclear, as when he defined virtue as a mean without saying in what sense we are to understand this. In an almost comical bit of diatribe, Plethon attempts to interpret Aristotle's doctrine in light of a single passage, where Aristotle said it would be unreasonable not to fear thunderstorms. This, to Plethon's mind, shows that Aristotle meant that virtue is a mean in the quantitative sense: in this case, too much or too little fear. It also shows that Aristotle had a distorted set of values, since in Plethon's Stoic-leaning version of Platonic ethics, we should fear only things that can harm the soul and that we can do something about. Thunderstorms don't meet either criterion.

One of Plethon's primary tactics is to use Aristotle against himself. He claims that Aristotle was prone to contradicting himself, as if this were "no big deal (οὐδὲν πρᾶγμα)."[42] He (supposedly) affirmed the immortality of the soul in the *De anima*—in this respect he was at least better than his commentator Averroes—but then wrote about ethics as if we should be concerned only with this earthly life. And he denied determinism, despite affirming two principles that imply it, namely, that nothing happens without a cause and that potentiality can only be realized by a prior actuality. This is, as Plethon observes, rather ironic. It was after all Aristotle who set out the rules of proper scientific demonstration in his *Posterior Analytics*, rules he regularly violates. Take for instance the paltry and irrelevant points Aristotle brought against Plato's theory of Forms: "If someone heard those things you stipulated in your work on demonstration, concerning the exactness of demonstration, he would never suppose that you could offer such lame, poor arguments."[43] Certainly Plethon condemns Aristotle for disagreeing with Plato on points of doctrine. As George Karamanolis has written, for Plethon, "Plato's philosophy represents the truth, or at least is very close to it; there is no point or room for progress further than Plato."[44] But it is striking how often Aristotle's failings are said to concern *methodology*, not just doctrine.

Plethon's polemic is like a funhouse mirror inversion of what we find in *On the Harmony of the Opinions of the Two Philosophers* ascribed to al-Fārābī and indeed what we find in the whole tradition of harmonizing commentary on Aristotle. Most obviously, Plethon leaps upon every divergence of Aristotle from Platonism instead of trying to explain them away. Less obviously, he turns traditional devices for exculpating Aristotle, and for harmonizing him with Plato, into items on a charge sheet. Earlier commentators had admitted that Aristotle was obscure, and purposefully so, which is exactly why we need commentary. For Plethon, by contrast, examples of unclarity and self-contradiction are just what they seem to be: proofs of incompetence. Where the harmonizers "read Aristotle through Aristotle" so as to let one passage illuminate another, Plethon *attacks* Aristotle through Aristotle, turning his own doctrines and methods against their author.

But Plethon accuses Aristotle of something still worse than incompetence: bad character. In that section on Aristotle's refutation of the theory of Forms, Plethon says that Aristotle failed to observe a crucial point due to "malice (βασκανία)."[45] And at the end of the work, he has a few choice words for Aristotle's way of dealing with our abiding concern, the status of authority.

> Plato evidently follows some of those who came before him, while refuting others. Aristotle, though, opposes and chastises all of them. In those cases where he does use the statements of those who came earlier, it's clear that he certainly doesn't want it to be evident that he is using the statements of others. This is very much the practice of the sophist, and entirely foreign to the way of the philosopher.

Plethon's unabashedly ad hominem attack provoked a response in kind from admirers of Aristotle. The initial backlash came from Gannadios Scholarius (d. 1472), who rose to the defense of Aristotle and in his post as patriarch in Ottoman Constantinople had works of Plethon posthumously burned. He justified this measure by charging Plethon with covert paganism. Whether he had good reason for this is a matter of controversy among today's scholars.[46] I myself tend to doubt it, since as I have said I see Plethon as siding with Greek Orthodoxy against the Western church.

But we are in any case more interested in the character assassinations perpetrated against Plato and Aristotle. Which brings us to George Trapezuntius (d. 1473). He was one of several scholars from the East (despite that moniker, he hailed from Crete, not Trebizond) who helped spark humanism in Italy by importing knowledge of Greek philology. He was at first happy to apply his skills to the Platonic corpus, translating the *Parmenides* and the *Laws*, but in time he became a severe critic of Plato. This may be due to the fact that Trapezuntius was deeply interested in rhetoric and was appalled by the attacks on this art in dialogues like the *Gorgias*.[47] Whatever the case, when he turned against Plato he turned hard, writing the *Comparison of the Philosophers Plato and Aristotle*, which adduced Plato's erotic dialogues and ancient biographical material as evidence that Plato was a depraved lover of boys. It's a far cry from the author of the *Harmony*, whom we saw fretting over the far less troubling prospect that Plato and Aristotle pursued two different ways of life, both of them virtuous.

Over the next century, admirers of Plato mounted a defense against this charge. They were so successful that we today use the phrase "Platonic love" to refer to *non*-sexual emotional attachment. A more high-minded, or if you prefer, bowdlerized, image of Plato was immediately put forth in response to Trapezuntius by another Greek émigré, Bessarion (d. 1472). He insisted that the erotic dialogues concerned themselves with "divine" love, in contrast to "earthly" love. Later Marsilio Ficino, in his commentary *Symposium*, goes so far as to exclude sexuality entirely from the realm of love (*eros*). For Ficino—and of course, for Ficino's version of Plato—love is always directed toward beauty, which can be grasped only through hearing, sight, and the mind. Pleasures of touch experienced through sex, therefore, are strictly speaking not "erotic." As he puts it, "The lust to touch the body is not a part of love, nor is it the desire of the lover, but rather a kind of wantonness and the derangement of a servile man."[48]

Yet it would be wrong to see Ficino as an heir of Plethon, at least as concerns the controversy over the merits of Aristotle and Plato.[49] For him, the best defense of Plato was not an attack on Aristotle but a life's work of translating and commenting on Plato and his late ancient followers. Admittedly, he did take exception to Aristotle's arguments against the Form of the Good in his commentary on the *Philebus*, showing that he was aware of disharmony between the two great authorities. But the "Aristotelian" position he found most troubling was not one Ficino would have ascribed to Aristotle himself. This was Averroes's notorious teaching on the unity of the human mind, which was finding support in fifteenth-century Italy to an alarming degree.

In fact, it would be fair to say that Italian humanists usually confined themselves to critique of individual theses put forward by Aristotle or later Peripatetics rather than arguing for the overall superiority of Plato to Aristotle, as Plethon had sought to do.[50] An earlier humanist like Leonardo Bruni (d. 1444) was capable of boiling Aristotle's philosophy down to one controversial thesis, namely, the aforementioned claim that external goods, like wealth and a prospering family (and maybe not being caught in thunderstorms), have genuine value and are needed for happiness.[51] This is not the Aristotle of the scholastic world, who has something to say, if not the last word, on every topic. It is Aristotle as he was known in Hellenistic philosophical literature, like the dialogues of Cicero, which not coincidentally were a major source for Bruni.

To my mind the most interesting case of this "reduced" version of Aristotle, where he appears only as a spokesman for one contentious thesis, comes in the Renaissance debate over the virtue of women. Today his sparse remarks on the inferiority of women to men are notorious in a way that would have stunned philosophers of the Islamic world and Byzantium, who barely engaged with this aspect of his thought. (One reason was that his *Politics*, which contains his most significant discussion of women, was apparently never available in Arabic and was not much discussed in the Greek East.) In Latin Christendom, though, medieval thinkers already made mention of Aristotle's misogyny, with some welcoming it and others lamenting it. That is the distant background for the last author I want to mention in this chapter, Lucrezia Marinella (d. 1653).

In her work *The Nobility and the Excellence of Women and the Defects and Shortcomings of Men*, printed in 1599, she repeatedly draws attention to one particular difference of opinion between Aristotle and Plato.[52] One was a misogynist, the other was not. Plato, as she puts it, claimed that women are "equal to men in valor and wit." Here she has in mind a famous discussion of women in the *Republic*, which gives both genders a role in guarding and ruling the ideal city while conveniently ignoring misogynistic passages like the one at the end of the *Timaeus*. Aristotle by contrast was an "enemy" of women who "was led by scorn, hate, or envy in many of his books, to vituperate and slander the female sex, just as on many occasions he reproved his master Plato."[53] She echoes some of the same strategies used by Plethon, for example, using Aristotle against himself. How can he be so scornful of women given that nature produces so many of them, and according to him nature almost always produces good results? Does not Aristotle's own account of the virtues make it obvious that women are more, not less, virtuous than men? Does not Aristotle himself admit in his *History of Animals* that females are more gentle and compassionate than males? Again like Plethon she also puts Aristotle's motives in question. She assumes that his hateful views must have been motivated by malice, perhaps because he had been spurned by a lover. Besides, he was "of small intelligence."

It may seem astonishing that a woman author of this era felt able to attack any male author with such ferocity, to say nothing of attacking the most influential philosopher of the previous two millennia. And Marinella is indeed a fairly astonishing case, perhaps the most frank and combative defender of women in the "long middle ages." But she was not unique. To the contrary, she stands at the end of another story that is worth telling, one that is intertwined with the story of the medieval debate over Plato and Aristotle. In this other story, the protagonists are women. Their project was not to identify authoritative authors and to decide how such authors should be used. It was to persuade a mostly male readership to treat *them* as being authoritative. How could they make this case in medieval society, which was hardly distinguished for its enlightened views about gender equality? Let's find out.

CHAPTER 6

Finding Their Voices

Women in Byzantine and Latin Christian Philosophy

In 1767 in my hometown of Boston, a poet named Phillis Wheatley published a volume of her verses. For a woman to publish anything at this time was unusual: Wheatley was only the fifth to do so in the American colonies. But for someone like Wheatley to appear in print was unheard of. She was an enslaved African, kidnapped as a child and transported to America only six years previously, in 1761. Readers would have been incredulous that a young, female slave could produce competent poetry whose style was close to that of Alexander Pope. So the volume was prefaced by a testimony from a number of worthies, including John Hancock, reassuring the reader that these works were indeed written by her. This highlights the unprecedented set of social disadvantages Wheatley faced as an author, being not only female and black but also considered the legal property of her masters.

She dealt with this threefold obstacle with a twofold strategy. Sometimes she accepted her supposed inferior status, only to exploit it by speaking truths to her supposed betters. A good example is an address she wrote to graduates of what was then the University of Cambridge, later Harvard University. Of course, the audience would have been made up of privileged white men. After reminding them of her less advantaged origins—"'Twas not long since I left my native shore, the land of errors, and Egyptian gloom"—she exhorted them to the avoidance of sin, adding "an Ethiop' tells you 'tis your greatest foe."[1] But in her poems she often adopted the opposite tactic of speaking from an elevated position, above that of her readers and, in a sense, above her own self. She presented herself as a mouthpiece of divine inspiration, invoking the angels as the source of her poetry, as when she prayed, "raise my mind to a seraphic strain"[2] or exalted poetry in general as a celestial language. Often she invoked the Muses, a classicizing element typical of her work. On occasion Wheatley combined the two strategies, as with this appeal to the Muses: "Inspire, ye sacred nine, your vent'rous Afric' in her great design."[3] Unable to occupy the authorial position that would have been easily available to a free, male, white author, Wheatley adopted variously a voice of humility—I, a mere girl from Africa, dare to say these things—and a voice of transcendence, drawing from a source above the merely human.[4]

It is appropriate that Wheatley used classical tropes in pursuing her twofold strategy, because these are themselves tropes that had been used by women centuries before. The two voices of humility and transcendence, respectively "lower" and "higher" than the discourse routinely employed by male authors, were characteristic of female medieval authors. One might even venture to say that these were the only two strategies open to such authors, excluded as they were from contributing to the literature being produced by schoolmen, churchmen, and men in general. It is a plausible hypothesis that female intellectuals in antiquity might have turned to the same strategies. But that's hard to prove, simply because of the lack of ancient texts written by women. As far as I know, there is not a single classical or late ancient text on an even remotely philosophical topic that can be securely ascribed to a female author. This is not to say that the historian of ancient philosophy will never encounter women. The most famous case is probably Diotima from Plato's *Symposium*; much later, Monica, the mother of Augustine, appeared prominently in her son's own dialogues and his *Confessions*. Augustine depicted Monica as a wise and holy figure who pushed him to accept Christianity and was even present during his decisive vision at Ostia, triggering his final conversion.[5]

This literary representation of Monica prefigures the use of what I have called the "voice of transcendence" in the medieval period. As does another figure who appears at the beginning of the Byzantine philosophical tradition and tellingly is another family member of a male Christian theologian: Gregory of Nyssa's sister Macrina (d. 379). In a work that deserves to be much better known than it is, titled *On Soul and Resurrection*, Gregory cast himself and his sister as the main characters in a restaging of Plato's *Phaedo*.[6] As Socrates was there depicted discussing the immortality of the soul just prior to his execution, so Macrina here lies on her deathbed in physical agony, yet still able to hold forth with Christian versions of the Platonist arguments for immortality.

As we know from a second work by Gregory, a hagiography of Macrina, he saw her as having effectively transcended her gender along with all other concerns of the body. He comments there that he is not even sure whether it is appropriate to call Macrina a woman, since she has passed beyond female nature.[7] In keeping with this, in the dialogue *On Soul and Resurrection* Macrina argues that the true self is the rational soul, which can survive bodily death because of its kinship to God. As she puts it:

> Anyone who says that the soul is a likeness of God should declare that all that is foreign to God falls outside the definition of the soul. For the similar is not preserved through deviations. Since, then, such things are not ascribed to the divine nature, one could reasonably suppose that they are not substantial for the soul either.[8]

The immediate topic here is emotion, which Macrina thinks is extraneous to the soul's nature. This is already relevant to questions of gender, since in antiquity women were commonly thought to be highly emotional. That's something we can see, in fact, in the *Phaedo*, both at the beginning when Socrates sends away his lamenting wife and at the end when he tells his companions to stop weeping over him like women. Gregory of Nyssa subverts that dynamic at the start of his own dialogue by contrasting his own distraught state to Macrina's calm confidence in the face of death. As the dialogue goes on, he subverts it in an even deeper way by making Macrina, a saintly woman, argue that the true self lacks all features associated with embodiment. This applies not only to emotion, but even to gender itself, since the soul is like God and God is neither male nor female.

As interesting as this dialogue is, it still hasn't provided us with an example of a woman writing in her own voice. We can find that later in the Byzantine tradition, though. Not that Byzantium was a particularly feminist culture. Far from it. Ancient Greek assumptions about women were still very much in force, and, as our look at Gregory already suggests, the highest achievement that could be fulfilled by women was to transcend the boundaries of their gender. Christian holiness provided the chief means of doing so. One hagiographical work about saintly women argued that such figures are even more admirable than holy men, because "they have a weaker nature and yet were not hindered by this from climbing up to the summit of virtue, but they made the female [element] male through a virile mind and accomplished the same and even more than the men."[9]

Yet some Byzantine texts suggest that women might excel through their intellectual capacities and not only through their piety. A kind of compromise, or perhaps conflict, between these two ideas about excellent women can be found in the encomium that the eleventh-century philosopher and scholar Michael Psellos composed for his mother, Theodote (d. 1054).[10] On the one hand, Psellos presents her as a holy figure devoted to God and committed to ascetic chastisement of the body. He talks about how her fasting made her seem almost dead, "like a shadow on a wooden board." Yet he also praises Theodote's rational perfection and mentions her view that men and women "possess reason equally." With the example of Macrina probably at the back of his mind, Psellos describes how his mother instructed his father on the afterlife following the death of their daughter, that is, Psellos's sister. This is the side of Theodote that Psellos relates to, since by his own admission he was never able to embrace the ascetic life himself. In this he fell short of her example, leading him ruefully to remark, "My devotion to philosophy is limited to its cloak."

All this provides us with a context to understand the most remarkable woman of Byzantine literature, Anna Komnene. As discussed in the previous chapter, she played an important role in the history of philosophy by gathering a circle of scholars to write commentaries on previously uncommented works by Aristotle. A funeral oration for Anna by George Tornikes informs us, "The works which philosophers of our time addressed to her bear witness to her love of learning, works concerning those writings of Aristotle on which commentaries had not been written until her time."[11] George also explains how Anna came to be so learned, even, as he puts it, "wiser than men." Despite the wariness of her parents, who feared exposing her to pagan literature, he says that "just as wise mothers of children often distrust match-makers, lest they inspire in maidens dishonorable passions," Anna "braced the weakness of [her] soul." "Like a maiden who takes a furtive glance at her bridegroom through some chink," she undertook independent study of the liberal arts.

The fruit of this assignation was not only the flowering of commentary on Aristotle, but Anna's own *Alexiad*, an epic historical work devoted to the exploits of her father, Alexios Komnene.[12] Anna Komnene was no Phillis Wheatley. As a royal princess she wielded obvious socioeconomic advantages that put her in the rare position to undertake such an ambitious literary project. Yet even she adopted the voice of humility, describing herself modestly in the preface to the *Alexiad* as one who is "not without some acquaintance with literature, having devoted the most earnest study to the Greek language, and being not un-practiced in rhetoric and having read thoroughly the treatises of Aristotle and the dialogues of Plato." Today, we would call this "humble-bragging." Leonora Neville has written about Anna's carefully crafted literary persona, which she calls "an exaggeratedly feminine persona of extreme emotionalism."[13] Yet Anna also emphasizes her own reliability as a historian and her ability to, for example, overcome grief over her father's death in order to tell her story. As Neville later adds:

> Anna's repeated practice of breaking out of the proper boundaries of history, breaking out of a masculinized historian's voice, to speak and participate in the discourses her culture marked as feminized, only to point out and apologize for her transgression, focuses attention both on her essentially female nature, and her ability to transcend that nature.[14]

Here we have, even in this most powerful and privileged of female authors, the dual strategy I've been describing. Since she could not just write as a woman and be taken seriously, she alternately abased herself by humbly calling attention to her limitations as a "mere woman" and suggested that she had somehow risen above her status as a woman altogether. This second aspect of her authorial persona recalls something Psellos says in the encomium for his mother: she "knew nothing feminine, except what was decreed by nature, but was in all other respects strong and manly in soul."[15]

Turning now to Latin Christendom, I might be expected to go through a series of authors who adopt the "voice of transcendence," given the fame of female mystics in the medieval West, figures like Hildegard of Bingen and Julian of Norwich. But that is only part of the story, and in terms of the broader culture, a pretty small part. Those mystical authors were obviously exceptional, not just in the sense that they were rare, but in the sense that they had removed themselves from the standard expectations and duties of the medieval woman. A case that is more representative, though still of course exceptional (given that mere literacy was exceptional, never mind actually writing works that survive to the present day), is that of the Carolingian author Dhuoda. Around 841, she wrote a letter to her son William, offering him practical and moral advice in a work that combined poetic and prose elements.[16] This is a widespread feature of medieval writings, inspired by Boethius's *Consolation of Philosophy*, only one sign of Dhuoda's learning. Yet the fundamentally domestic occasion of the text reminds us of the role standardly played by medieval women, whose sphere of competence was restricted to overseeing her household and family. In this sense Dhuoda is the medieval heir of the anonymous, possibly female authors of antiquity who wrote letters on such domestic matters as raising children and coping with a husband's adultery, which have come down to us spuriously ascribed to female figures from the Pythagorean tradition.[17]

As for the aforementioned famous names from the mystical tradition, we find them combining the two strategies I have been describing, sometimes even in the same passage. Take Hildegard of Bingen (d. 1179). More obvious in her writings is the voice of transcendence, as she reports on visions she received from God, whom she calls the "living light," and implicitly claims special authority to interpret those visions. In a work like her *Scivias*, she not only relates the vision—as when she saw an iron mountain used as a seat by a luminous winged giant—but also explains the symbolic meaning of each of its details.[18] This looks like a bold assertion of theological authority. Yet the very explanation of her authoritative position is given in the voice of humility. These things have been possible for Hildegard as a mere woman, because despite "remaining in the fragility of the weaker rib," that is, despite the fact that woman was formed from Adam's side and is thus inferior to man, "she is filled with mystical inspiration."[19]

A model for this nuanced self-presentation—weaker than men, yet given insight beyond the ken of humans—would have been the Virgin Mary. The point is well made by a poem that Hildegard herself devoted to Mary.

> O great the wonder that in a female body a king entered. God did this as humility rises above all. And O great the happiness in that woman, because the evil that came from woman [Eve], this one [Mary] then swept away.[20]

Hildegard, like Mary, was a humble woman exalted above the rest of humankind after being chosen by God. She took advantage of this status in her dealings with men, as when she presumed to pronounce on a piece of technical scholastic philosophy put forth by Gilbert of Poitiers, despite being, in her own words, not "imbued with human doctrine."[21] Her general verdict on the scholastics was severe, as she wrote in a letter, "The teachers and the masters (*doctores et magistri*) do not wish to sing with the trumpet of the justice of God." On another occasion she was annoyed by the archbishop of Mainz and did not hesitate to tell him so. The voice of transcendence rang out as she effectively claimed identity with God. With pointed use of the first person, she intimidated the archbishop with the words, "I am the height and the depth, the circle and the descending light."[22]

Few medieval women asserted the right to speak like this, even among those who claimed to have enjoyed mystical experiences. Beginning in the thirteenth century, we see such authors instead employing the tropes of courtly romance literature. In a kind of gender swap, the role of the pining male lover was played by the female mystic, while God or Christ was the remote and mostly unattainable love object. One central author in this literature of *minne*, meaning "love," was Mechthild of Magdeburg (d. 1282), whose German vernacular writings figure her intermittent union with God as an exquisitely agonizing erotic relationship. This was daring stuff and provoked criticism, as we can see from a passage in Mechthild's *Flowing Light of Divinity* (*Das fließende Licht der Gottheit*), where she responds to a threat to burn her book. Sounding not unlike Hildegard, she admits that she is no "spiritually learned man (*geleret geistliche man*)," but precisely because of her humble status, she claims to be an ideal vessel for God's grace. Sure enough, a vision comes from God to reassure her: "no one can burn the truth." Again recalling Hildegard and her bold critique of the schoolmen from a position of self-conscious modesty, Mechthild reflected on this episode by saying that "learned tongues are taught by the unlearned mouth."[23]

One of the rules for this dialectic between humility and transcendence is that the female author should at least pose as a passive recipient of God's illumination. Thus Mechthild, looking back on the time before "God's word came into her soul," says that she never sought to receive this revelatory gift.[24] And this is another reason why Mechthild and comparable authors like Hadewijch (early to mid-thirteenth century) described their relation to God by using the language of courtly love poetry. The lover, here the female mystic, never knows when the beloved, here God, will appear, so that desperate longing may be satisfied with a union that outstrips the power of human thought and language. Hadewijch daringly evoked the doctrine of the Trinity to describe this encounter with the divine.

> The Father took the Son to himself with me and took me to himself with the Son. And in this unity into which I was taken and where I was enlightened, I understood this essence and knew it more clearly than, by speech, reason, or sight, one can know anything that is knowable on earth.[25]

In a more frankly erotic application of the same idea, Mechthild spoke of her soul as "naked," with nothing between it and God.[26]

One author who followed the logic of humility and transcendence to its logical conclusion was Marguerite Porete (d. 1310), burned to death by the Parisian authorities after she refused to disavow her supposedly heretical book, *The Mirror of Simple Souls*.[27] It is another dialogue, in which characters representing the author's soul and abstract notions like Love and Reason discuss the possibility and meaning of union with God. Marguerite's doctrine is put especially in the mouth of the character Love, who explains that the soul reaches God by achieving a state of maximal humility, which can also be called "annihilation."[28] This happens when the soul's will is extinguished to the point of wanting nothing at all, not even union with God. Annihilation is a form of self-knowledge in which the soul, as a created entity, comes to see herself as being nothing at all in comparison to the infinity of God. Here the voice of humility has become the voice of outright self-abnegation. Marguerite says that the soul "does not seek for knowledge of God among the teachers of this world, but by truly despising this world and herself."[29]

That sounds like a rationale for punishing asceticism, as pursued by Psellos's mother, Theodote, and any number of saintly Christian women going back to late antiquity. But actually Marguerite Porete was rather unimpressed by asceticism and indeed by all attempts to exercise "virtue" in this world.[30] She thought that the annihilated soul can transcend virtue, one of the teachings that appalled the church and was quoted in the documents of the trial leading to her execution. Of course, her point is not that one should live hedonistically, or engage in worldly vice. Rather, the mystic "takes leave" of the whole arena of practical morality. She does not virtuously resist desire but ceases to have desire at all. She does not tame her will but aligns her will entirely with that of God, to the point that there is no difference between them. Marguerite's rather abstract approach to the humility of the mystic puts her close to a figure like Meister Eckhart, who also emphasized the "nothingness" of created things and proposed that we should learn to subsume our will entirely within the divine will. He may even have been influenced by Marguerite, though this remains a matter of scholarly debate.[31]

By contrast, prominent women thinkers of the later fourteenth century, like Catherine of Siena (d. 1380) and Julian of Norwich (d. after 1416), pursued union with God using the tools of what has been called "affective mysticism."[32] This style of mysticism is anything but abstract. It can involve spectacular forms of self-chastisement. Famously, Catherine starved to death after nourishing herself on nothing but the eucharistic host. Other affective mystics went in for such practices as eating the scabs and drinking the pus of lepers. This should provoke more than lurid curiosity. What was the intellectual or spiritual rationale behind such behavior? An answer has been provided by Caroline Walker Bynum's *Holy Fast and Holy Feast*, one of the more influential books in medieval studies from the past several decades.[33] Bynum set out to explain why medieval women authors, and medieval male authors writing about holy women, so frequently referred to food and used other images having to do with the body, as when they had visions of themselves nursing Christ or saw him before them on the wall, drenched in blood.

At the risk of oversimplifying, Bynum's answer was that medieval women embraced the close association of women with embodiment, sexual reproduction, food production, and bodily fluids like blood and breast milk. Taking their cue from the doctrines of the Incarnation and the Eucharist, where the divine literally manifests in physical form, they located spirituality and even sacredness in such physical phenomena. Bynum says, "In a religiosity where wounds are the source of a mother's milk, fatal disease is a bridal chamber, pain or insanity clings to the breast like perfume, physicality is hardly rejected or transcended. Rather, it is explored and embraced."[34] This is a plausible and fruitful proposal that has been carried forward in significant ways by other scholars like Amy Hollywood and Christina Van Dyke. I don't want to attempt anything that ambitious here but only to tease out an implication already present in Bynum's original study, namely, that the phenomenon she identified represents a perfect synthesis of the dialectic of humility and transcendence that I have been discussing.

In fact, affective mysticism and the more abstract doctrine of annihilation found in Marguerite Porete represent two alternative ways to speak simultaneously with the voices of humility and transcendence. If, as Marguerite argues, the mystic is nothing at all apart from God, then self-knowledge is becoming simultaneously aware of her infinite humility *and* her infinite transcendence. And if, as the affective mystics seem to be suggesting, the divine is immanent in the most despised and lowly aspects of our physical experience, then the supposedly humble roles allowed to women in medieval culture, like the preparation of food or the birthing and nursing of children, can be reconceived as exalted activities that bring women into contact with God.

It makes perfect sense that the most ambitious, and most philosophically challenging, achievements of medieval women authors would take this form. Excluded from the philosophical discourse of scholastic thinkers, they could speak from a position of inferiority to those thinkers, emphasizing their weak femininity. Or they could speak from a position of superiority, not thanks to any personal achievement, of course, but thanks to the passive reception of a divine gift. This rhetorical posture went together with admissions of inability to do "rational" philosophy in the fashion of an Aristotelian scholastic, or a refusal to do so. This kind of philosophy is either too elevated for our women authors, or beneath their contempt, or both at the same time. We've seen examples already in Hildegard and Mechthild. Marguerite offers another one. In her dialogue Reason herself is one of the personifications, and this character consistently fails to understand the teachings of Love, which are found in "no book." Reason thus raises a series of objections against Marguerite's central idea of eliminating will. But ultimately Reason's "death" is declared and she departs the scene.[35]

Marguerite is, as usual, exceptional in her frank disdain for the discourse of the schoolmen, which was so important to the life and institutions of the church at this time and beyond. Given that women could not attend the universities, there was little or no prospect of a female thinker taking the reverse approach and embracing scholastic discourse. Yet before long, women authors would get the opportunity to write on more or less equal terms with men. This happened thanks to another movement that was opposed to the methods and the very language of the schoolmen: humanism. The seeds were already being planted in the fourteenth century, as Dante (d. 1321), a contemporary of Marguerite Porete, and somewhat later Petrarch (d. 1374) and Boccaccio (d. 1375), engaged in many of the activities that would become characteristic of humanism in the Italian Renaissance, like writing in the vernacular and devoting philological effort to editing and translating long unread works of antiquity. These efforts already played a role in shifting attitudes toward the role of women in intellectual life. To write in the vernacular was to write for a wider audience, including women, as explicitly recognized by Dante in his *Banquet* (*Convivio*).[36] And one classicizing genre that became popular in the Renaissance was the catalog of famous or virtuous women, pioneered by Boccaccio in 1361.

Among those who followed his lead were several women authors who likewise enumerated admirable pagan and Christian women from ancient history. *The City of Ladies* by Christine de Pizan (d. ca. 1430) and later works by figures of the Italian Renaissance like Moderata Fonte (d. 1592), Lucrezia Marinella (d. 1653), and Arcangela Tarabotti (d. 1652), rebutted the calumnies of misogynists and went so far as to say that women are *more* virtuous than men, in fact more excellent than men in every way. They even argued that women should after all be allowed to pursue scholastic learning. Lucrezia Marinella had a strong suspicion about why women weren't being trained in the sciences: "Man does not permit women to apply herself to such studies, fearing, with reason, that she will surpass him in them."[37]

Here we see women abandoning the strategies of humility and transcendence, claiming instead that women are capable of engaging, and excelling, in the same sorts of discourse and speculation pursued by men. But I think the main breakthrough, the one that allowed Renaissance women to move past the two tactics that had animated and facilitated the writing of medieval women, was not actually the so-called *querelle des femmes*, or debate about women. It was, rather, the introduction of a new standard for measuring intellectual ability: eloquence. In the first half of the fifteenth century humanists like Coluccio Salutati (d. 1406), Leonardo Bruni, and most aggressively, Lorenzo Valla (d. 1457) started to polemicize against scholasticism and fetishize the use of excellent Latin. They wanted to drop the barbarisms used in medieval translations of Aristotle and usher in a new age of rhetorical refinement reviving the language of Cicero.

The reason this is relevant for us is that women had much better chances of acquiring superb Latin than receiving an advanced training in scholasticism. The humanists were explicitly in favor of offering their brand of education to women. Bruni wrote a letter to a noblewoman of his acquaintance advising her that the study of classical rhetoric was appropriate for those of her sex, even if women would have no opportunity to engage in public oratory. Such study encourages virtue, so it is good for everyone. Besides, as another author observed, these days the better class of men wanted to marry educated ladies.[38] But it seems that male humanists did not anticipate the result, which was the emergence of at least some women who could write Latin as well as they could. We see this especially in published collections of letters by authors like Isotta Nogarola (d. 1466), Laura Cereta (d. 1499), and Cassandra Fedele (d. 1558).[39]

Admittedly, these figures do still tactically employ the voice of humility to soften up their audience, as when Fedele calls herself a "bold little woman" or "insignificant girl," Nogarola apologizes for her "girlish" letters, and Cereta refers to herself as "a mere female, inept at literary matters." But this is clearly just false modesty, of the sort typical of all humanist writing, and is coupled with straightforward declarations of ambition. These women unabashedly stated their aim to achieve "fame" and "glory" through their writings, just as male humanists wished to do. And it worked. Cassandra Fedele was particularly celebrated in her own time, with one observer proclaiming that she was an "ornament for the greatness of [Venice's] empire" and had won glory for her own sex rivaling that claimed by men.[40] Isotta Nogarola was somewhat less famous, but after being praised by the humanist Guarino Guarini, she wrote to him, "I have now achieved immortality and need no longer be anxious about the public's opinion and estimation of me," something she compared to the lasting reputation given to Socrates thanks to the defense offered by Plato.[41]

Perhaps alluding to her daring attempt to play on a level field with men, Nogarola several times refers to stories from antiquity involving cross-dressing: Euclides was banned from Athens as a citizen of Megara and disguised himself as a woman in order to study with Socrates; Axiothea donned men's clothing in order to visit Plato's Academy.[42] As these allusions also imply, women humanists were interested in attaining a philosophical education, with their excellent Latin giving them the right to do so. They would graduate, so to speak, from rhetoric to dialectic. Nogarola was encouraged by a male correspondent to study Aristotle and his heirs, including not only scholastics of Latin Christendom but also authors from the Islamic world like Avicenna, al-Ghazālī, and Averroes.[43] Fedele spoke of long nights spent awake reading the "Peripatetic philosophers." Cereta too was burning the candle at both ends, as she complained that domestic chores left her little time to study and write, and advised her readers not to "waste nights sleeping."[44]

That biographical detail reveals why the women humanists were not really competing on a level field with men. The leading expert on these figures, Margaret King, has pointed out that they usually peaked early as young, unmarried women and then faced a fateful choice: marry and give up scholarship or adopt a life of religious asceticism to justify their single status.[45] Nogarola took the latter course, which enabled her to keep living the life of the mind, whereas her similarly talented sister, Ginevre, gave up that life to marry. Cereta married but was able to keep writing thanks to the early death of her husband. This recalls a line in Christine de Pizan, consoling herself about the death of her own husband: at least it gave her more time for her studies! Despite the silver lining, both women were distraught over their husbands' deaths. Cereta's intellectual outlook seems to have changed fundamentally after her harsh encounter with mortality. She cited the death of her husband as a lesson in the unpredictability of fortune and wrote, "Since this mortal life of ours will live on after death, I have renounced—for it is holier to do so—that glory, transitory and slipping, which being full of the contrariness of earthly beings, separates us from the true religion of pious faith."[46]

So it would be an exaggeration to say that fifteenth- or sixteenth-century women achieved equal opportunity with men when it came to intellectual pursuits. Indeed, it would be an exaggeration to say that even now in the twenty-first century. But as twenty-first-century readers I think we can learn a lesson from the story I've just told, one that bears on the themes of this book. We have been concerned with questions of authority and belief formation and have seen that the answer to such questions lies at least partially in giving a good second-order account about the formation of first-order beliefs. For instance, even if we do not have expertise in a given scientific field, we may be able to satisfy ourselves that someone else has such expertise, for example, by looking at their track record or their credentials. Women in the medieval period suffered from a phenomenon that Miranda Fricker has dubbed "epistemic injustice": their authority was down-rated simply because they were women.[47] To inflict epistemic injustice on someone is to use a faulty rule of second-order belief formation. It might make sense to distrust someone's views about who is likely to win the World Series if you find out she has never actually watched a baseball match, but it wouldn't make sense to distrust someone's views on this matter simply because she is a woman.

My discussion of women authors from the medieval period has shown how well they already understood the phenomenon of epistemic injustice. Being subjected to a particularly severe form of it, they realized that they needed to push back at the level of second-order belief. They did so through a kind of tactical retreat, in which what we might call "normal authority" was ceded to men. Hildegard, Mechthild, and Marguerite did not claim authoritative expertise in matters of religion and science, at least not the kind of expertise claimed by clerics and scholastics. Instead, they found ways to speak persuasively even as they entirely disclaimed authority. A first part of this strategy was to adopt what I have called the voice of humility: I may be a mere woman, but you should listen to me anyway. This could underscore that the truths being conveyed are in principle open to absolutely everyone, the point made by Phillis Wheatley exhorting those Cambridge graduates to a more Christian way of life. Or it could involve restricting themselves to the domestic realm, where even Aristotle had granted them an authoritative role.

The second part of the strategy was more daring and more cunning. They presented themselves as passive conduits for an authority higher than any churchman or schoolman. The more abject the woman's standing, the more fitting she would be as a locus for God to reveal his grace. Thus Mechthild speaks of allowing her soul to "sink to the lowest place where God rules."[48] On this basis the voice of humility could be fused with a voice of transcendence, with which these women would speak for God himself. On the one hand, this was a bold demand that others take them seriously. On the other hand, since the truth was claimed to come from God and not the woman herself, listeners did not have to concede epistemic standing to the woman herself. Indeed, medieval assumptions about the inferiority of women made it all the more plausible to see them as passive vessels for divine inspiration.

With the rise of humanism, new strategies offered themselves. Now women could dare to contend openly for literary renown. Cassandra Fedele even commented, "It is a very sweet victory indeed to outstrip men of eloquence."[49] As a result, the second-order dispute over women's testimony started to come into the open. Laura Cereta, speaking rhetorically to men about their refusal to let women have a proper education despite their equal talent, wrote: *vestra est auctoritas, nostrum ingenium*, meaning "you have the authority, but we have the inborn ability."[50] One could cite any number of similar passages from the women authors of the sixteenth and seventeenth centuries who wrote against misogyny. They insisted that sex was irrelevant to intellectual ability and even claimed that women have more potential than men. Thus Moderata Fonte, writing in 1592, said, "We have just as much right to speak about [scientific] subjects as they have, and if we were educated properly as girls, we'd outstrip men's performance in any science or art you care to name."[51]

But of course the transition from the medieval age to the Renaissance was a gradual one. It's not as if the pope sent a letter to the rest of Europe in the year 1500 telling everyone to start reading Cicero and get ready for the arrival of the printing press. If I had to name a single author who best represents the shift I've just been describing, I would choose Christine de Pizan. Her life spanned the fourteenth and fifteenth centuries, and her works display both the typically "medieval" and the typically "Renaissance" rhetorical strategies. Early in her writing career, she showed herself an adept user of the voice of humility in the famous dispute she incited over the *Romance of the Rose*. This was right around the turn of the fifteenth century. Christine complained of the misogyny in this famous poem, written more than a hundred years previously by Jean de Meun and already celebrated as a classic of medieval French literature, and containing passages where characters said things like, "You [women] are all now, will be, and have been, whores, in deed or intention."[52] To justify her impertinent attack on a widely admired text, Christine pointed out that this was a rare topic on which she could indeed speak with authority. Being female herself, she could claim some insight into the moral psychology of other women. So this was an occasion where men might want to listen to her despite her being, as she self-deprecatingly described herself, a "woman of untrained intellect." She was right to anticipate this reaction. One of the men who rose in defense of Jean de Meun sneeringly described her as "not lacking in intelligence within the limits of her female capacity."[53]

Some years later, in works like the *City of Ladies* and the *Vision*, Christine sounds more like the women humanists of the Renaissance. She claims competence in traditionally male fields like scholastic thought and even the history of ancient philosophy, which is summarized in the second part of the *Vision* along with an allegorical description of herself moving through the halls of the University at Paris. The beginning of the *City of Ladies* dramatizes her own emerging confidence. A fictional version of Christine in the dialogue laments the inferiority of her sex after reading a misogynist book. But she is then visited by several "Ladies," personifications of Reason, Justice, and Rectitude, who go on to present her with an avalanche of historical evidence for the virtue of womankind. As Fonte and Marinella will later do, Christine de Pizan here embraces Boccaccio's project of cataloging "famous women" and uses it to mount a frontal assault in the battle of the sexes. She has found her voice, and she uses it to say things that it's hard to imagine finding in the writings of a "medieval" woman. My favorite example comes from Christine's *Vision*: "One day, a man criticized my desire for knowledge, saying that it was inappropriate for a woman to be learned, as it was so rare, to which I replied that it was even less fitting for a man to be ignorant, as it was so common."[54]

CHAPTER 7

The Rule of Reason

Human and Animal Nature

As we've seen in this book, medieval thinkers devoted enormous time and effort to considering the nature of acceptable belief. Not in the sense that we usually associate with the medievals, where the question would be which beliefs are religiously, or perhaps politically, acceptable. Rather, in the sense of *rationally* acceptable. Do you need to ensure for yourself that your beliefs are definitely true or at least well justified? Or can you depend for your beliefs on authoritative figures and texts? If so, which authorities should you take as reliable? And how might you establish yourself as a reliable authority for others, especially if you are a member of an oppressed group, like women? In all this it has been taken more or less for granted that it is a good thing to take care forming one's beliefs or, even better, to attain full-blown knowledge. Intellectuals looked down on the sizable majority of humans who failed to manage this, or at least failed to manage it as well as the intellectuals could.

But why exactly was it better to be a member of the elite, to have beliefs that had been formed in the "acceptable" way? It's unlikely that this was a matter of sheer utility or practicality. For one thing, medieval philosophers were rarely utilitarians. For another, they standardly followed Aristotle's division of philosophy into theoretical and practical spheres. It would seem odd, or even incoherent, to explain the value of *theoretical* philosophy in terms of *practical* utility. Then too, worries of epistemic luck notwithstanding, it might be just as practically useful to be the follower of a reliable authority as to be the authority oneself. This is a version of a point already made in Plato's *Meno*: true belief about how to travel to a certain destination will get you there just as well as knowledge would, so the true belief is "no less useful" (97b–c). But the medievals clearly held that, even in a situation where expertise and slavish acceptance of instruction from an expert will get you equally good results, it is still preferable to be the expert.

In a medieval context this attitude was not just in need of justification, but downright problematic. Moses, Christ, and Muḥammad offered prophetic truth and salvation to everyone, not just to experts, scientists, and intellectuals. In their Bibles the Christians could read Saint Paul saying that "God has made foolish the wisdom of the world (τὴν σοφίαν τοῦ κόσμου)" (1 Corinthians 1:20), a line seized upon by late ancient and medieval authors who wanted to put pagan philosophers, and contemporaries who admired them, in their place.[1] At the other end of the spectrum were the hard-core rationalists of the Islamic world, men like al-Fārābī and Averroes, who were more or less "professionally" committed to the study of Aristotle. These *falāsifa*, and elitists of the *kalām* tradition like al-Ghazālī, saw themselves as having the obligation of the *mujtahid* to think for himself, just as ordinary folk have the obligation of the *muqallid* to accept the judgment of authority. Both kinds of person are "doing what they ought to," but of course the *mujtahid* is superior to the *muqallid*, even if both are carrying out their epistemic and religious duties.

In this final chapter, I want to focus on one medieval rationale for this preference, for valuing reason and knowledge so highly: namely, that it is only by this means that we fully realize human nature itself. The locus classicus (in every sense of the phrase) for this idea is Aristotle, *Nicomachean Ethics* 1.7. Here we find the famous *ergon*, or function, argument, which contends that happiness lies in the excellent performance of the distinctive human function, namely, the use of reason. Aristotle explicitly contrasts humans to plants and to animals, who are incapable of reason and so do not share that function, though they do have in common with us the "life of sense perception." "What remains," he says, "is the active life of that which has reason (λείπεται δὴ πρακτική τις τοῦ λόγον ἔχοντος), on the one hand that which can obey reason (ἐπιπειθὲς λόγῳ), on the other hand that which can think (διανοούμενον)" (1098a3–5).

According to Aristotle, then, the most happy life will be the life that is most fully human. This will be the life in which the capacity for reason is used excellently, since it is the capacity for reason that makes us humans and not mere animals, or even worse, plants. So here we have our justification for valuing superior use of reason. It is constitutive of the happy life, and the happy life is the best life.

As Aristotle says in the final phrase just quoted, the rationality that is proper to humanity has two aspects, defined in terms of obedience and thinking. Both aspects became important in medieval discussions about how humans differ from other animals. To understand the aspect of human nature that is obedient to reason, the medievals looked back to the same author Aristotle himself surely had in mind, Plato. In his dialogues, especially the *Republic*, *Phaedrus*, and *Timaeus*, Plato described the human soul as having three parts, namely, reason, spirit, and desire.[2] This account is pervasive in discussions of moral psychology in the Islamic world. As mentioned in chapter 5, the transmission of Plato's dialogues into Arabic was rather incomplete, but the works of Galen were translated on a massive scale. Through Galen's paraphrases of dialogues, including the *Timaeus*, and through Galen's own works, the theory of the tripartite soul was well known in Arabic.

An excellent example is Abū Bakr al-Rāzī's debate with his fellow townsman Abū Ḥātim. As we saw in chapter 5, al-Rāzī considered himself a follower of Plato, albeit one who reserved the right to make up his own mind. This attitude is well illustrated by his ethical treatise the *Spiritual Medicine*.[3] It devotes some pages to explaining the theory of the tripartite soul, which is ascribed to both Plato and Socrates. In this case al-Rāzī does not have to choose between endorsing the authority of Plato and Aristotle. In a syncretic move often found in Arabic philosophical works of the formative period, he simply assumes that the tripartite soul of the *Republic* and *Timaeus* can be conflated with the three faculties of soul in Aristotle. Thus he speaks of an "irascible and animal soul" and a "vegetative, growth, appetitive" soul as aspects of the human soul that are lower than the rational soul.[4]

The reason this theory of soul is so important in an ethical context is that, from al-Rāzī's point of view, defects of character typically stem from a failure of reason to dominate the lower souls. He makes this point the centerpiece of his whole ethical teaching.

> The most noble and greatest principle, and the most useful in reaching the goal of this book of ours, is the subduing of desire, opposing what nature calls us to do in most cases.[5]

He repeatedly states that the rational restraint of natural desire is a distinctively human capacity, indeed *the* distinctive human capacity, as in the immediate sequel of the quotation just above.

> This is the primary respect in which people are superior to beasts: the sovereignty of volition and unleashing action only after deliberation (*rawiyya*). For beasts are not capable of checking themselves from what nature calls them to do, and they act without restraining themselves or deliberating over it.

And again later on, with reference to the tendencies of the irascible or "animal" soul:

> One should control oneself so that, at a moment of anger, one acts only after thought (*fikr*) and deliberation. . . . [O]ne should not, in common with beasts, unleash action with no deliberation.[6]

At the very outset of the *Spiritual Medicine* al-Rāzī has extolled reason (*ʿaql*) as a great gift to humans from God, already indicating that it is through reason that we are better than "irrational animals."[7] The "medicine" offered in the work thus consists of advice for strengthening one's reason to keep the lower soul in check, extirpating tendencies like wrathfulness, gluttony, licentiousness, and even fidgeting. On this last topic al-Rāzī tells the story of a king who was shamed into not toying with his beard, a case of the rational soul being supported by the irascible soul, which values honor, to defeat the appetitive soul.[8]

The *Refinement of Character*, an influential work on ethics written by Miskawayh (d. 1030), draws more heavily on Aristotle's *Ethics* than al-Rāzī had done. But Miskawayh likewise uses the Platonic theory of the tripartite soul and defines virtue in terms of reason's control over the lower parts of the soul.[9] Also like al-Rāzī and Galen before him, Miskawayh draws an extended analogy between the training of character and the sort of regime recommended by doctors for bodily health. Ethical advice is, in other words, medicine for the soul rather than the body.[10] Neither author recommends extirpating the desires of the lower souls entirely. The desire for physical pleasure, for example, is rooted in the lowest, "appetitive" soul. It plays an important function by leading us to pursue what our bodies need, whether this be food and drink or sex.[11] So it is not always animalistic to have lower desires and act on them, even if Miskawayh calls the appetitive soul "bestial (*bahīmiyya*)." Surrendering oneself to pleasure, though, does mean acting like a pig or a worm and falling below the rank of the properly human.[12] When people of this sort do use their rational soul, it is instrumentalized for the sake of pursuing pleasure.

Similarly, the middle soul and its capacity to feel anger can be useful. Much as al-Rāzī suggested that its sensitivity to dishonor can motivate us to act well, for instance, by not fidgeting, Miskawayh says that agitation of the irascible soul can help quell cowardice.[13] But both authors think that excessive anger is a disease of the soul and provide advice on how to avoid this. Miskawayh's discussion of anger is, in fact, a good illustration of his more generally harmonizing approach to ancient ethics. He identifies anger as an agitation of the irascible soul, as Platonic psychology would suggest. But he also urges us to cultivate an Aristotelian virtue with respect to irascibility. We ought to strike a mean between two vicious extremes, in this case feeling neither too much nor too little anger. And he adds that anger involves the boiling of blood around the heart, also mentioned by Aristotle.[14] Finally, Miskawayh takes a leaf from Galen by talking about the way different bodily temperaments lead to greater or lesser irascibility. The point of controlling anger, again, is to ensure that we are "amenable to reason," for instance, capable of taking good advice, which would be impossible in a furious mood.[15] (People who write books of ethical advice tend to emphasize the importance of being able to take advice about ethics.)

So al-Rāzī and Miskawayh both endorsed what the Hellenistic philosophical tradition called *metriopatheia*, or moderation of the passions, rather than *apatheia*, the extirpation or complete subdual of the passions. While Islam has of course not been without its ascetic tendencies, it was common for Muslim intellectuals to criticize Christians for being overly hostile to bodily desire. Thus Yaḥyā Ibn ʿAdī, a Christian thinker discussed in previous chapters, who worked between the times of al-Rāzī and Miskawayh, felt the need to respond to (presumably Muslim) critics of the Christian ideal of monastic chastity (*ʿiffa*).[16] Ibn ʿAdī saw total domination of bodily desire as a kind of heroic, perhaps supererogatory feat that is to be pursued by a spiritual elite, an equivalent in the moral sphere of the epistemic elite so often discussed in this book. This is how he deals with the objection that chastity would lead to the extinction of the human race: only a select few will be capable of this virtue, so the honoring of chastity will have little or no impact on overall population. Similar ideas can be found in late ancient pagan ethics, for example, in Porphyry's *On Abstinence*, which discourages the killing and eating of animals but aims its arguments only at philosophers.

Indeed, for all their theological disagreements, Neoplatonists and late ancient Christian intellectuals had this in common: they were attracted by the ideal of *apatheia*, in which the lower soul and its desires would be not just moderated and overseen by reason, but entirely eliminated as sources of effective motivation. A paradigm example is the "desert father" Evagrius (d. 399), who understood the passions (*pathe*) of the lower soul to be the vulnerable point at which demonic influence can turn us away from God.[17] Moving forward into the medieval Christian traditions, we have already seen with the example of Psellos's encomium of his mother how Byzantine piety could manifest itself as extreme asceticism. Psellos even calls his mother's ascetic lifestyle "philosophy," a usage that itself goes back to late antiquity. And of course this kind of "philosophy" was not only for women. The Hesychast movement, which culminated in the work of the late Byzantine theologian Gregory Palamas, drew on earlier figures like Maximus the Confessor (d. 662) and Symeon the New Theologian (d. 1022) who portrayed bodily asceticism as a preparation for a mystical vision of God.[18]

The same general idea, in which desires bubble up from the lower parts of our psychology and need to be restrained by reason, is something we also find in Latin Christendom. One idea, which goes all the way back to Stoic authors such as Seneca, was that emotional reactions and affective desires are more or less spontaneous "motions" that may or may not lead to action, depending on whether the rational mind allows itself to be incited.[19] The sight of an attractive member of the opposite sex might provoke a lustful instinctive reaction in the soul, but we are not forced to act in accordance with that reaction. In early medieval thought there was a debate as to whether these initial motions are themselves sinful. At a minimum they are a *consequence* of sin, because in our prelapsarian state the affective motions would have been effortlessly subject to the rational will. But whether each wicked, "instinctive" desire counts as a new sin would depend on whether they are subject to rational control, if only by planning ahead. Knowing that you have lustful urges when you see members of the opposite sex, you might retreat to a monastery or convent to get away from them. This topic gave rise to another version of the contrast between humans and animals. Animals are incapable of sin, because in their case, neither their initial urges nor the actions they perform as a result are subject to their deliberate control.

Ethics, like just about every other area of philosophy, was transformed in the thirteenth century as readers of Latin gained access to a wider range of works by Aristotle.[20] The Aristotelian understanding of virtue as a mean between extremes had to be either rejected or adapted for the Christian context. The latter was a challenge, since central Christian values like faith and charity don't seem to fit the Aristotelian scheme of virtues as means between extremes (surely it is not unvirtuous to be excessively charitable, or have too much faith). Thomas Aquinas handled this problem by distinguishing between natural and theological virtues, the former conceived as means between extremes, the latter not.[21] In keeping with this, he moved away from the more ascetic tendencies of the Christian tradition. The ideal to be followed in respect of bodily desire is moderation and control, not elimination.

Aquinas goes into these issues in a question of his *Summa theologiae* devoted to the desires of the sensitive soul. In an echo of the Platonic tripartite theory, he distinguishes between two kinds of sensitive desire: irascible and concupiscent.[22] He makes it clear that these desires are indeed useful, since they are really just tendencies to pursue what is suitable and avoid what is unsuitable. For them to play their appropriate role they need to be guided by reason. Predictably, Aquinas thus contrasts our situation with that of animals. We are not moved by desire alone but only once reason judges and the will decides. As for animals, they simply respond automatically to whatever attracts or repels them: a hungry sheep will instinctively go for fresh grass and turn up its nose at steak.

We've seen this point already in al-Rāzī, but Aquinas alludes to a different thinker of the Islamic world to explain how it works: Avicenna.

He repeats Avicenna's famous example, pervasive in scholastic and even early modern European philosophy, of the sheep that is afraid of the wolf.[23] Since the wolf's hostility is not visible, or audible, or accessible by any of the five external senses, Avicenna thought that the sheep must be perceiving the hostility through some other capacity, which he called *wahm*.[24] In English this is usually called the "estimative" faculty, in imitation of the Latin translation, *aestimatio*. By invoking the estimative faculty, Avicenna and Aquinas after him could explain how animals are able to form preferences that would be otherwise inexplicable, like the sheep that flees the wolf but shows affection toward the lamb. Of course, animals have no rational control over these reactions. How could they, since they are not rational?[25]

A standard way to think about the difference between human cognition and the cognition enjoyed by animals through estimation, and their perceptive faculties in general, is that animal cognition is limited to grasping particulars, whereas humans can use reason to think about universals. This is true of desires, as Robert Miner has pointed out in the case of Aquinas: "The sensitive appetite tends toward concrete singulars that are apprehended by the senses, whereas the rational appetite tends toward universal goods that are perceived by the intellect."[26] This is why sheep can only fear one wolf at a time and not consider the fact that wolves in general really seem to have it in for sheep in general. But the point also applies outside the sphere of motivation, to cognition in general. The sheep can perceive that some given grass is green, remember the grass it saw yesterday, and so on. But it cannot think about the color green or the nature of grass as such. The dividing line between human and animal thus runs along a set of binary contrasts: rational versus irrational; intellectual soul versus sensory soul; universal concepts versus particular impressions.[27]

It would be a large endeavor to trace the history of this opposition, but in the medieval part of that story it is again Avicenna who would play a leading role. Not only did he devise the influential theory just discussed in order to explain the complexity of animal behavior while stopping short of ascribing reason to them. He also used the contrast between particular and universal to establish a fundamental metaphysical divide between human souls and animal souls. He argued that humans could not entertain universal concepts or make universal judgments if their intellects were seated in a bodily organ.[28] Here too his ideas were taken up by many later thinkers, not least in the Latin Christian world. The result was that rational thought, ever since Aristotle the basis for defining the best human life in opposition to a life "fit for beasts," now also became the basis for showing that humans are beings of a fundamentally different kind from animals. We are in part immaterial beings, with souls that are united to bodies but able to survive bodily death and exercise some capacities without using any bodily organ. Animals by contrast are nothing more than ensouled bodies.

This brings us back to our initial question: Why is it valuable to make good of use one's reasoning and one's capacity for intellective reflection? Because, no less than using reason to constrain desire, it is definitive of what it means to be human. Someone who doesn't use reason, and use it well, in both practical *and* theoretical contexts, is not living a fully human life. There is a passage in Averroes that makes this point in dramatic terms.

> The name "human" is predicated equivocally of a human being who is perfected by a speculative science and of one who is not perfected by it or who does not have aptitude to be perfected by it. Similarly the name "human" is predicated equivocally of a living and dead human being, or of a rational human being and one that is made of stone.[29]

In other words, if you aren't a philosopher, then you might as well be an animal. And of course most people are not philosophers. Indeed, the Renaissance Averroist Pietro Pomponazzi remarked that "almost an infinite number of men seem to have less intellect than many beasts."[30]

We already know what Averroes and his followers would understand by being a philosopher, or being "perfected by speculative science." As explained above in chapter 2, it involves grasping universal and necessary truths. If you go through life failing to do this, just perceiving and pursuing (or avoiding) particular objects and never engaging in universal science, you are not fully human. Was there any way to avoid this conclusion, to adopt a less damning verdict on the non-philosophers from within this medieval anthropology? We might explore the possibility that there are psychological faculties unique to humans that fall short of full-blown intellection. Using these could be a way of leading a properly human life, without needing to engage in theoretical inquiry. Averroes himself offered a candidate for such a faculty, in the shape of the "cogitative power (*al-quwwa al-fikriyya*)."[31] This power enables us to engage in thought (*fikr*) about particulars.[32] Like Avicenna, Averroes assumes that if this power grasps particulars it must itself be particular. Thus cogitation, unlike intellection, is a function carried out in a bodily organ, the brain (to be specific, the middle ventricle).

While this might suggest that animals too could be capable of cogitation—after all, they would not need immaterial, intellective souls to do so—Averroes denies this, holding that engaging in cogitation is possible only for beings endowed with reason.[33] It is our possession of this function, then, that makes it possible for us to think rationally without thinking at a universal level. Which certainly makes sense. Clearly all humans, even philosophers, spend plenty of time thinking without engaging in scientific inquiry. Even if all you are doing is thinking rationally about what to have for dinner (as opposed to merely desiring food, seeing food, or remembering what you ate last night), you are still doing more than any animal can manage. Thus even if humans who do not pursue intellection and scientific knowledge are not, by Averroes's reckoning, fully realizing the potentialities given to humans by nature, they would still be living distinctively human lives.

In that same question from the *Summa* that I mentioned earlier, Aquinas brings up the cogitative faculty posited by Averroes. He explains that it is the human analogue of what, in animals, is mere estimation.[34] But the difference between the animal and human cases is a telling one, because it still turns on the use of universals. Aquinas says that cogitation is sometimes called "particular reasoning (*ratio particularis*)" because it deals with particular properties called "intentions," just as does the sheep's estimative faculty, which grasps the "intention" of hostility (the Arabic word for this is *maʿnā*). The sensitive desire can be moved by such an intention, which again is just the same as in an animal. The difference is that in humans, universal reason can step in as a guide. Aquinas alludes here to Aristotle's theory of the practical syllogism. The basic idea would be that if a person is thinking about what to have for dinner, they might reason as follows: all healthy things are to be eaten, that salad in the fridge is healthy, so I should eat the salad.

This is all the work of reason, not intellect, since the latter deals exclusively with universal intelligibles, whereas everyday rational thought gets to particular conclusions from universal principles (*deducere universalia principia in conclusiones singulares, non est opus simplicis intellectus, sed rationis*). While this illustration involves a practical decision, it's obvious that this theory can be generalized to cases that do not call for action. Indeed, if you couldn't apply universal truths to particular cases, then universal science could never be deployed at all. I need, for instance, to know that *this* is a triangle to use my knowledge that all triangles have internal angles equal to two right angles (an example used in the opening chapter of Aristotle's *Posterior Analytics*).

There is a fine line to be walked here. If we admit that "thinking" could be a much less exalted thing, the sort of thing every person does all day, we run the risk of having to admit that thinking is not unique to humans after all. After all, don't animals evidently "think" about things like what to eat, how to get at food, where to build their nests, and the like? Aquinas's discussion of cogitation shows how to avoid admitting this. He insists that all "thinking" involves universals to some extent, so if animals have no grasp of universals, they cannot think. And indeed, unlike the human power of cogitation, animal estimation never involves the actual use of a universal or grasp of a universal as such.[35] But some medievals disagreed with this. Al-Rāzī mentions an observation already made in antiquity, that a mouse can use its tail to extract oil from a bottle. He finds it unbelievable that the mouse could do this without "thought" and "reflection" (*fikr, rawiyya*).[36] A contemporary of Aquinas, Roger Bacon (d. ca. 1292), discusses the similar case of a cat draining water out of a vessel to get at a fish. But he stops short of saying that the cat has something like human reasoning, classifying such animal behaviors as *quasi*-reasoning: "*as if* they were inferring a conclusion from premises."[37]

Critics of scholasticism detected a weak point here, and duly pressed it. In the Islamic world, post-Avicennan thinkers wondered whether it is really true that the estimative faculty (*wahm*) can function without using universals. Thus Fakhr al-Dīn al-Rāzī wrote:

> True, what exists outside the mind [e.g., hostility] is something particular, and in something particular, namely a certain wolf. But the

> scope by which I know it is something universal, just as, when someone knows that there is one man in this house, what he knows is something universal. For "man who is in this house" can be said interchangeably of numerous [men], even though this man is in himself particular, and this house too is in itself particular.[38]

This objection seems pretty plausible: the sheep is after all spurred to run away by any manifestation of hostility in a predator, not by anything special about the unique hostility manifested by *this* wolf. Why not then suppose that the sheep is operating with a general concept of hostility, that is, a universal? Another example discussed by Avicenna is even more susceptible to this objection. He mentions how a dog may fear all sticks, because of having been beaten by one stick in the past.[39] That certainly suggests that the dog can generalize from one experience to a universal rule ("Sticks are dangerous!").

In the Latin Christian world we find the humanist Lorenzo Valla mounting, within his wide-ranging attack on Aristotelian scholasticism, a refutation of the whole contrast between rational humans and irrational animals. Characteristically he traces the mistake to a philological problem, which is that the Greek word *aloga*, applied to animals, can mean both "irrational" and "non-speaking." It's true that animals don't *talk*, but it was from the beginning an error to suppose that they cannot *reason*.[40] Animals can also make choices, according to Valla, something we've seen philosophers consistently denying because they thought that animals react instinctively to each stimulus. Valla is, admittedly, a rather special case because of his unusually strong animus against scholasticism. But quite a few thinkers of the Italian Renaissance questioned whether it is possible to draw a firm boundary between animal and human.[41] Tommaso Campanella went so far as to say that some animals can "syllogize," as when a dog infers from the smell of its prey which way it should run in pursuit. Having said this, even Campanella reserves rationality properly speaking to humans.

The gradual blurring of the line between human and animal is apt to strike us as an obvious case of philosophical progress. These medieval and Renaissance thinkers seem to have been inching their way toward the gradualism we now take for granted in the wake of Darwinism. When we see apes and monkeys being described as being strikingly similar to humans—another, very early medieval example is Isidore of Seville (d. 636), who explains that the Latin for "apes" is *simia* "because one can see a strong similarity (*similitudo*) to human reason in them"[42]—we want to urge the medievals to take the next step, giving up altogether on a sharp divide between "higher" animals and humans. But there was a significant downside to gradualism too. It opened the possibility of consigning some humans to a kind of intermediate class, not really animal but not fully human and so not deserving of normal moral consideration or respect.

Here one might think of Maimonides's remarks on irreligious peoples, mentioned in the introduction to this book, or in chapter 4, Niketas of Byzantium's accusation that Islam makes its adherents "similar to the irrational animals." Or consider the charge made by Christians against Jews for being preoccupied with the concerns of the body, which I discussed in chapter 3. In light of the ideas I've been discussing in this final chapter, it becomes clear that this was in effect an accusation of being, if not actually irrational, then insufficiently dominated by properly rational concerns. Jews, in other words, are living less fully human lives than Christians, a sentiment that may easily be connected to more overt and often violent persecution of Jews in medieval Christian culture.

A more curious and, in terms of its direct practical consequences, innocuous example is pygmies. They were notoriously discussed by Albert the Great as a marginal case straddling the human/animal divide.[43] Not that Albert ever met a pygmy, of course. But based on literary reports about these semi-mythical beings, he concluded that they are not genuinely rational and are thus animals, not humans. They do, however, have a "shadow of reason" that makes them superior to all other animals like monkeys, which simply have a very strong estimative power. Like his student Aquinas, Albert thought the decisive criterion is the use of universals. He assumed that even if pygmies manage to communicate with one another, they must never use language that designates universals, since they are not really human.

Albert's discussion foreshadowed a debate with far more momentous consequences, which was provoked by the Europeans' encounter with the so-called Indians of the Americas. This event provided matter for centuries' worth of philosophical controversy and theological speculation. Were the "Indians" descended from Adam and Eve? Were they subject to original sin, and if so, why had they been allowed to live for so long without being offered redemption through the sacrifice of Christ? Were they capable of morally good actions, like pre-Christian pagans arguably had been?[44] And, most germane to our purposes, should the native Americans be considered proper human beings at all? Were they, in other words, rational?

A passionate advocate for the welfare of the native Americans was Bartolomé de las Casas (d. 1566). He was a Spanish Dominican who lived in the Americas and participated in the *encomienda* system, even owning slaves, until he became convinced that the violence exercised by his countrymen against the "Indians" was unacceptable. As he tells us, his stance was anticipated by Antonio de Montesinos, another friar who denounced the Spaniards in a speech delivered in 1511. Tellingly, Montesinos framed his polemic as follows: "Are these not men? Do they not have rational souls? Are you not obliged to love them as yourselves?"[45] Taking his cue from this, Las Casas determined to disabuse his fellow Spaniards of their "error of thinking that the Indians were not rational beings."[46] He argued that they were in fact "truly men" and indeed gentle, upright folk whose language and civil society proved that they were even admirable members of the human race. Referring to the care with which native parents raised their children, he wrote:

> Did Plato, Socrates, Pythagoras, or even Aristotle leave us better or more natural or more necessary exhortations to the virtuous life than these barbarians delivered to their children? Does the Christian religion teach us more, save the faith and what it teaches us of invisible and supernatural matters? Therefore, no one may deny that these people are fully capable of governing themselves and of living like men of good intelligence and more than others well ordered, sensible, prudent, and rational.[47]

In his extensive reportage of the cruelties borne by the "Indians," Las Casas frequently observed that they were nonetheless treated by the Spanish as if they were mere animals. When he tried to persuade his countrymen that this was evil, they reacted as if "it was a bad dream, hearing the strange news that they could not hold Indians in service without sinning, as if telling them that they couldn't use beasts of the field."[48]

But Las Casas was opposed by defenders of the conquistadors, most prominently the Aristotelian scholar Juan Gínes de Sepúlveda (d. 1573). In writings and in an oral debate with Las Casas, held in Valladolid in 1550–51, Sepúlveda argued that the "Indians" were indeed in some sense subhuman. He did not, however, argue that they were literally *non*human, if only because the excuse for the depravities being inflicted in the New World was that its inhabitants needed to be converted to Christianity. As Las Casas pointed out, this goal was pursued more in the breach than in the observance: "I can attest that neither then nor in subsequent years was there any more effort to bring Christianity to these people than there was to teach the Faith to the mares and horses and other beasts of the field."[49] Still, the rhetoric of conversion presupposed that the native Americans did in fact have human souls to save.

Sepúlveda duly acknowledged this, as when he fobbed off praise of their orderly communities by asking what this proved, "except that they are not bears or monkeys and that they are not completely devoid of reason?"[50] Still he needed to argue that the native Americans fell below even the status of European children. After all, the Spaniards did not think it was all right to enslave their own children to work in silver mines, or beat them to death for the slightest resistance or even for sport, as they were doing to the peoples they had encountered in the Americas. Knowing his Aristotle, Sepúlveda appealed to a concept he could find in the latter's *Politics*, "natural slavery."[51] Again, the notion that rationality is definitive of proper humanity was central here. Natural slaves are in a sense like children who will never grow up. Their rational faculty is so underdeveloped that they need guidance from the outside to live good lives, or rather, the best lives possible for them. Sepúlveda argued that it was a positive boon for the native Americans to be Christianized and dominated by Europeans. They had thereby been "converted from barbarians and *barely men* into humans and civilized men to the extent that they can be."[52] In fact, they were already born as slaves, so by taking possession of them the conquistadors were simply ratifying in law what was already true by nature.[53]

Sepúlveda, who by the way never set foot in the New World, thought the natural slavery of the "Indians" was clear from reports about their practices, for example, human sacrifice. From this it was evident that the native Americans were incapable of grasping the "natural law," an inborn sense of right and wrong that, according to none other than Thomas Aquinas, should guide each person through their rational faculty.[54] Las Casas, no less a devotee of Aquinas, countered that obedience to the natural law would require benevolence to the native Americans, not cruelty and enslavement.[55] In fact, he argued, it was the Spanish who were behaving like wild beasts. As this aspect of the debate shows, medieval notions of rationality were still operative in a literally life-and-death controversy of the sixteenth century. As, indeed, was the notion that grasping universals is a constitutive part of human reasoning. When laying out the natural law, Aquinas explained that this law consists of principles that are the same for everyone, though their application may vary from one situation to another.[56] Which should sound familiar. His account of natural law and its application has the same structure as his account of cogitation, which applies to particulars the universal judgments performed by the intellect. Thus moral reasoning in accordance with the natural law is, according to Aquinas, indeed *reasoning*. It should come as no surprise that animals cannot do it.[57] In this respect, Sepúlveda saw the native Americans as being human in body and in soul but animalistic in their way of life and their cognitive capacities, and thus in need of guidance by the more rational Europeans.

One of the things that we can learn from this sorry episode is that the medievals tended to see a close analogy between social hierarchy and a hierarchy of powers within the soul.[58] I began this chapter by asking why it is so important to be rational anyway and said in answer that it is rationality that makes humans *properly* human. This means having reason rule within the soul, by controlling or entirely suppressing the lower soul faculties, and by drawing on lower forms of cognition to arrive at rationally well-justified beliefs and, ideally, scientific knowledge. In just the same way, the most "rational" members of society—meaning well-educated adult men—were expected to rule over other humans, the women and children in their families, the peasants and the slavish in wider society. This authority was both political and epistemic.

A particularly clear expression of the attitude can be found, once again, in Aquinas. He discusses the topic of "implicit faith," which is usefully defined by J. A. Dinoia as follows: "the dispositions of one who is a member of the [religious] community, who accepts what is taught in it as right . . . even though he may not be able fully to articulate all the teachings of his community in their totality and complexity."[59] As Aquinas explains (*ST* 2.2, Q. 2, art. 6), revelation must "reach the worse people through the better people (*ad inferiores pervenit per superiores*)," with the latter relating to the former as angels do to humans. This frees the simple believer from any expectation that they can explain their faith in words or, as Aquinas notes (ad. obj. 1), have to answer difficult questions on religious topics (*non sunt examinandi de subtilitatibus fidei*). One should expect of them only that they not cling obstinately to error (ad. obj. 3).

Aquinas's forbearing approach is analogous to the Muslim theologians who encouraged, or even required, the adoption of *taqlīd* by common believers: his contrast between "better" and "worse" people is reminiscent of that between the *mujtahid* and the *muqallid*. His discussion of implicit faith is also relevant to the topic I've just been discussing, the status occupied by non-Christians, in the New World or otherwise. As John Marenbon has pointed out, Aquinas applied the notion of implicit faith to the case of wise non-Christians who followed the teachings of Jewish prophets or simply believed in divine providence.[60] But this does not mean that the condition of the simple Christian is no different from, and no better than, that of the virtuous pagan. Once the "New World" was discovered, Christian authorities had a new and urgent reason to insist on this point. In the sixteenth century, even as the Spanish were forcing Christianity on inhabitants of the "New World," the Inquisition in Spain itself was condemning the doctrine that "many barbarians and Gentiles and Turks and Moors, although they have no knowledge of our faith, just by believing and understanding that there was but one God and by living in accordance with natural law, could be saved."[61]

In general, then, and notwithstanding occasional objections from figures like the women humanists discussed in the previous chapter, or moral crusaders like Las Casas, the medievals typically took for granted that the elite had a monopoly on both the tools of violence and the means of knowledge. I've been arguing in this book that we have valuable things to learn about authority and belief from the medievals. This, clearly, is not one of them. Nor is the fundamental contrast they drew between humans and animals really sustainable. For example, the ubiquitous claim that animals cannot withstand desire turns out to be false. Monkeys and large-brained birds will restrain themselves from eating food if put in an experimental situation where they know they will get more, or preferable, food if they wait instead of eating what has already been given to them. Indeed, they do about as well on tests like this as human children (and probably better than I would do, to be honest).[62] Then too, as we've already seen, some medievals already noticed that animals seem to be capable of rational thought, since they can make plans, solve unfamiliar problems, and make apparent use of universal concepts and judgments.

These facts are inconvenient for the medieval anthropology, which invested so much in defining humans in opposition to animals. But there may still be ideas we can take from the Aristotelian tradition that remain attractive today. One strategy could be to focus attention, not on the general capacity for thought or the deployment of universal concepts, since these are arguably present in other animals too. We could instead suggest that animals do not engage in *second-order* reflection on their beliefs. A cat might believe that the best way to get at a fish is to drain the water from the fishbowl, but it presumably does not ask itself whether this belief is well justified or whether the belief counts as knowledge. Animals can also learn from each other, but it is plausible to suppose that they don't operate with conscious criteria for deciding which other animals are worth imitating. If this is right, then the epistemological policies I looked at earlier in this book, when I talked about justified *taqlīd*, turn out to be policies that only humans are capable of instituting. To the extent that we place value on the cognitive capacities that are unique to humans, we now have another reason to make intelligent use of authority: this is a kind of intelligence that is uniquely human.

But here's a second thought. If we go all the way back to Aristotle's function argument, we may wonder (as many commentators have done) why it should be so important that rationality, or some more specific application of intelligence, is *unique* or *peculiar* to humans.[63] If it turns out that, say, apes are also rational or capable of second-guessing which other apes are worth treating as authoritative, would that really undermine the value we place on reason or on having a discerning attitude toward authority? What if we took the less exclusive approach of supposing that *everything* about human nature is valuable to us as humans, without worrying which aspects of human nature can be found elsewhere in the natural world?

It might seem that this approach would be alien to the medieval mind-set, given how much stress we've seen being placed on reason at the expense of lower capacities. But here we should recall that many, though not all, of the thinkers I've discussed were in favor of *moderating* the passions and not extirpating them, so that lower psychological powers are allowed to play a role in the best human life. These powers will play that role well just so long as they follow the lead of reason, much as the *muqallid* is a valuable member of society and the religious community but needs to follow the lead of the expert. This fits with another significant idea in medieval anthropology, namely, that all created natures are contained within human nature. Often this was expressed by describing humans as a "microcosm," that is, a version of the whole universe in miniature. Examples of this idea are too numerous to mention, but from the Islamic world one could refer to al-Kindī, who ends one of his cosmological works by comparing the human body to the universe. He arguably goes into more detail than strictly necessary, as he mentions how caves are like intestines, pools and wells like the stomach and bladder.[64] The concept of the microcosm then becomes a central theme in the writings of the Brethren of Purity, who devoted an entire treatise to the idea, and another to the inverse claim that the cosmos is a "great human."[65]

In the Christian tradition one should at least mention Hildegard of Bingen, who explores the theme at length in her *On the Works of God.*[66] Rather than dismiss the body and its functions, Hildegard extols the value of such things as breath, the heat in the heart, our eyes and brain, as images of different parts of the wider universe. The most famous example from Christian Europe, though, comes later with the short oration by Pico Della Mirandola (d. 1494), posthumously called *On the Dignity of Man.*[67] In this speech Pico argues that God already created all natures before finally making humans and thus decided to fuse all these natures in Adam. It is this that makes humans the "most happy of animals" and indeed the creature most worthy of admiration.

Not that these works are without any trace of the hierarchical thinking we've seen throughout this chapter. Pico extols human nature for containing all things but insists that it is then up to us to choose the *better* part of this comprehensive nature, which of course is our rationality. And the Brethren of Purity, following the Platonic tradition, claim that the cosmos has a single soul and that this soul rules over the whole universe like a king or householder. My point is rather that the microcosm theme was one way the medievals could show appreciation for such phenomena as sensation or digestion in humans, precisely the respects in which we are like animals. I will bring this chapter and the book to a close by giving just one more example, which comes from the very same work with which I began: Ibn Ṭufayl's *Ḥayy ibn Yaqẓān*.

As you'll recall, this text is a narrative whose title character begins as an infant on an island with no other humans and matures to become a philosopher and mystic. Something I left unmentioned in the introduction is that Ḥayy's progress is not merely a matter of emerging rationality. To the contrary, his animal nature is clearly marked, as is his plant nature, if we take this to be an implication of his being spontaneously generated from the earth. Ḥayy's survival as an exposed infant on the island is thanks to a gazelle who adopts him, and he goes on to learn to imitate animal calls and even to garb himself like an animal.[68] Now, this is only an early stage in Ḥayy's development, and he goes on to what we would recognize as more distinctively human levels of maturation. But this does not mean his "animal" phase is forgotten or rejected as valueless. In general, it is a central and difficult interpretive question whether the earlier phases of Ḥayy's story are fully transcended by subsequent phases, in which case all his philosophical discoveries would themselves be rendered obsolete by Ḥayy's progression to Sufi-style mystic insight. I would lean toward a reading on which Ibn Ṭufayl recognizes the value of each stage, and hence of every aspect of Ḥayy's nature, even while recognizing that the later stages are "higher" or more advanced. That would take from the story a message similar to what we have gleaned from uses of the microcosm theory, a theory that, by the way, Ibn Ṭufayl himself endorses.[69]

This, I think, is a final message worth taking to heart. Rationality in belief, in the search for knowledge, and in the critical use of authority are all valuable. They were well worth the attention lavished on them by the medievals, and well worth the time you and I have invested in writing and reading this book. But there is, after all, more to life than being rational.

FURTHER READING

What follows is a brief guide to further reading in English on the figures and topics discussed in this volume. I have not mentioned editions or translations of primary texts here, as these are found in the notes to chapters. Note that this is not an attempt to provide a complete bibliography but only to give tips for where to start reading if my discussion has, as I hope, prompted the desire to read more deeply about medieval thought.

Abelard

J. E. Brower and K. Guilfoy, *The Cambridge Companion to Abelard* (Cambridge: Cambridge University Press, 2004).

J. Marenbon, *The Philosophy of Peter Abelard* (Cambridge: Cambridge University Press, 1997).

C. J. Mews, *Abelard and Heloise* (New York: Oxford University Press, 2005).

Anna Komnene

T. Gouma-Peterson, ed., *Anna Komnene and Her Times* (New York: Routledge, 2000).

L. Neville, *Anna Komnene: The Life and Work of a Medieval Historian* (Oxford: Oxford University Press, 2016).

Animals in Medieval Philosophy

P. Adamson and G. F. Edwards, eds., *Animals: A History* (New York: Oxford University Press, 2018).

C. Muratori, *Renaissance Vegetarianism: The Philosophical Afterlives of Porphyry's "On Abstinence"* (Cambridge: Cambridge University Press, 2020).

A. Oelze, *Animal Rationality: Later Medieval Theories 1250–1350* (Leiden: Brill, 2018).

D. Perler, "Why Is the Sheep Afraid of the Wolf? Medieval Debates on Animal Passions," in *Emotion and Cognitive Life in Medieval and Early Modern Philosophy*, ed. M. Pickavé and L. Shapiro (Oxford: Oxford University Press, 2012), 32–52.

Averroes (Ibn Rushd)

P. Adamson and M. Di Giovanni, eds., *Interpreting Averroes: Critical Essays* (Cambridge: Cambridge University Press, 2018).

T.-A. Druart, "Averroes on the Harmony of Philosophy and Religion," in *Averroes and the Enlightenment*, ed. M. Wahba and M. Abousenna (Amherst, NY: Prometheus, 1996), 253–62.

R. C. Taylor, "Averroes on the *Sharīʿah* of the Philosophers," in *The Muslim, Christian, and Jewish Heritage: Philosophical and Theological Perspectives in the Abrahamic Traditions*, ed. R. C. Taylor and I. Omar (Milwaukee, WI: Marquette University Press, 2012), 283–304.

Avicenna (Ibn Sīnā)

P. Adamson, ed., *Interpreting Avicenna: Critical Essays* (Cambridge: Cambridge University Press, 2013).

D. Gutas, *Avicenna and the Aristotelian Tradition: Introduction to Reading Avicenna's Philosophical Works* (Leiden: Brill, 1988; 2nd revised ed. 2014).

J. McGinnis, *Avicenna* (New York: Oxford University Press, 2010).

J. McGinnis, ed., *Interpreting Avicenna* (Leiden: Brill, 2004).

Byzantine Philosophy

B. Bydén and K. Ierodiakonou, eds., *The Many Faces of Byzantine Philosophy* (Athens: Norwegian Institute at Athens, 2012).

K. Ierodiakonou, ed., *Byzantine Philosophy and Its Ancient Sources* (Oxford: Oxford University Press, 2002).

A. Kaldellis and N. Siniossoglou, eds., *The Cambridge Intellectual History of Byzantium* (Cambridge: Cambridge University Press, 2017).

N. Wilson, *Scholars of Byzantium* (London: Duckworth, 1983).

Christian Apologetic Literature in the Near East

H. Goddard, *A History of Christian-Muslim Relations* (Edinburgh: Edinburgh University Press, 2000).

S. H. Griffith, *The Beginning of Christian Theology in Arabic* (Burlington, VT: Ashgate, 2002).

S. H. Griffith, "Disputes with Muslims in Syriac Christian Texts: From Patriarch John (d. 648) to Bar Hebraeus (d. 1286)," in *Religionsgespräche im Mittelalter*, ed. F. Niewohner (Wiesbaden: Harassowitz, 1992), 251–73.

S. L. Husseini, *Early Christian-Muslim Debate on the Unity of God: Three Christian Scholars and Their Engagement with Islamic Thought (9th century C.E.)* (Leiden: Brill, 2014).

Christine de Pizan

R. Brown-Grant, *Christine de Pizan and the Moral Defence of Women: Reading Beyond Gender* (Cambridge: Cambridge University Press, 1999).

C. Cannon Willard, *Christine de Pizan: Her Life and Works* (New York: Persea, 1984).

N. Margolis, *An Introduction to Christine de Pizan* (Gainesville: University Press of Florida, 2011).

M. Zimmermann and D. De Rentiis, eds., *The City of Scholars: New Approaches to Christine de Pizan* (Berlin: de Gruyter, 1994).

Demonstration and Certainty

D. L. Black, "Knowledge *(ʿilm)* and Certitude (*yaqīn)* in al-Fārābī's Epistemology," *Arabic Sciences and Philosophy* 16 (2006): 11–46.

R. Pasnau, *After Certainty: A History of Our Epistemic Ideals and Illusions* (Oxford: Oxford University Press, 2017).

Ethiopian Philosophy

C. Sumner, *Ethiopian Philosophy*, 5 vols. (Addis Ababa: Central Printing Press, 1974–82).

C. Sumner, "The Light and the Shadow: Zera Yacob and Walda Heywat: Two Ethiopian Philosophers of the Seventeenth Century," in *A Companion to African Philosophy*, ed. K. Wiredu (Malden, MA: Blackwell, 2004), 172–82.

al-Fārābī

P. Adamson, "Plotinus Arabus and Proclus Arabus in the *Harmony of the Two Philosophers* Ascribed to al-Fārābī," in *Reading Proclus and the Book of Causes*, vol. 2, ed. D. Calma (Leiden: Brill, 2021), 184–99.

T.-A. Druart, "Al-Fārābī, Ethics and First Intelligibles," *Documenti e studi sulla tradizione filosofica medievale* 7 (1996): 403–23.

M. Mahdi, *Alfarabi and the Foundations of Islamic Political Philosophy* (Chicago: University of Chicago Press, 2001).

M. Rashed, "On the Authorship of the Treatise *On the Harmonization of the Opinions of the Two Sages* Attributed to al-Fārābī," *Arabic Sciences and Philosophy* 19 (2009): 43–82.

Hallevi

Y. T. Langermann, "Science and the *Kuzari*," *Science in Context* 10 (1997): 495–522.

Y. Silman, *Philosopher and Prophet: Judah Halevi, the Kuzari and the Evolution of His Thought* (Albany: SUNY Press, 1995).

Hildegard of Bingen

C. Burnett and P. Dronke, eds., *Hildegard of Bingen: The Context of Her Thought and Art* (London: Warburg Institute, 1998).

S. Flanagan, *Hildegard of Bingen 1098–1179: A Visionary Life* (London: Routledge, 1998).

B. M. Kienzle, D. Stoudt, and G. Ferzoco, eds., *A Companion to Hildegard of Bingen* (Leiden: Brill, 2014).

Ibn Ṭufayl

L. I. Conrad, ed., *The World of Ibn Ṭufayl: Interdisciplinary Perspectives on Ḥayy Ibn Yaqẓān* (Leiden: Brill, 1996).

T. Kukkonen, *Ibn Tufayl: Living the Life of Reason* (London: Oneworld, 2014).

Islamic Law

A. El Shamsy, *The Canonization of Islamic Law: A Social and Intellectual History* (Cambridge: Cambridge University Press, 2013).

W. B. Hallaq, *A History of Islamic Legal Theories* (Cambridge: Cambridge University Press, 1997).

W. B. Hallaq, *The Origins and Evolution of Islamic Law* (Cambridge: Cambridge University Press, 2005).

C. Melchert, *The Formation of the Sunni Schools of Law* (Leiden: Brill, 1997).

J. Schacht, *An Introduction to Islamic Law* (Oxford: Oxford University Press, 1982).

Jewish Medieval Philosophy

D. H. Frank and O. Leaman, *The Cambridge Companion to Medieval Jewish Philosophy* (Cambridge: Cambridge University Press, 2003).

D. H. Frank and O. Leaman, *History of Jewish Philosophy* (London: Routledge, 1997).

C. Sirat, *A History of Jewish Philosophy in the Middle Ages* (Cambridge: Cambridge University Press, 1985).

John of Damascus

A. Louth, *St. John Damascene: Tradition and Originality in Byzantine Theology* (Oxford: Oxford University Press, 2009).

P. Schadler, *John of Damascus and Islam: Christian Heresiology and the Intellectual Background to Earliest Christian-Muslim Relations* (Leiden: Brill, 2018).

al-Kaʿbī (Abū l-Qāsim al-Balkhī)

R. El Omari, *The Theology of Abū l-Qāsim al-Balkhī/al-Kaʿbī (d. 319/931)* (Leiden: Brill, 2016).

al-Kindī

P. Adamson, *Al-Kindī* (New York: Oxford University Press, 2007).

P. Adamson, *Studies on Plotinus and al-Kindī* (Aldershot: Ashgate, 2014).

C. D'Ancona, "Aristotelian and Neoplatonic Elements in Kindī's Doctrine of Knowledge," *American Catholic Philosophical Quarterly* 73 (1999): 9–35.

Llull

A. Bonner, *The Art and Logic of Ramon Llull: A User's Guide* (Leiden: Brill, 2007).

A. Fidora and J. E. Rubio, eds., *Raimundus Lullus: An Introduction to His Life, Works and Thought* (Turnhout: Brepols, 2008).

Mechthild of Magdeburg

A. Hollywood, *The Soul as Virgin Wife: Mechthild of Magdeburg, Marguerite Porete, and Meister Eckhart* (Notre Dame, IN: University of Notre Dame Press, 1995).

S. S. Poor, *Mechthild of Magdeburg and Her Book: Gender and the Making of Textual Authority* (Philadelphia: University of Pennsylvania Press, 2004).

F. Tobin, *Mechthild of Magdeburg: A Medieval Mystic in Modern Eyes* (Columbia, SC: Camden House, 1995).

Plato vs. Aristotle

B. Bydén, "'No Prince of Perfection': Byzantine Anti-Aristotelianism from the Patristic Period to Plethon," in *Power and Subversion in Byzantium*, ed. D. Angelov and M. Saxby (Farnham: Ashgate, 2013), 147–76.

C. D'Ancona, "The Topic of the 'Harmony Between Plato and Aristotle': Some Examples in Early Arabic Philosophy," in *Wissen über Grenzen: Arabisches Wissen und lateinisches Mittelalter*, ed. A. Speer and L. Wegener (Berlin: de Gruyter, 2006), 379–405.

E. Del Soldato, *Early Modern Aristotle: On the Making and Unmaking of Authority* (Philadelphia: University of Pennsylvania Press, 2020).

G. Karamanolis, *Plato and Aristotle in Agreement? Platonists on Aristotle from Antiochus to Porphyry* (Oxford: Oxford University Press, 2006).

G. Karamanolis, "Plethon and Scholarios on Aristotle," in *Byzantine Philosophy and Its Ancient Sources*, ed. K. Ierodiakonou (Oxford: Oxford University Press, 2002), 253–82.

Plethon

V. Hladký, *The Philosophy of Gemistos Plethon: Platonism in Late Byzantium, between Hellenism and Orthodoxy* (Farnham: Ashgate, 2014).

N. Siniossoglou, *Radical Platonism in Byzantium: Illumination and Utopia in Gemistos Plethon* (Cambridge: Cambridge University Press, 2011).

C. M. Woodhouse, *George Gemistos Plethon: The Last of the Hellenes* (Oxford: Oxford University Press, 1986).

Marguerite Porete

D. Kangas, "Dangerous Joy: Marguerite Porete's Good-bye to the Virtues," *Journal of Religion* 91 (2011): 299–319.

S. Kocher, *Allegories of Love in Marguerite Porete's "Mirror of Simple Souls"* (Turnhout: Brepols, 2008).

J. Maguire Robinson, *Nobility and Annihilation in Marguerite Porete's "Mirror of Simple Souls"* (Albany: SUNY Press, 2002).

M. G. Sargent, "The Annihilation of Marguerite Porete," *Viator* 28 (1997): 253–79.

Psellos

C. Barber and D. Jenkins, eds., *Reading Michael Psellos* (Leiden: Brill, 2006).

A. Kaldellis, *Mothers and Sons, Fathers and Daughters: The Byzantine Family of Michael Psellos* (Notre Dame, IN: University of Notre Dame Press, 2006).

D. J. O'Meara, "Michael Psellos," in *Interpreting Proclus from Antiquity to the Renaissance*, ed. S. Gersh (Cambridge: Cambridge University Press, 2014), 165–81.

al-Rāzī

P. Adamson, *Al-Rāzī* (New York: Oxford University Press, 2021).

S. Stroumsa, *Freethinkers of Medieval Islam: Ibn al-Rāwandī, Abū Bakr al-Rāzī, and Their Impact on Islamic Thought* (Leiden: Brill, 1999).

Saadia Gaon

I. Efros, *Studies in Medieval Jewish Philosophy* (New York: Columbia University Press, 1974).

H. A. Wolfson, "Saadia on the Trinity and Incarnation," in H.A. Wolfson, *Studies in the History of Philosophy and Religion*, vol. 2 (Cambridge, MA: Harvard University Press, 1977), 394–414.

Skepticism in the Middle Ages

D. G. Denery, K. Ghosh, and N. Zeeman, eds., *Uncertain Knowledge: Scepticism, Relativism and Doubt in the Middle Ages* (Turnhout: Brepols, 2014).

R. Haliva, ed., *Scepticism and Anti-Scepticism in Medieval Jewish Philosophy and Thought* (Berlin: de Gruyter, 2018).

H. Lagerlund, ed., *Rethinking the History of Skepticism: The Missing Medieval Background* (Leiden: Brill, 2010).

H. Lagerlund, *Skepticism in Philosophy: A Comprehensive, Historical Introduction* (London: Routledge, 2020).

D. Perler, "Skepticism," in *The Cambridge History of Medieval Philosophy*, 2 vols., ed. R. Pasnau (Cambridge: Cambridge University Press, 2010), 384–96.

Syriac Philosophy

Y. Arzhanov, "Plato in Syriac Literature," *Le muséon* 132 (2019): 1–36.

S. Brock, *Syrian Perspectives on Late Antiquity* (London: Variorum, 1984).

H. Takahashi, "Between Greek and Arabic: The Sciences in Syriac from Severus Sebokht to Barhebraeus," in *Transmission of Sciences: Greek, Syriac, Arabic and Latin*, ed. H. Kobayashi and M. Kato (Tokyo: Waseda University, 2010), 16–39.

J. W. Watt, *Rhetoric and Philosophy from Greek into Syriac* (Farnham: Ashgate, 2010).

Taqlīd and *Ijtihād*

A. El Shamsy, "Rethinking *Taqlīd* in the Early Shāfiʿī School," *Journal of the American Oriental Society* 128 (2008): 1–23.

M. Fadel, "The Social Logic of *Taqlīd* and the Rise of the *Mukhtaṣar*," *Islamic Law and Society* 3 (1996): 193–233.

R. M. Frank, "Knowledge and *Taqlīd*: The Foundations of Religious Belief in Classical Ashʿarism," *Journal of the American Oriental Society* 109 (1989): 37–62.

W. B. Hallaq, "Was the Gate of *Ijtihād* Closed?," *International Journal of Middle East Studies* 16 (1984): 3–41.

A. F. Ibrahim, "Rethinking the *Taqlīd–ijtihād* Dichotomy: A Conceptual-Historical Approach," *Journal of the American Oriental Society* 136 (2016): 285–303.

al-Ṭūsī

P. Fatoorchi, "On Intellectual Skepticism: A Selection of Skeptical Arguments and Ṭūsī's Criticisms, with Some Comparative Notes," *Philosophy East and West* 63 (2013): 213–50.

West African Islam

O. O. Kane, *Beyond Timbuktu: An Intellectual History of Muslim West Africa* (Cambridge, MA: Harvard University Press, 2006).

D. van Dalen, *Doubt, Scholarship and Society in 17th-Century Central Sudanic Africa* (Leiden: Brill, 2016).

Women Humanists

M. L. King, *Humanism, Venice and Women: Essays on the Italian Renaissance* (Aldershot: Ashgate, 2005).

L. Panizza, ed., *Women in Italian Renaissance Culture and Society* (Oxford: Oxford University Press, 2000).

Women in Medieval Philosophy

C. W. Bynum, *Holy Feast and Holy Fast: The Religious Significance of Food to Medieval Women* (Berkeley: University of California Press, 1987).

C. Dinshaw and D. Wallace, *Cambridge Companion to Medieval Women's Writing* (Cambridge: Cambridge University Press, 2003).

P. Dronke, *Women Writers of the Middle Ages* (Cambridge: Cambridge University Press, 1984).

A. B. Mulder-Bakker, ed., *Seeing and Knowing: Women and Learning in Medieval Europe 1200–1550* (Turnhout: Brepols, 2004).

B. Neil and L. Garland, eds., *Questions of Gender in Byzantine Society* (London: Routledge, 2016).
R. Roded, *Women in Islam and the Middle East: A Reader* (London: Tauris, 2008).
A. Sayeed, *Women and the Transmission of Religious Knowledge in Islam* (Cambridge: Cambridge University Press, 2013).

Yaḥyā Ibn ʿAdī

P. Adamson, "Yaḥyā Ibn ʿAdī against al-Kindī on the Trinity," *Journal of Eastern Christian Studies* 72 (2020): 241–71.
C. Schöck, "The Controversy between al-Kindī and Yaḥyā b. ʿAdī on the Trinity," *Oriens* 40 (2012): 1–50; 42 (2014): 220–53.
H. A. Wolfson, "The Philosopher Kindi and Yahya ibn ʿAdi on the Trinity," in *Études philosophiques offertes au Dr. Ibrahim Madkour*, ed. U. Amin (Cairo: al-Hayʾa al-Miṣrīyah al-ʿĀmmah li-l-Kitāb, 1974), 49–64.

NOTES

INTRODUCTION

1. On Ibn Ṭufayl, see T. Kukkonen, *Ibn Tufayl: Living the Life of Reason* (London: Oneworld, 2014); and for the text in English, see *Ibn Tufayl's Hayy ibn Yaqzān*, trans., introd., and notes L. E. Goodman (Chicago: University of Chicago Press, 2009).

2. This would connect *Ḥayy* to a tradition of worry over "vicious" states and the plight of good men in them, which goes back to Plato by way of al-Fārābī and is thematized in the tellingly named *Regime of the Solitary*, a work by Ibn Bājja, another Andalusian philosopher whose works were well known to Ibn Ṭufayl.

3. M. Meyerhof and J. Schacht, ed. and trans., *The Theologus autodidactus of Ibn al-Nafīs* (Oxford: Clarendon, 1968). See N. Fancy, "The Virtuous Son of the Rational: A Traditionalist's Response to the *Falāsifa*," in *Avicenna and His Legacy: A Golden Age of Science and Philosophy*, ed. Y. T. Langermann (Turnhout: Brepols, 2009), 219–47.

4. Here I should mention a book that came to my attention only while revising the manuscript: A. R. Booth, *Islamic Philosophy and the Ethics of Belief* (London: Palgrave Macmillan, 2016). Booth investigates some of the same issues I do. He even uses the phrase "epistemic elite" (41) and talks about the problem of expertise (59). However, his conclusions are rather different from mine, for a number of reasons. For one thing he focuses only on the *falāsifa* (in fact mostly on al-Fārābī), whereas the present book is much more wide-ranging. More important, he seeks to spell out the epistemology of al-Fārābī and other *falāsifa* in the language of contemporary epistemology, which I think leads to some distortions. In particular, the concepts "evidence" and "justification," which play a central role in Booth's account, are not concepts that were used by the *falāsifa*. They were foundationalists who thought that knowledge must be of *necessary* truths, which will be either indubitable first principles or derived from such principles (on this, see below, ch. 2). So it is rather misleading to suggest that the epistemic norm accepted by the *falāsifa* is to ensure that one's beliefs are "justified" by an "epistemic reason" (5). In most if not all cases the "reason" would simply be that the proposition one is believing is necessarily true and

cannot be doubted by anyone who grasps it properly. This helps explain the absence of discussions about justification in medieval Islamic epistemology.

5. M. Maimonides, *The Guide of the Perplexed*, vol. 1, trans., introd., and notes by S. Pines (Chicago: University of Chicago Press, 1963), §3.51.

CHAPTER 1

1. This notorious quotation is also cited at the outset of U. Coope, "Free to Think? Epistemic Authority and Thinking for Oneself," *Journal of the British Academy* 7 (2019): 1–23, which looks at issues like the ones I raise in the book but in the context of the ancient thinkers Plato, Cicero, and Olympiodorus. She reaches a conclusion similar to mine in chapter 3 below, namely, that responsible use of authority requires that one "engage critically with expert testimony without having expert knowledge oneself" and "evaluate the credentials of an alleged expert, even though you lack expert knowledge yourself" (19).

2. A. El Shamsy, "Rethinking *Taqlīd* in the Early Shāfiʿī School," *Journal of the American Oriental Society* 128 (2008): 1–23, at 4–5.

3. I give the death date for each medieval author at first mention, always using the AD or CE date to facilitate chronological comparison between Jewish, Muslim, and Christian authors.

4. See D. Gutas, "Avicenna and After: The Development of Paraphilosophy. A History of Science Approach," in *Islamic Philosophy from the 12th to the 14th Century*, ed. S. Conermann and A. Al Ghouz (Bonn: Bonn University Press, 2018), 19–72.

5. On this, see A. El Shamsy, *The Canonization of Islamic Law: A Social and Intellectual History* (Cambridge: Cambridge University Press, 2013).

6. A. F. Ibrahim, "Rethinking the *Taqlīd–ijtihād* Dichotomy: A Conceptual-Historical Approach," *Journal of the American Oriental Society* 136 (2016): 285–303, at 292.

7. El Shamsy, "Rethinking *Taqlīd*," 4.

8. W. B. Hallaq, "Was the Gate of *Ijtihād* Closed?," *International Journal of Middle East Studies* 16 (1984): 3–41.

9. S. A. Jackson, "*Taqlīd*, Legal Scaffolding and the Scope of Legal Injunctions in Post-Formative Theory: *Muṭlaq* and *ʿāmm* in the Jurisprudence of Shihāb al-Dīn al-Qarāfī," *Islamic Law and Society* 3 (1996): 165–92, at 167.

10. On this in the Mālikī school, see M. Fadel, "The Social Logic of *Taqlīd* and the Rise of the *Mukhtaṣar*," *Islamic Law and Society* 3 (1996): 193–233.

11. Ibrahim, "Rethinking the *Taqlīd–ijtihād* Dichotomy," 286, 296; R. Peters, "*Ijtihād* and *Taqlīd* in 18th and 19th Century Islam," *Die Welt des Islams* 20 (1980): 131–46, at 140.

12. N. Calder, "Doubt and Prerogative: The Emergence of an Imāmī Shīʿī Theory of *Ijtihād*," *Studia Islamica* 70 (1989): 57–78, at 61.

13. Hasan b. Yusuf al-ʿAllamā, quoted in Calder, "Doubt and Prerogative," 75.

14. Quoted in R. El Omari, *The Theology of Abū l-Qāsim al-Balkhī/al-Kaʿbī (d. 319/931)* (Leiden: Brill, 2016), 152–53; the following quote on al-Kaʿbī's view is from 159.

15. R. M. Frank, "Al-Ašʿarī's Conception of the Nature and Role of Speculative Reasoning in Theology," in *Proceedings of the VIth Congress of Arabic and Islamic Studies* (Stockholm: Almquist och Wiksell, 1972), 136–54, at 144.

16. R. M. Frank, "Knowledge and *Taqlīd*: The Foundations of Religious Belief in Classical Ashʿarism," *Journal of the American Oriental Society* 109 (1989): 37–62, at 45.

17. Frank, "Knowledge and *Taqlīd*," 50.

18. See, e.g., D. Pritchard, *Epistemic Luck* (Oxford: Clarendon Press, 2005).

19. Frank, "Knowledge and *Taqlīd*," 48.

20. Frank, "Knowledge and *Taqlīd*," 53.

21. Jalāl al-Dīn Dawānī, *Nūr al-Hidāya*, in *al-Rasāʾil al-mukhāra az ʿAllāma Muḥaqqiq Dawānī wa Mīr Dāmād*, ed. S. A. Toysirkānī (Isfahan: Imām ʿAlī Public Library, 1983), 105–28, at 110–11. My thanks to Hanif Amin Beidokhti for help with the Persian text.

22. K. El-Rouyaheb, *Islamic Intellectual History in the Seventeenth Century: Scholarly Currents in the Ottoman Empire and the Maghreb* (Cambridge: Cambridge University Press, 2015), 176, 182.

23. See P. Adamson, *A History of Philosophy Without Any Gaps: Philosophy in the Islamic World* (Oxford: Oxford University Press, 2016), 419, where I explain this as an "externalist" criterion as opposed to al-Sanūsī's "internalist" constraint that the believer must have certain knowledge that his belief is true.

24. For what follows, see D. van Dalen, *Doubt, Scholarship and Society in 17th-Century Central Sudanic Africa* (Leiden: Brill, 2016).

25. El Shamsy, "Rethinking *Taqlīd*," 10. For the relation between consultation and *taqlīd*, see also B. G. Weiss, *The Search for God's Law: Islamic Jurisprudence in the Writings of Sayf al-Dīn al-Āmidī* (Salt Lake City: University of Utah Press, 2010), ch. 17.

26. Frank, "Knowledge and *Taqlīd*," 58.

27. R. M. Frank, "Al-Ghazālī on *Taqlīd*: Scholars, Theologians, and Philosophers," *Zeitschrift für Geschichte der arabisch-islamischen Wissenschaften* 7 (1991–92): 207–52.

28. F. Griffel, "*Taqlīd* of the Philosophers: al-Ghazālī's Initial Accusation in His *Tahāfut*," in *Ideas, Images, and Methods of Portrayal: Insights into Classical Arabic Literature and Islam*, ed. S. Günther (Leiden: Brill, 2005), 273–96, at 281.

29. al-Ghazālī, *The Incoherence of the Philosophers*, ed. and trans. M. E. Marmura (Provo, UT: Brigham Young University Press, 1997), 226.

30. See P. Adamson, "On Knowledge of Particulars," *Proceedings of the Aristotelian Society* 105 (2005): 273–94.

31. F. Bouhafa, "Ethics and *Fiqh* in al-Fārābī's Philosophy," in *Philosophy and Jurisprudence in the Islamic World*, ed. P. Adamson (Berlin: de Gruyter, 2019), 11–27.

32. Abū Naṣr al-Fārābī, *Kitāb al-Milla wa nuṣūṣ ukhrā*, ed. M. Mahdi (Beirut: Dār al-Mashriq, 1968), 47.

33. al-Fārābī, *Kitāb al-Milla*, 47–48.

34. For the use of this term in Islamic law, as meaning a "recognized" report about the sayings of the Prophet agreed by consensus, see A. Zysow, *The Economy of Certainty: An Introduction to the Typology of Islamic Legal Theory* (Atlanta, GA: Lockwood, 2013), 17–22.

35. For more on the significance of this title, relating the work to the concerns of Islamic jurisprudence, see U. Rudolph, "Reflections on al-Fārābī's *Mabādi arā' ahl al-madīna al-fāḍila*," in *In the Age of al-Fārābī: Arabic Philosophy in the Fourth/Tenth Century*, ed. P. Adamson (London: Warburg Institute, 2008), 1–14.

36. I here differ from A. R. Booth, *Islamic Philosophy and the Ethics of Belief* (London: Palgrave Macmillan, 2016), 42, who holds that for al-Fārābī *only* the prophet belongs to the epistemic elite. I do not see anything in al-Fārābī to rule out the possibility of a philosopher who has comprehensive demonstrative understanding. But such a figure could not play the vital political role carried out by the prophet, since the non-prophet philosopher has no revelatory text for presenting truths to the masses in a persuasive fashion.

37. Fadel, "The Social Logic of *Taqlīd*," 203–4.

38. On the Aristotelian source of this slogan, see R. C. Taylor, "Truth Does Not Contradict Truth: Averroes and the Unity of Truth," *Topoi* 19 (2000): 3–16.

39. For this, see my forthcoming paper "Averroes' *Decisive Treatise* (*Faṣl al-maqāl*) and *Exposition* (*Kashf*) as Dialectical Works," in *Contextualizing Premodern Philosophy: Explorations of the Greek, Hebrew, Arabic, and Latin Traditions*, ed. K. Krause, L. X. López Farjeat, and N. Oschman (London: Taylor and Francis).

40. Averroes, *Faṣl al-maqāl fī taqrīr mā bayna l-sharīʿa wa-l-ḥikma min al-ittiṣāl*, ed. M.ʿA. Jābirī (Beirut: Markaz Dirāsāt al-Waḍah al-ʿArabiyya, 1997), 89.

41. Averroes, *Faṣl al-maqāl*, 107.

42 Ibn Rushd, *Naṣṣ talkhīṣ manṭiq Arisṭū, Kitāb al-jadṭal wa-l-mughālaa*, ed. J. Rajhāmī (Beirut: Dār al-Fikr al-Lubnānī, 1992), §1.9.

43. Averroes, *al-Kashf ʿan manāhij-l-adilla fī ʿaqāʾid al-milla*, ed. M. Qāsim (Cairo: Maktabat al-Anjilū al-Miṣriyya, 1964), 168.

44. Averroes, *al-Kashf*, 138.

45. In addition to the discussion of women intellectuals later in this book (ch. 6), I should add that some philosophers took an unusally generous position on women's intellectual capacities. The most famous example is Averroes, who endorses Plato's view that women can be philosophers: R. Lerner, ed. and trans., *Averroes on Plato's Republic* (Ithaca, NY: Cornell University Press, 1974), 58. On this point, Deborah Black has also reminded me that al-Fārābī says women and men are equal in respect of reason: Al-Fārābī, *On the Perfect State* (*Mabādiʾ ārāʾ ahl al-madīnat al-fāḍilah*), ed. and trans. R. Walzer (Oxford: Oxford University Press, 1985), §12.8.

46. As pointed out by Hallaq, "Gate of *Ijtihād*," 7.

47. El Shamsy, "Rethinking *Taqlīd*," 19.

48. Peters, "*Ijtihād* and *Taqlīd* in 18th and 19th Century Islam."

CHAPTER 2

1. L. Bonjour, *Structure of Empirical Knowledge* (Cambridge, MA: Harvard University Press, 1985), 15.

2. See M. Frede, "Stoics and Skeptics on Clear and Distinct Impressions," in his *Essays in Ancient Philosophy* (Oxford: Oxford University Press, 1987), 151–78.

3. A. A. Long and D. N. Sedley, *The Hellenistic Philosophers* (Cambridge: Cambridge University Press, 1987), 40 ff.

4. *Posterior Analytics* 1.8, 75b21–25; my trans. For a commentary on the work, see Aristotle, *Posterior Analytics*, trans. J. Barnes (Oxford: Oxford University Press, 1996).

5. *Posterior Analytics* 2.19, on which see, e.g., D. Hamlyn, "Aristotelian *Epagoge*," *Phronesis* 21 (1976): 167–80; T. Engberg-Pedersen, "More on Aristotelian *Epagoge*," *Phronesis* 24 (1979): 301–17, at 314; L. A. Kosman, "Understanding, Explanation and Insight in Aristotle's *Posterior Analytics*," in *Exegesis and Argument*, ed. E. N. Lee et al. (Assen: Van Gorcum, 1973), 374–92; P. Adamson, "*Posterior Analytics* II.19: A Dialogue with Plato?," in *Aristotle and the Stoics Reading Plato*, ed. V. Harte, M. M. McCabe, R. W. Sharples, and A. Sheppard (London: Institute of Classical Studies, 2010), 1–19.

6. See on this the classic paper by M. Burnyeat, "Aristotle on Understanding Knowledge," in *Aristotle on Science: The Posterior Analytics*, ed. E. Berti (Padua: Antenore, 1981), 97–139.

7. See further P. Adamson, "Eternity in Medieval Philosophy," in *Eternity: A History*, ed. Y. Melamed (Oxford: Oxford University Press, 2016), 75–116.

8. *On the Quantity of Aristotle's Books* §V.7, 6–7, in *The Philosophical Works of al-Kindī*, trans. P. Adamson and P. E. Pormann (Karachi: Oxford University Press, 2012). See further P. Adamson, *Al-Kindī* (New York: Oxford University Press, 2007), 127–35.

9. *On the Quantity of Aristotle's Books* §VI.1.

10. H. A. Davidson, "John Philoponus as a Source of Medieval Islamic and Jewish Proofs of Creation," *Journal of the American Oriental Society* 89 (1969): 357–91.

11. For an English translation, see Saadia Gaon, *The Book of Beliefs and Opinions*, trans. S. Rosenblatt (New Haven, CT: Yale University Press, 1948). I quote the work from the Arabic edition, Saadia Gaon, *Kitāb al-Amānāt wa l-iʿtiqādāt*, ed. S. Landauer (Leiden: Brill, 1880).

12. Saadia, *Kitāb al-Amānāt*, 12–13. See also I. Efros, "Saadia's Theory of Knowledge," *Jewish Quarterly Review* 33 (1942): 133–70.

13. Saadia, *Kitāb al-Amānāt*, 73–74.

14. Saadia, *Kitāb al-Amānāt*, 74.

15. Saadia, *Kitāb al-Amānāt*, 7.

16. Saadia, *Kitāb al-Amānāt*, 10.

17. Translation and study in P. Adamson and P. E. Pormann, "More than Heat and Light: Miskawayh's Epistle on Soul and Intellect," *Muslim World* 102 (2012): 478–524.

18. Adamson and Pormann, "More than Heat and Light," 489.

19. al-Fārābī, *On the Conditions of Certainty* (*al-Sharā'it al-yaqīn*), in *Manṭiq 'inda 'l-Fārābī*: *Kitāb al-Burhān wa-Kitāb Sharā'it al-yaqīn*, ed. M. Fakhry (Beirut: Dar el-Machreq, 1987). See further D. Black, "Knowledge (*'ilm*) and Certainty (*yaqīn*) in al-Fārābī's Epistemology," *Arabic Sciences and Philosophy* 16 (2006): 11–45.

20. al-Fārābī, *Conditions of Certainty*, 98.

21. Black, "Knowledge (*'ilm*) and Certainty (*yaqīn*)," 20.

22. Al-Fārābī qualifies these as *lā 'alā l-iṭlāq*, i.e., the negation of his Arabic phrase corresponding to Aristotle's ἁπλῶς, at *Conditions of Certainty*, 104. Compare his willingness to describe both philosophical demonstration and the symbolic presentation of truth in religion as "understanding" (*ma'rifa*) but in a higher and lower sense, in Al-Fārābī, *On the Perfect State*, ed. and trans. R. Walzer (Oxford: Oxford University Press, 1985), §17.2. He goes on to say (§2.2) that the lower "understanding" of religious belief is susceptible to being undermined, a worry considered in chapter 1 of this book.

23. al-Fārābī, *Conditions of Certainty*, 101.

24. al-Fārābī, *Conditions of Certainty*, 100. On this, see Black, "Knowledge (*'ilm*) and Certainty (*yaqīn*)," 29. The point was repeated by Maimonides, who was strongly influenced by al-Fārābī. Maimonides explained certainty as having a belief such that no other belief is considered possible and that does not come about accidentally. See C. Manekin, "Scepticism and Anti-Scepticism: The Case of Maimonides," in *Scepticism and Anti-Scepticism in Medieval Jewish Philosophy and Thought*, ed. R. Haliva (Berlin: de Gruyter, 2018), 86–106, at 99–100.

25. D. Black, "Certitude, Justification, and the Principles of Knowledge in Avicenna's Epistemology," in *Interpreting Avicenna: Critical Essays*, ed. P. Adamson (Cambridge: Cambridge University Press, 2013), 120–42.

26. Black, "Certitude, Justification," 124.

27. Black, "Certitude, Justification," 128.

28 Avicenna, *al-Shifā'—al-Burhān*, ed. A. Afīfī and I. Madkour (Cairo: Organisation Generale Egyptienne, 1956), 249.

29. Avicenna, *al-Burhān*, 73.

30. P. Adamson, "On Knowledge of Particulars," *Proceedings of the Aristotelian Society* 105 (2005): 273–94, discusses the passages just cited from the *Burhān* in greater detail.

31. There are numerous English translations available, including W. M. Watt, *The Faith and Practice of al-Ghazālī* (London: George Allen, 1951); and R. J.

McCarthy, *Freedom and Fulfillment* (Boston: Twayne, 1980). I have used the Arabic edition in al-Ghazālī, *al-Munqidh min al-dalāl* (*Erreur et déliverance*), ed. and trans. F. Jabre (Beirut: Commission Libanaise pour la Traduction des Chefs-d'oeuvre, 1959). On the skeptical crisis described in this work, see S. Menn, "The *Discourse on the Method* and the Tradition of Intellectual Autobiography," in *Hellenistic and Early Modern Philosophy*, ed. J. Miller and B. Inwood (Cambridge: Cambridge University Press, 2003), 141–91; T. Kukkonen, "Al-Ghazālī's Skepticism Revisited," in *Rethinking the History of Skepticism: The Missing Medieval Background*, ed. H. Lagerlund (Leiden: Brill, 2010), 29–59.

32. al-Ghazālī, *al-Munqidh min al-dalāl*, 11.

33. al-Ghazālī, *al-Munqidh min al-dalāl*, 13.

34. al-Ghazālī, *al-Munqidh min al-dalāl*, 13.

35. This point has also been made by Kukkonen, "Al-Ghazālī's Skepticism," 49.

36. See al-Ghazālī, *al-Munqidh min al-dalāl*, 21; al-Ghazālī, *The Incoherence of the Philosophers*, ed. and trans. M. E. Marmura (Provo, UT: Brigham Young University Press, 1997), 4.

37. Which of these positions is endorsed by al-Ghazālī is a matter of dispute. For a reading with which I am in sympathy, that he is open to either option in this context since either would suit his argument, see F. Griffel, *Al-Ghazālī's Philosophical Theology* (New York: Oxford University Press, 2009).

38. al-Ghazālī, *Incoherence of the Philosophers*, 171.

39. Averroes, *Tahāfut al-Tahāfut*, trans. S. Van Den Burgh (Cambridge: Cambridge University Press, 1954), 319.

40. I was made aware of these passages by P. Fatoorchi, "On Intellectual Skepticism: A Selection of Skeptical Arguments and Ṭūsī's Criticisms, with Some Comparative Notes," *Philosophy East and West* 63 (2013): 213–50. For al-Rāzī more generally, see A. Shihadeh, *The Teleological Ethics of Fakhr al-Dīn al-Rāzī* (Leiden: Brill, 2006).

41. Naṣīr al-Dīn al-Ṭūsī, *Talkhīs al-Muḥaṣṣal*, ed. A. Nūrānī (Tehran: Institute of Islamic Studies, 1980), 41.

42. Fatoorchi, "On Intellectual Skepticism," 228.

43. These examples come from Nicholas Aston, as discussed in L. A. Kennedy, "Philosophical Scepticism in England in the Mid-Fourteenth Century," *Vivarium* 21 (1983): 35–57. An earlier thinker to discuss God changing the past was Peter Damian: see I. M. Resnick, *Divine Power and Possibility in St. Peter Damian's "De divina omnipotentia"* (Leiden: Brill, 1992). For medieval reactions to the problem that Aristotelian philosophy introduced unrealistic expectations of arriving at certainty, see more generally, R. Pasnau, *After Certainty: A History of Our Epistemic Ideals and Illusions* (Oxford: Oxford University Press, 2017).

44. See J. R. Weinberg, *Nicholas of Autrecourt: A Study in 14th-Century Thought* (Princeton, NJ: Princeton University Press, 1948); T. K. Scott, "Nicholas of Autrecourt, Buridan and Ockhamism," *Journal of the History of Philosophy* 9 (1971): 15–41; J. M. M. H. Thijssen, "The Quest for Certain Knowledge in the

Fourteenth Century: Nicholas of Autrecourt against the Academics," in *Ancient Scepticism and the Sceptical Tradition*, ed. J. Sihvola (Helsinki: Philosophical Society of Finland, 2000), 199–223; C. Grellard, "Nicholas of Autrecourt's Skepticism: The Ambivalence of Medieval Epistemology," in Lagerlund, *Rethinking the History of Skepticism*, 119–32.

45. A. Krause, "Nikolaus von Autrecourt über das erste Prinzip und die Gewißheit von Sätzen," *Vivarium* 47 (2009): 407–20, at 413.

46. P. King, "Jean Buridan's Philosophy of Science," *Studies in History and Philosophy of Science* 18 (1987): 109–32; J. Zupko, "Buridan and Skepticism," *Journal of the History of Philosophy* 31 (1993): 191–221.

47. I take this point from H. Lagerlund, *Skepticism in Philosophy: A Comprehensive, Historical Introduction* (London: Routledge, 2020); I am grateful to him for showing me an advance copy of some chapters. For more general studies on medieval skepticism, see D. Perler, *Zweifel und Gewissheit: Skeptische Debatten im Mittelalter* (Frankfurt: Klostermann, 2006); D. G. Denery, K. Ghosh, and N. Zeeman, eds., *Uncertain Knowledge: Scepticism, Relativism and Doubt in the Middle Ages* (Turnhout: Brepols, 2014).

48. As pointed out by D. Perler, "Skepticism," in *The Cambridge History of Medieval Philosophy*, 2 vols., ed. R. Pasnau (Cambridge: Cambridge University Press, 2010), 384–96, at 389.

CHAPTER 3

1. The quotations in this paragraph are taken, respectively, from *Ibn Taymiyya Against the Greek Logicians*, trans. W. B. Hallaq (Oxford: Clarendon Press, 1993), 253; J. R. Sommerfeldt, *Bernard of Clairvaux on the Life of the Mind* (New York: Paulist Press, 2004), 126; H. Alfeyev, *St. Symeon the New Theologian and Orthodox Tradition* (Oxford: Oxford University Press, 2000), 40.

2. Quoted from R. M. Frank, "Al-Ghazālī on *Taqlīd*: Scholars, Theologians, and Philosophers," *Zeitschrift für Geschichte der arabisch-islamischen Wissenschaften* 7 (1991–92): 207–52, at 212.

3. Again, I cite from the Jabre edition, in my own translations: al-Ghazālī, *al-Munqidh min al-dalāl* (*Erreur et déliverance*), ed. and trans. F. Jabre (Beirut: Commission Libanaise pour la Traduction des Chefs-d'oeuvre, 1959).

4. al-Ghazālī, *al-Munqidh min al-dalāl*, 43.

5. al-Ghazālī, *al-Munqidh min al-dalāl*, 45.

6. On this, see B. G. Weiss, *The Search for God's Law: Islamic Jurisprudence in the Writings of Sayf al-Dīn al-Āmidī* (Salt Lake City: University of Utah Press, 2010), 703.

7. al-Ghazālī, *al-Munqidh min al-dalāl*, 10–11.

8. Judah Hallevi, *al-Kitāb al-Khazarī, Kitāb al-radd wa-l-dalīl fī dīn al-dhalīl*, ed. N. Bashir (Freiberg: al-Kamel, 2012), cited by section number in my own

translations. Translation in Judah b. Samuel Ha-Levi, *Judah Hallevi's Kitāb al-Khazari*, trans. H. Hirschfeld (London: Routledge, 1905), which has the same section numbers.

9. D. H. Baneth, "Judah Hallevi and al-Ghazali," in *Studies in Jewish Thought*, ed. A. Jospe (Detroit, MI: Wayne State University Press, 1981), 181–99; B. Kogan, "Al-Ghazali and Hallevi on Philosophy and the Philosophers," in *Medieval Philosophy and the Classic Tradition in Islam, Judaism and Christianity*, ed. J. Inglis (Richmond: Curzon Routledge, 2002), 64–80.

10. Hallevi, *al-Kitāb al-Khazarī*, §1.5.

11. Hallevi, *al-Kitāb al-Khazarī*, §1.8.

12. Hallevi, *al-Kitāb al-Khazarī*, §1.48.

13. For this theme in Hallevi, see Y. T. Langermann, "Science and the *Kuzari*," *Science in Context* 10 (1997): 495–522.

14. Hallevi, *al-Kitāb al-Khazarī*, §1.76–77.

15. Hallevi, *al-Kitāb al-Khazarī*, §3.53. See also §4.9, which says that humans do not understand such processes "in detail."

16. Hallevi, *al-Kitāb al-Khazarī*, §3.73.

17. This should be compared to the use of transmitted testimony in the Islamic tradition. Sophisticated discussions were devoted to the question in Islamic law under the heading *tawātur*, the transmission of *ḥadīth*, where great care needed to be taken to establish the reliability of a report. In this context it was allowed that testimony could in some cases generate necessary or certain knowledge, but most sound *ḥadīth* reports were seen as "probable." See on this, W. B. Hallaq, "The Authenticity of Prophetic *Ḥadīth*: A Pseudo-Problem," *Studia Islamica* 89 (1999): 75–90. For al-Ghazālī's discussion of the problem, which draws on both Avicennan epistemology and the legal tradition, see B. G. Weiss, "Knowledge of the Past: The Theory of *Tawātur* According to Ghazali," *Studia Islamica* 61 (1985): 81–105. My thanks to Amin Ehtashami for these references.

18. Hallevi, *al-Kitāb al-Khazarī*, §1.65.

19. I use the translation in S. Harvey, trans., *Falaquera's Epistle of the Debate: An Introduction to Jewish Philosophy* (Cambridge, MA: Harvard University Press, 1987), cited by page number; this quote is at 23.

20. *Epistle of the Debate*, 33.

21. *Epistle of the Debate*, 27–28.

22. *Epistle of the Debate*, 43.

23. *Epistle of the Debate*, 18.

24. Hallevi, *al-Kitāb al-Khazarī*, §1.89.

25. Hallevi, *al-Kitāb al-Khazarī*, §2.48.

26. For what follows, see M. Kellner, *Dogma in Medieval Jewish Thought: From Maimonides to Abravanel* (Oxford: Oxford University Press, 1986).

27. See K. Ierodiakonou, "The Anti-Logical Movement in the Fourteenth Century," in *Byzantine Philosophy and Its Ancient Sources*, ed. K. Ierodiakonou (Oxford: Oxford University Press, 2002), 219–36.

28. B. Radice and M. T. Clanchy, *The Letters of Abelard and Heloise* (London: Penguin, 2003), 21-22.

29. William of Conches, *Glosae super Platonem*, ed. E. Jeauneau (Paris: Vrin, 1965), §74.

30. William of Conches, *Glosae super Platonem*, §71.

31. I translate from Ostlender's edition, reprinted in *Peter Abelard, Theologia summi boni: Tractatus de unitate et trinitate divine*, trans. U. Niggili (Hamburg: Felix Meiner, 1988), at §1.5.

32. Cited by section number from the English version in Peter Abelard, *Ethical Writings*, trans. P. V. Spade (Indianapolis, IN: Hackett, 1995). I quote in Spade's translation and give his section numbers, as well as the sections from the Latin text in the *Patrologia Latina*, vol. 178.

33. *Dialogue* §4, 1614A (cf. §157); §13, 1615C.

34. *Dialogue* §25, 1616B.

35. *Dialogue* §171, 1641A.

36. *Dialogue* §164, 1639B–C; emphasis mine.

37. *Dialogue* §35, 1617C.

38. *Dialogue* §207, 1644C.

39. *Dialogue* §157, 1638B.

40. *Dialogue* §285, 1656D.

41. I cite by page number from the translation of *The Book of the Gentile and Three Wise Men* in *Doctor Illuminatus: A Ramon Llull Reader*, ed. and trans. A. Bonner (Princeton, NJ: Princeton University Press, 1993); see also Ramon Llull, *Selected Works of Ramon Llull*, 2 vols., trans. A. Bonner (Princeton, NJ: Princeton University Press, 1985).

42. Llull, *Book of the Gentile*, 167.

43. Llull, *Book of the Gentile*, 90.

44. Llull, *Book of the Gentile*, 168.

45. Llull, *Book of the Gentile*, 116.

46. A. Bonner, *The Art and Logic of Ramon Llull: A User's Guide* (Leiden: Brill, 2007), 281.

47. I take the translation and my knowledge of the passage, which is from Llull's *Liber de acquisitione Terrae Sanctae*, from A. Giletti, "An Arsenal of Arguments: Arabic Philosophy at the Service of Christian Polemics in Ramón Martí's *Pugio fidei*," in *Mapping Knowledge: Cross-Pollination in Late Antiquity and the Middle Ages*, ed. C. Burnett and P. Mantas-España (London: Warburg Institute, 2014), 153–65, at 163–64.

48. Llull, *Book of the Gentile*, 120.

49. Llull, *Book of the Gentile*, 120.

50. Llull, *Book of the Gentile*, 144.

51. The problem of conflicting authorities was intensely discussed in Islamic law, with reference to the slogan "every *mujtahid* is correct (*muṣīb*)," which seems to suggest that even when two jurists draw opposing conclusions, both are in some

sense right. See on this, A. Zysow, *The Economy of Certainty: An Introduction to the Typology of Islamic Legal Theory* (Atlanta, GA: Lockwood, 2013), ch. 5.

52. This in the context of discussing the writings of Joshua Reynolds, at *The Complete Poetry and Prose of William Blake*, ed. D. V. Erdman (Berkeley: University of California Press, 1982), 639.

CHAPTER 4

1. ʿĔnbāqom, *Anqaṣa Amin (La porte de la foi)*, ed. and trans. E. Z. van Donzel (Leiden: Brill, 1969).

2. B. E. Perry, ed., *Secundus the Silent Philosopher* (Ithaca, NY: Cornell University Press, 1964). For more on the reception of Greek philsophy in Geʾez, see C. Sumner, *Ethiopian Philosophy*, 5 vols. (Addis Ababa: Central Printing Press, 1974–82).

3. In N. G. Wilson, ed., *Saint Basil on the Value of Greek Literature* (London: Duckworth, 1975); and with facing-page Italian translation, M. Naldini, ed. and trans., *Basilio di Cesarea, Discorso ai giovani* (Florence: A. Mondadori, 1984).

4. *To the Youth*, §4. The image of the bees goes back to Seneca: see M. R. Graver, "Honeybee Reading and Self-Scripting: *Epistulae morales 84*," in *Seneca Philosophus*, ed. M. L. Colish and J. Wildberger (Berlin: de Gruyter, 2014), 269–93.

5. On him, see A. Louth, *St. John Damascene: Tradition and Originality in Byzantine Theology* (Oxford: Oxford University Press, 2009); and for an edition and translation of his works, P. B. Kotter, ed., *Die Schriften des Johannes von Damaskos*, 6 vols. (Berlin: de Gruyter, 1969–88); Saint John of Damascus, *Writings*, trans. F. H. Chase (Washington, DC: Catholic University of America Press, 1958). On the *Philosophical Chapters*, see G. Richter, *Die Dialektik des Johannes von Damaskos: Eine Untersuchung des Textes nach seinen Quellen und seiner Bedeutung* (Ettal: Buch-Kunst Verlag, 1964).

6. D. Thomas, ed. and trans., *Anti-Christian Polemic in Early Islam: Abū ʿĪsā al-Warrāq's Against the Trinity* (Cambridge: Cambridge University Press, 1992) and *Early Muslim Polemic Against Christianity: Abū ʿĪsā al-Warrāq's Against the Incarnation* (Cambridge: Cambridge University Press, 2002), with this characterization of Abū ʿĪsā at 74 in the latter volume. I quote the work in Thomas's translation with occasional modification.

7. On the Christian background of a dialectical locution typical of this work and of *kalām* in general ("if they say . . . then we say"), see F. Benevich, "'Wenn sie sagen . . . , dann sagen wir . . .': Die Ursprünge des dialektischen Verfahrens des *Kalām*," *Le muséon* 128 (2015): 181–201.

8. Thomas, *Abū ʿĪsā al-Warrāq's Against the Trinity*, §70.

9. Thomas, *Abū ʿĪsā al-Warrāq's Against the Trinity*, §62, 65.

10. For discussions of universals, see, e.g., Thomas, *Abū ʿĪsā al-Warrāq's Against the Incarnation*, 160, 187–78, 219, 284, 300.

11. On him, see V. Calzolari and J. Barnes, eds., *L'oeuvre de David l'Invincible* (Leiden: Brill, 2009).

12. On this argument in Avicenna, see T. Mayer, "Faḫr ad-Dīn ar-Rāzī's Critique of Ibn Sīnā's Argument for the Unity of God in the *Išārāt* and Naṣīr ad-Dīn aṭ-Ṭūsī's Defence," in *Before and After Avicenna*, ed. D. C. Reisman (Leiden: Brill, 2003), 199–218; P. Adamson, "From the Necessary Existent to God," in *Interpreting Avicenna: Critical Essays*, ed. P. Adamson (Cambridge: Cambridge University Press, 2013), 170–89.

13. For another important example of *kalām* influence on Avicenna, see R. Wisnovsky, "Notes on Avicenna's Concept of Thingness (*shay'iyya*)," *Arabic Sciences and Philosophy* 10 (2000): 181–221.

14. Thomas, *Abū ʿĪsā al-Warrāq's Against the Incarnation*, §159. Notice that *ḥujja* was also the term used to describe the legal evidence or proof needed to justify an independent judgment, as we saw in chapter 1.

15. See P. Adamson, "Yaḥyā Ibn ʿAdī against al-Kindī on the Trinity," *Journal of Eastern Christian Studies* 72 (2020): 241–71, which includes a translation of al-Kindī's argument with Ibn ʿAdī's response. Al-Kindī's side of the dispute was already translated in *The Philosophical Works of al-Kindī*, trans. P. Adamson and P. E. Pormann (Karachi: Oxford University Press, 2012); and Ibn ʿAdī's, in A. Périer, "Un traité de Yahyâ ben ʿAdî: Défense du dogme de la Trinité contre les objections d'al-Kindî," *Revue de l'orient chrétien*, ser. 3, 2 (1920–21): 3–21.

16. Adamson and Pormann, *The Philosophical Works of al-Kindī*, 80.

17. See A. Périer, ed. and trans., *Petite traités apologétiques de Yaḥyā ben ʿAdī* (Paris: Vrin, 1920), 21–22.

18. §Y10, in Adamson, "Yaḥyā Ibn ʿAdī against al-Kindī on the Trinity."

19. The work is in Yaḥyā Ibn ʿAdī, *Philosophical Treatises*, ed. S. Khalifat (Amman: al-Jamīʿa al-Urduniyya, 1988), 375–404, with this passage at 404.

20. Thomas, *Abū ʿĪsā al-Warrāq's Against the Trinity*, §106.

21. Thomas, *Abū ʿĪsā al-Warrāq's Against the Trinity*, §115.

22. Saadia Gaon, *Kitāb al-Amānāt wa l-iʿtiqādāt*, ed. S. Landauer (Leiden: Brill, 1880), 79.

23. Saadia, *Kitāb al-Amānāt wa 'l-Iʿtiqādāt*, 86.

24. S. T. Keating, ed. and trans., *Defending the "People of Truth" in the Early Islamic Period: The Christian Apologies of Abū Rāʾiṭah* (Leiden: Brill, 2006).

25. *First Epistle on the Trinity* §10, in Keating, *Defending the "People of Truth."*

26. *First Epistle on the Trinity* §21, in Keating, *Defending the "People of Truth."*

27. *First Epistle on the Trinity* §23, in Keating, *Defending the "People of Truth."*

28. For interreligious literature and attitudes in this cultural context, see J. Meyendorff, "Byzantine Views of Islam," *Dumbarton Oaks Papers* 18 (1964): 113–32; A. Cameron, *Arguing It Out: Discussion in Twelfth-Century Byzantium* (Budapest: Central European University Press, 2016).

29. H. Goddard, *A History of Christian-Muslim Relations* (Edinburgh: Edinburgh University Press, 2000), 57.

30. M. Trizio, "A Neoplatonic Refutation of Islam from the Time of the Komneni," in *Knotenpunkt Byzanz: Wissensformen und kulturelle Wechselbeziehungen*, ed. A. Speer and P. Steinkrüger (Berlin: de Gruyter, 2012), 145–66.

31. Quoted from Trizio, "A Neoplatonic Refutation," 150.

32. Quoted from Trizio, "A Neoplatonic Refutation," 158.

33. Quoted from N. M. El Cheikh, *Byzantium Viewed by the Arabs* (Cambridge, MA: Harvard University Press, 2004), 106.

34. See D. Gutas, *Greek Thought, Arabic Culture: The Graeco-Arabic Translation Movement in Baghdad and Early Society (2nd–4th / 8th–10th Centuries)* (London: Routledge, 1998).

35. "The Apology of Timothy the Patriarch before Caliph Mahdi," in *Christian Documents in Syriac, Arabic and Garshuni*, ed. and trans. A. Mingana (Cambridge: W. Heffer and Son, 1928); M. Heimgartner, trans., *Timotheos I., ostsyrischer Patriarch: Disputation mit dem Kalifen al-Mahdī* (Leuven: Peeters, 2011). For the history of Syriac interreligious disputation, see also S. H. Griffith, "Disputes with Muslims in Syriac Christian Texts: From Patriarch John (d. 648) to Bar Hebraeus (d. 1286)," in *Religionsgespräche im Mittelalter*, ed. F. Niewohner (Wiesbaden: Harassowitz, 1992), 251–73.

36. D. Gutas, *Greek Thought, Arabic Culture, 61.*

37. See H. P. J. Cheikho, *Dialectique du langage sur Dieu: Letter de Timothée I (728–823) à Serge* (Rome: Pontificia Studiorum Universitas, 1983).

38. *Disputation mit dem Kalifen al-Mahdī*, 76.

39. *Disputation mit dem Kalifen al-Mahdī*, 22–23; for a similar passage, see 81–82.

40. See, e.g., Dexippus, *On Aristotle Categories*, trans. J. Dillon (London: Duckworth, 1990), 53; and for the Arabic reception, C. Ferrari, "Der Duft des Apfels: Abū l-Faraǧ ʿAbdallāh ibn aṭ-Ṭayyib und sein Kommentar zu den *Kategorien* des Aristoteles," in *Aristoteles e i suoi esegeti neoplatonici: Logica e ontologia nelle interpretazioni greche e arabe*, ed. V. Celluprica and C. D'Ancona (Pisa: Bibliopolis, 2003), 87–106.

41. *Disputation mit dem Kalifen al-Mahdī*, 89.

42. *Disputation mit dem Kalifen al-Mahdī*, 96.

43. *Disputation mit dem Kalifen al-Mahdī*, 79; ʿĔnbāqom, *Anqaṣa Amin*, 175.

44. ʿĔnbāqom, *Anqaṣa Amin*, 245–55; quotation at 249 (I translate from van Donzel's French version). Earlier cases of this strategy are listed in van Donzel's introduction at 106–12.

45. Translation from Adamson and Pormann, *The Philosophical Works of al-Kindī*, 271 (*Sayings of Socrates* §27).

46. For example, the texts in *Die Doxographie des Pseudo-Ammonios: Ein Beitrag zur neuplatonischen Überlieferung im Islam*, ed. and trans. U. Rudolph (Stuttgart: Franz Steiner, 1989); and E. Wakelnig, *A Philosophy Reader from the Circle*

of Miskawayh (Cambridge: Cambridge University Press, 2014). On the genre more generally, see D. Gutas, "Classical Arabic Wisdom Literature: Nature and Scope," *Journal of the American Oriental Society* 101 (1981): 49–86.

47. For the works, see C. Sumner, *The Treatise of Zär'a Ya'əqob and of Wäldä Ḥəywat: Text and Authorship* (Addis Ababa: Central Printing Press, 1976). For discussions of the authenticity, see A. Mbodj-Pouye and A. Wion, "L'histoire d'un vrai faux traité philosophique (*Ḥatatā* Zar'a Yā'eqob et *Ḥatatā* Walda Ḥeywat)," *Afriques, Débats et lectures* [online journal] (2013); G. Haile, "*The Discourse of Wärqe*, Commonly Known as *Ḥatäta zä-Zär'a Ya'əqob*," in *Ethiopian Studies in Honour of Amha Asfaw*, ed. G. Haile (New York: Tipografia Centrala, 2017), 51–71.

48. Translation from Sumner, *The Treatise*, 6.

49. *Johannes Damaskenos und Theodor Abū Qurra: Schriften zum Islam*, trans. R. Glei and A. T. Khoury (Würzburg: Echtler, 1995), 94.

CHAPTER 5

1. Abū Ḥātim al-Rāzī, *The Proofs of Prophecy*, ed. and trans. T. Khalidi (Provo, UT: Brigham Young University Press, 2011).

2. al-Rāzī, *Proofs* 24–25; trans. taken, with modifications, from S. Stroumsa, *Freethinkers of Medieval Islam: Ibn al-Rāwandī, Abū Bakr al-Rāzī, and Their Impact on Islamic Thought* (Leiden: Brill, 1999), 97.

3. P. Adamson, *Al-Rāzī* (New York: Oxford University Press, 2020), ch. 7.

4. al-Rāzī, *Proofs* 26; my trans.

5. For the Ismā'īlīs in general, see F. Daftary, *The Ismailis: Their History and Doctrines* (Cambridge: Cambridge University Press, 1990) and *Mediaeval Ismaili History and Thought* (Cambridge: Cambridge University Press, 1996).

6. al-Rāzī, *Proofs* 8.

7. al-Rāzī, *Doutes sur Galien*, ed. and trans. P. Koetschet (Berlin: de Gruyter, 2019).

8. al-Rāzī, *Doutes sur Galien, §2.1.*

9. al-Rāzī, *Proofs* 13.

10. See P. Adamson and A. Lammer, "Fakhr al-Dīn al-Rāzī's Platonist Account of the Essence of Time," in *Philosophical Theology in Islam: The Later Ash'arī Tradition*, ed. A. Shihadeh and J. Thiele (Leiden: Brill, 2020), 95–122, at 109.

11. Suhrawardī, *The Philosophy of Illumination*, ed. and trans. J. Walbridge and H. Ziai (Provo, UT: Brigham Young University Press, 1999), §1.4; my trans. See also J. Walbridge, *The Wisdom of the Mystic East: Suhrawardi and Platonic Orientalism* (Albany: SUNY Press, 2001).

12. G. Karamanolis, "Porphyry: the First Platonist Commentator on Aristotle," in *Philosophy, Science and Exegesis in Greek, Arabic and Latin Commentaries*, 2 vols., ed. P. Adamson, H. Baltussen and M. W. F. Stone (London: Institute of Classical Studies, 2004), vol. 1, 97–120. For the topic more generally, see G. Karamanolis's

Plato and Aristotle in Agreement? Platonists on Aristotle from Antiochus to Porphyry (Oxford: Oxford University Press, 2006).

13. *Simplicii in Aristotelis categorias commentarium*, ed. K. Kalbfleisch (Berlin: G. Reimer, 1907), 7. Translation taken from *Simplicius: On Aristotle Categories 1–4*, trans. M. Chase (Ithaca, NY: Cornell University Press, 2003). See also H. Baltussen, *Philosophy and Exegesis in Simplicius* (London: Bloomsbury, 2008), 33.

14. *A Concise and Brief Statement about the Soul*, in *The Philosophical Works of al-Kindī*, ed. P. Adamson and P. E. Pormann (Karachi: Oxford University Press, 2012). See further C. D'Ancona, "The Topic of the 'Harmony Between Plato and Aristotle': Some Examples in Early Arabic Philosophy," in *Wissen über Grenzen: Arabisches Wissen und lateinisches Mittelalter*, ed. A. Speer and L. Wegener (Berlin: de Gruyter, 2006), 379–405.

15. P. Adamson, "Aristotelianism and the Soul in the Arabic Plotinus," *Journal of the History of Ideas* 62 (2001): 211–32.

16. I cite from the section numbers of al-Fārābī, *L'Harmonie entre les Opinions de Platon et d'Aristote, texte et traduction*, ed. and trans. F. W. Najjar and D. Mallet (Damascus: Institut français de Damas, 1999). See also al-Fārābī, *L'Armonia delle opinioni dei due sapienti il divino Platone et Aristotele*, ed. and trans. C. Martini Bonadeo (Pisa: Pisa University Press, 2008). English translation in Alfarabi, *The Political Writings: "Selected Aphorisms" and Other Texts*, trans. C. E. Butterworth (Ithaca, NY: Cornell University Press, 2001).

17. M. Rashed, "On the Authorship of the Treatise *On the Harmonization of the Opinions of the Two Sages* Attributed to al-Fārābī," *Arabic Sciences and Philosophy* 19 (2009): 43–82.

18. al-Fārābī, *Harmonie* §2.

19. al-Fārābī, *Harmonie* §4.

20. al-Fārābī, *Harmonie* §1.

21. al-Fārābī, *Harmonie* §4.

22. al-Fārābī, *Harmonie* §8.

23. This, by the way, does recall a tactic used by the real al-Fārābī, who in a treatise defending Aristotle from the criticisms of Galen wrongly claimed that Aristotle was well aware of the nervous system but simply used different words to refer to the nerves. See F. W. Zimmermann, "Al-Fārābī und die philosophische Kritik an Galen von Alexander zu Averroes," in *Abhandlungen der Akademie der Wissenschaften in Göttingen*, phil.-hist. Klasse, Dritte Folge, Nr. 98 (Göttingen: Vandenhoeck & Rüprecht, 1976), 401–14; for the treatise in Arabic, see *Rasā'il falsafiyya li-l-Kindī wa-l-Fārābī wa-Ibn Bājja wa-Ibn ʿAdī*, ed. A. Badawī (Beirut: Dār al-Andalus, 1980).

24. al-Fārābī, *Harmonie* §41, 71.

25. al-Fārābī, *Harmonie* §55.

26. I discuss this point, and the following example, in "Plotinus Arabus and Proclus Arabus in the *Harmony of the Two Philosophers* Ascribed to al-Fārābī," in *Reading Proclus and the Book of Causes*, ed. D. Calma (Leiden: Brill, 2021), vol. 2, 184–99.

27. §I.54 in G. Lewis's translation of the *Theology of Aristotle*, in *Plotini Opera, Tomus II: Enneades IV–V*, ed. P. Henry and H.-R. Schwyzer (Paris: Desclée de Brouwer, 1959).

28. On her, see T. Gouma-Peterson, ed., *Anna Komnene and Her Times* (Abingdon: Routledge, 2000); L. Neville, *Anna Komnene: The Life and Work of a Medieval Historian* (Oxford: Oxford University Press, 2016).

29. M. Trizio, "Neoplatonic Source-Material in Eustratios of Nicaea's Commentary on Book VI of the *Nicomachean Ethics*," in *Medieval Greek Commentaries on the Nicomachean Ethics*, ed. C. Barber and D. Jenkins (Leiden: Brill, 2009), 72–109, at 93.

30. Quoted from H. P. F. Mercken, "The Greek Commentators on Aristotle's *Ethics*," in*Aristotle Transformed: The Ancient Commentators and Their Influence*, ed. R. Sorabji (London: Duckworth, 1990), 407–43, at 418. See also K. Giocarinis, "Eustratius of Nicaea's Defense of the Doctrine of Ideas," *Franciscan Studies* 24 (1964): 159–204.

31. B. Bydén, "'No Prince of Perfection': Byzantine Anti-Aristotelianism from the Patristic Period to Plethon," in *Power and Subversion in Byzantium*, ed. D. Angelov and M. Saxby (Farnham: Ashgate, 2013), 147–76. The following quote is taken from 152.

32. J. Anton, "Neoplatonic Elements in Arethas' Scholia on Aristotle and Porphyry," in *Néoplatonisme et philosophie médiévale*, ed. L. G. Benakis (Turnhout: Brepols, 1995), 291–306, at 294.

33. Bydén, "'No Prince of Perfection,'" 169.

34. See M. Jeffreys and M. D. Lauxtermann, eds., *The Letters of Psellos: Cultural Networks and Historical Realities* (Oxford: Oxford University Press, 2017), 151–52.

35. B. Bydén, *Theodore Metochites' Stoicheiosis astronomike and the Study of Natural Philosophy and Mathematics in Early Palaiologan Byzantium* (Göteborg: Acta Universitatis Gothoburgensis, 2003), 50–54.

36. B. Bydén, "The Criticism of Aristotle in Nikephoros Gregoras' *Florentius*," in ΔΩΡΟΝ ΡΟΔΟΠΟΙΚΙΛΟΝ: Studies in Honour of Jan Olof Rosenqvist, ed. D. Searby et al. (Uppsala: Uppsala Universitet, 2012), 107–22.

37. Greek edition in B. Lagarde, "Le *De differentiis* de Pléthon d'après l'autographe de la Marcienne," *Byzantion* 43 (1973): 312–43. For a full English translation, see C. M. Woodhouse, *George Gemistos Plethon: The Last of the Hellenes* (Oxford: Clarendon, 1986), 192–214. I provide page numbers from Lagarde's edition followed by section numbers from Woodhouse's translation. Newer, partial translation and commentary in B. Bydén, "George Gemistos (Plethon), *On Aristotle's Departures from Plato* 0–19," in *The Aristotelian Tradition: Aristotle's Works on Logic and Metaphysics and Their Reception in the Middle Ages*, ed. B. Bydén and C. T. Thörnqvist (Toronto: Pontifical Institute of Mediaeval Studies, 2017), 267–344.

38. *Departures* 321, §1.

39. Woodhouse, *George Gemistos Plethon*, 146.

40. For this as the true meaning of Ficino's famous remark that Plethon inspired Cosimo de' Medici to set up a Platonic "Academy" in Florence, see J. Hankins, "Cosimo de' Medici and the 'Platonic Academy,'" *Journal of the Warburg and Courtauld Institutes* 53 (1990): 144–62.

41. For a good example of this, see the response to Aristotle's criticism of Plato's theory of Forms at *Departures* 334–37, §37–43. For the following criticisms, see 322, §4 (untoward interest in shellfish); 324, §9 (inadequate theology); 327, §18 (thoughtless); 328, §21 (unclear about virtue, thunderstorm example).

42. *Departures* 325, §12. The following examples are at 327–28, §20 (immortality and ethics); 333–34, §34–35 (determinism).

43. *Departures* 335, §38.

44. G. Karamanolis, "Plethon and Scholarios on Aristotle," in *Byzantine Philosophy and Its Ancient Sources*, ed. K. Ierodiakonou (Oxford: Oxford University Press, 2002), 253–82, at 261.

45. *Departures* 339, §47; and for the following passage, 342–43, §55.

46. N. Siniossoglou, *Radical Platonism in Byzantium: Illumination and Utopia in Gemistos Plethon* (Cambridge: Cambridge University Press, 2011), accepts that Plethon had pagan sympathies, whereas V. Hladký, *The Philosophy of Gemistos Plethon: Platonism in Late Byzantium, between Hellenism and Orthodoxy* (London: Routledge, 2017), denies it.

47. This is the hypothesis of J. Monfasani, *George of Trebizond: A Biography and a Study of His Rhetoric and Logic* (Leiden: Brill, 1976).

48. Translation from S. Jayne, trans., *Marsilio Ficino's Commentary on Plato's Symposium* (Columbia: University of Missouri Press, 1944), §2.9.

49. See J. Monfasani, "Marsilio Ficino and the Plato-Aristotle Controversy," in *Marsilio Ficino: His Theology, His Philosophy, His Legacy*, ed. M. J. B. Allen and V. Rees (Leiden: Brill, 2002), 179–202.

50. One notable exception is Pico della Mirandola whose list of 900 theses, which he proposed to debate against all comers in Rome, reconciled many authorities, including Plato and Aristotle. About them he wrote, "There is no natural or divine question in which [they] do not agree in meaning and substance, although in their words they seem to disagree"; S. A. Farmer, *Syncretism in the West: Pico's 900 Theses (1486)* (Tempe, AZ: Medieval and Renaissance Texts and Studies, 1998), §1.1. Note again the contrast between surface and deeper meaning.

51. See his ethical *Introduction*, in *The Humanism of Leonardo Bruni*, trans. G. Griffiths et al. (Binghamton: Medieval and Renaissance Texts and Studies, 1987).

52. Translations taken from Lucrezia Marinella, *The Nobility and the Excellence of Women and the Defects of Men*, trans. A. Dunhill (Chicago: University of Chicago Press, 1999).

53. Marinella, *Nobility and the Excellence of Women*, 40. For the following points, see 68 (nature); 115 (virtue); 143 (*History of Animals*); 120 (spurning of Aristotle and his small intelligence).

CHAPTER 6

1. Phillis Wheatley, *The Collected Works of Phillis Wheatley*, ed. J. C. Shields (Oxford: Oxford University Press, 1988), 15–16.

2. Wheatley, *Collected Works*, 43.

3. Wheatley, *Collected Works*, 62.

4. A similar point has been made about a somewhat later black woman author, Maria W. Stewart. Marilyn Richardson, in *Maria W. Stewart: America's First Black Woman Political Writer* (Bloomington: Indiana University Press, 1988), comments that one of Stewart's public lectures "opened with the full-fledged conjuring of an apocalyptic vision and concluded with homely advice to wives and mothers," showing "Stewart speaking in first one and then the other of the two voices of her antiphonal mode."

5. Augustine, *Confessions*, trans. H. Chadwick (Oxford: 1991), §9.10.24.

6. Gregory of Nyssa, *De Anima et resurrectione*, ed. A. Spira (Leiden: Brill, 2014); English version, Gregory of Nyssa, *The Soul and the Resurrection*, trans. C. Roth (Crestwood, NY: St. Vladimir's Seminary Press, 1993). What follows summarizes part of the argument of P. Adamson, "Macrina's Method: Reason and Reasoning in Gregory of Nyssa's *On Soul and Resurrection*," in *Women and the Female in Neoplatonism*, ed. J. Schulz and J. Wilberding (Leiden: Brill, 2022), 255–75.

7. Grégoire de Nysse, *Vie de sainte Macrine*, ed. P. Maraval (Paris: Editions du Cerf, 1971), 1; English version, Gregory, Bishop of Nyssa, *The Life of Saint Macrina*, trans. K. Corrigan (Eugene, OR: Wipf & Stock, 2001).

8. Gregory of Nyssa, *De Anima et resurrectione*, 34.

9. C. Rapp, "Figures of Female Sanctity: Byzantine Edifying Manuscripts and Their Audience," *Dumbarton Oaks Papers* 50 (1996): 313–44, at 324; trans. modified.

10. A. Kaldellis, ed. and trans., *Mothers and Sons, Fathers and Daughters: The Byzantine Family of Michael Psellos* (Notre Dame, IN: University of Notre Dame Press, 2006). Quotes in the following are from sections 17b, 25b, and 26a of this version.

11. R. Browning, "An Unpublished Funeral Oration on Anna Comnena," in *Aristotle Transformed: The Ancient Commentators and Their Influence*, ed. R. Sorabji (London: Duckworth, 1990), 393–406, §4.

12. English version, Anna Komnene, *The Alexiad*, rev. ed., ed. P. Frankopan, trans. E. R. A. Sewter (London: Penguin Classics, 2009).

13. L. Neville, *Anna Komnene: The Life and Work of a Medieval Historian* (Oxford: Oxford University Press, 2016), 8.

14. Neville, *Anna Komnene*, 73.

15. Kaldellis, *Mothers and Sons, Fathers and Daughters*, §7b.

16. Dhuoda, *Handbook for Her Warrior Son: Liber Manualis*, ed. and trans. M. Thiébaux (Cambridge: Cambridge University Press, 1998).

17. A. B. Huizenga, *Moral Education for Women in the Pastoral and Pythagorean Letters* (Leiden: Brill, 2013).

18. Hildegard of Bingen, *Selected Writings*, trans. M. Atherton (London: Penguin, 2001); Hildegard of Bingen, *Scivias*, trans. C. Hart and J. Bishop (New York: Paulist Press, 1990).

19. Hildegard, *Selected Writings*, 9; see also 31.

20. Cited from S. Flanagan, *Hildegard of Bingen, 1098–1179: A Visionary Life* (London: Routledge, 1998), 110.

21. J. Stover, "Hildegard, the Schools and Their Critics," in *A Companion to Hildegard of Bingen*, ed. B. M. Kienzle, D. Stoudt, and G. Ferzoco (Leiden, Brill: 2014), 109–35.

22. Hildegard, *Selected Writings*, 51.

23. Mechthild von Magdeburg, *Das fließende Licht der Gottheit*, ed. and trans. G. Vollmann-Profe (Berlin: Deutscher Klassiker Verlag, 2010), §2.26. English version, Mechthild of Magdeburg, *The Flowing Light of the Godhead*, trans. F. Tobin (New York: Paulist Press, 1998).

24. Mechthild, *Das fließende Licht*, §4.2.

25. *Hadewijch: The Complete Works*, trans. C. Hart (London: SPCK, 1980), 17.

26. Mechthild, *Das fließende Licht*, §1.44.

27. Marguerite Porete, *The Mirror of Simple Souls*, trans. E. Colledge, J. C. Marler, and J. Grant (Notre Dame, IN: University of Notre Dame Press, 1999).

28. See M. G. Sargent, "The Annihilation of Marguerite Porete," *Viator* 28 (1997): 253–79.

29. Porete, *Mirror of Simple Souls*, 5.

30. D. Kangas, "Dangerous Joy: Marguerite Porete's Good-bye to the Virtues," *Journal of Religion* 91 (2011): 299–319.

31. See the remarks of Lydia Wegener in J. M. Hackett, ed., *A Companion to Meister Eckhart* (Leiden: Brill, 2013), 433–41.

32. On this tradition, see C. Van Dyke, "'Many Know Much, but Do Not Know Themselves': Self-Knowledge, Humility, and Perfection in the Medieval Affective Contemplative Tradition," *Proceedings of the Society for Medieval Logic and Metaphysics* 14 (2018): 89–106.

33. C. W. Bynum, *Holy Feast and Holy Fast: The Religious Significance of Food to Medieval Women* (Berkeley: University of California Press, 1987).

34. Bynum, *Holy Feast*, 249–50.

35. Porete, *Mirror of Simple Souls*, 7, 87.

36. Dante, *The Banquet*, trans. C. Ryan (Saratoga, NY: Anma Libri, 1989), §1.9.

37. Lucrezia Marinella, *The Nobility and the Excellence of Women and the Defects of Men*, ed. and trans. A. Dunhill (Chicago: University of Chicago Press, 1999), 140.

38. P. F. Grendler, *Schooling in Renaissance Italy: Literacy and Learning, 1300–1600* (Baltimore: Johns Hopkins University Press, 1989), 87–88.

39. Cassandra Fedele, *Letters and Orations*, ed. and trans. D. Robin (Chicago: University of Chicago Press, 2000); Isotta Nogarola, *Complete Writings: Letterbook, Dialogue on Adam and Eve, Orations*, ed. and trans. M. L. King and D. Robin

(Chicago: University of Chicago Press, 2004); Laura Cereta, *Collected Letters of a Renaissance Feminist*, ed. and trans. D. Robin (Chicago: University of Chicago Press, 1997).

40. Fedele, *Letters and Orations*, 54.

41. Nogarola, *Complete Writings*, 51.

42. Nogarola, *Complete Writings*, 38, 74.

43. Fedele, *Letters and Orations*, 76–77; Nogarola, *Complete Writings*, 107–13.

44. Cereta, *Collected Letters*, 24, 31, 55.

45. M. L. King, *Humanism, Venice and Women: Essays on the Italian Renaissance* (Aldershot: Ashgate, 2005).

46. Cereta, *Collected Letters*, 105.

47. See M. Fricker, *Epistemic Injustice: Power and the Ethics of Knowing* (Oxford: Oxford University Press, 2009). In particular medieval women were victims of what Fricker calls "pre-emptive testimonial injustice," in which "social groups who are subject to identity prejudice and are thereby susceptible to unjust credibility deficit will, by the same token, also tend simply not to be asked to share their thoughts, their judgements, their opinions. (If the word of people like you is generally not taken seriously, people will tend not to ask for it)" (30).

48. Mechthild, *Das fließende Licht*, §5.4.

49. Fedele, *Letters and Orations*, 71.

50. Cereta, *Collected Letters*, 79.

51. Moderata Fonte, *The Worth of Women: Wherein Is Clearly Revealed Their Nobility and Their Superiority to Men*, ed. and trans. V. Cox (Chicago: University of Chicago Press, 1997), 238.

52. Christine of Pizan, *Debate of the "Romance of the Rose,"* ed. and trans. D. F. Hult (Chicago: University of Chicago Press, 2010), 38; see 50 and 103 for the following quotes.

53. Christine of Pizan, *Debate of the "Romance of the Rose,"* 103.

54. Christine de Pizan, *Christine's Vision*, trans. G. McLeod (New York: Garland, 1993), 118.

CHAPTER 7

1. Nice examples from the two Christian cultures are Nicholas of Methone, who quotes it in his critical commentary on Proclus's *Elements of Theology* (at proposition 195), and Lorenzo Valla, scourge of Aristotle and his scholastic heirs, who alludes to the verse in his *On Free Will*: trans. C. Trinkaus, in *The Renaissance Philosophy of Man*, ed. E. Cassirer et al. (Chicago: University of Chicago Press, 1948), 181.

2. For a collection of studies on the Platonic theory and its late ancient reception, see R. Barney, T. Brennan, and C. Brittain, eds., *Plato and the Divided Self* (Cambridge: Cambridge University Press, 2012).

3. Arabic edition, Abū Bakr al-Rāzī, *Rasāʾil falsafiyya*, ed. P. Kraus (Cairo: Fouad University, 1939); English version in *The Spiritual Physick of Rhazes*, trans. A. J. Arberry (London: John Murray, 1950).

4. al-Rāzī, *Rasāʾil falsafiyya*, 27.

5. al-Rāzī, *Rasāʾil falsafiyya*, 20.

6. al-Rāzī, *Rasāʾil falsafiyya*, 20, 56.

7. al-Rāzī, *Rasāʾil falsafiyya*, 18.

8. al-Rāzī, *Rasāʾil falsafiyya*, 78.

9. Miskawayh, *Tahdhīb al-akhlāq*, ed. C. Zurayk (Beirut: al-Jāmiʿa al-Amīrīkiyya, 1966); the tripartite soul is introduced at 15–16, see also 51–55. For an English version, see Miskawayh, *The Refinement of Character*, trans. C. Zurayk (Beirut: American University of Beirut, 1968).

10. On this analogy, see P. Adamson, "Health in Arabic Ethical Works," in *Health: A History*, ed. P. Adamson (New York: Oxford University Press, 2019), 103–35.

11. Miskawayh makes this point at *Tahdhīb al-akhlāq*, 185–86; and al-Rāzī defends a policy of moderation and not asceticism with regard to bodily pleasure in his *Philosophical Life*. For his views on sex as conducive to bodily health, see P. E. Pormann, "Al-Rāzī (d. 925) on the Benefits of Sex: A Clinician Caught between Philosophy and Medicine," in *O Ye Gentlemen: Arabic Studies on Science and Literary Culture, in Honour of Remke Kruk*, ed. A. Vrolijk and J. P. Hogendijk (Leiden: Brill, 2007), 115–27.

12. Miskawayh, *Tahdhīb al-akhlāq*, 44–46.

13. Miskawayh, *Tahdhīb al-akhlāq*, 206.

14. Miskawayh, *Tahdhīb al-akhlāq*, 193–94, cf. Aristotle, *Nicomachean Ethics* 403a30–b1.

15. Miskawayh, *Tahdhīb al-akhlāq*, 194, 196.

16. For the text, see V. Mistrih, "Traité sur la continence de Yaḥyā Ibn ʿAdī, édition critique," *Studia orientalia christiana* 16 (1981): 1–137. Studies in S. H. Griffith, "Yaḥyā Ibn ʿAdī's Colloquy *On Sexual Abstinence and the Philosophical Life*," in *Arabic Theology, Arabic Philosophy*, ed. J. E. Montgomery (Leuven: Peeters, 2006), 299–333; T.-A. Druart, "An Arab Christian Philosophical Defense of Religious Celibacy against Its Islamic Condemnation: Yaḥyā Ibn ʿAdī," in *Chastity: A Study in Perception, Ideals, Opposition*, ed. N. Van Deusen (Leiden: Brill, 2008), 77–85.

17. For relevant passages, see the translations in A. M. Casiday, *Evagrius Ponticus* (London: Routledge, 2006), 5–7, 14, 91–93, 106, 115; at 100 he concedes, like Miskawayh, that anger may be useful in stirring us up toward moral striving.

18. See D. Bradshaw, *Aristotle East and West: Metaphysics and the Division of Christendom* (Cambridge: Cambridge University Press, 2004), 197; H. Alfeyev, *St. Symeon the New Theologian and Orthodox Tradition* (Oxford: Oxford University Press, 2000), 122. It should however be noted that in Hesychasm the vision is seen as a gift of grace, not a kind of "automatic" reward for heroic self-abnegation. See

A. N. Williams, *The Ground of Union: Deification in Aquinas and Palamas* (Cambridge: Cambridge University Press, 1999), 116.

19. For what follows, see S. Knuuttila, *Emotions in Ancient and Medieval Philosophy* (Oxford: Oxford University Press, 2004), ch. 3.

20. For this process regarding the *Ethics*, see G. Wieland, *Ethica-scientia practica: Die Anfänge der philosophischen Ethik im 13. Jahrhundert* (Münster: Aschendorff, 1981); A. J. Celano, *Aristotle's Ethics and Medieval Philosophy* (Cambridge: Cambridge University Press, 2015); and for the exegetical tradition, I. P. Bejczy, ed., *Virtue Ethics in the Middle Ages: Commentaries on Aristotle's Nicomachean Ethics, 1200–1500* (Leiden: Brill, 2008).

21. Aquinas, *Disputed Questions on the Virtues*, ed. and trans. E. M. Atkins and T. Williams (Cambridge: 2005), art. 13. See further R. Konyndyk DeYoung, C. McCluskey and C. Van Dyke, *Aquinas's Ethics: Metaphysical Foundations, Moral Theory, and Theological Context* (Notre Dame, IN: University of Notre Dame Press, 2009); T. Hoffmann, J. Müller, and M. Perkams, eds., *Aquinas and the "Nicomachean Ethics"* (Cambridge: Cambridge University Press, 2013).

22. *Summa theologiae* I, Q. 81, art. 2. The distinction was already drawn before the Latin scholastic tradition: Aquinas cites the Greek Christian authors Gregory of Nyssa and John of Damascus for it and could also have found it in Avicenna. For further discussion, see D. Perler, "Why Is the Sheep Afraid of the Wolf? Medieval Debates on Animal Passions," in *Emotion and Cognitive Life in Medieval and Early Modern Philosophy*, ed. M. Pickavé and L. Shapiro (Oxford: Oxford University Press, 2012), 32–52. On emotions in Aquinas, see also M. D. Jordan, "Aquinas's Construction of a Moral Account for the Passions," *Freiburger Zeitschrift für Philosophie und Theologie* 33 (1986): 71–97; P. King, "Aquinas on the Passions," in *Aquinas's Moral Theory*, ed. S. MacDonald and E. Stump (Ithaca, NY: Cornell University Press, 1999), 101–32; R. Miner, *Thomas Aquinas on the Passions* (Cambridge: Cambridge University Press, 2009).

23. *Summa theologiae* I, Q. 81, art. 3.

24. For discussion, see D. L. Black, "Estimation in Avicenna: The Logical and Psychological Dimensions," *Dialogue* 32 (1993): 219–58; D. L. Black, "Imagination and Estimation: Arabic Paradigms and Western Transformations," *Topoi* 19 (2000): 59–70; P. E. Pormann, "Avicenna on Medical Practice, Epistemology, and the Physiology of the Inner Senses," in *Interpreting Avicenna: Critical Essays*, ed. P. Adamson (Cambridge: Cambridge University Press, 2013), 91–108.

25. See on this *Summa theologiae* II-1, Q. 26, art. 1.

26. Miner, *Thomas Aquinas on the Passions*, 21.

27. As nicely pointed out by A. Oelze, *Animal Rationality: Later Medieval Theories 1250–1350* (Leiden: Brill, 2018), 42.

28. For this argument and criticisms it provoked in the Islamic world, see P. Adamson, "From Known to Knower: Affinity Arguments for the Mind's Incorporeality in the Islamic World," *Oxford Studies in the Philosophy of Mind* 1 (2020): 373–96.

29. Averroes, *Commentarium in libros Physicorum Aristotelis*, proemium, fol. 1b, h–I, trans. J. Toivanen. As I have pointed out in "Human and Animal Nature in the Philosophy of the Islamic World," in *Animals: A History*, ed. P. Adamson and G. F. Edwards (New York: Oxford University Press, 2018), 90–113, at 92–93, there is a similar statement to be found in Ibn ʿAdī's commentary on Aristotle, *Metaphysics* Alpha Elatton.

30. Quoted in R. Lo Presti, "(Dis)embodied Thinking and the Scale of Beings: Pietro Pomponazzi and Agostino Nifo on the 'Psychic' Processes in Men and Animals," in *Human and Animal Cognition in Early Modern Philosophy and Medicine*, ed. S. Buchenau and R. Lo Presti (Pittsburgh, PA: University of Pittsburgh Press, 2017), 37–54, at 47. As Lo Presti remarks, Pomponazzi "attaches men (or at least a majority of them) to the beasts rather than to the gods" (46).

31. See R. C. Taylor, "Remarks on *cogitatio* in Averroes' *Commentarium magnum in Aristotelis De anima libros*," in *Averroes and the Aristotelian Tradition*, ed. G. Endress and J. A. Aertsen (Leiden: Brill, 1999), 217–55, for the development of the idea throughout Averroes's career.

32. Its uniqueness to humans is confirmed in Averroes's *Paraphrase of the Parva Naturalia*; see R. Hansberger, "Averroes and the 'Internal Senses,'" in *Interpreting Averroes: Critical Essays*, ed. P. Adamson and M. Di Giovanni (Cambridge: Cambridge University Press, 2018), 138–57, at 150.

33. Taylor, "Remarks on *Cogitatio*," 122.

34. *Summa theologiae* I, Q. 81, art. 3; cf. Q. 78, art. 4, for the restriction of estimation to animals. It should be noted that Averroes eliminates the estimative power completely. For him, all animal behavior can be explained by appealing to their capacity for imagination, and humans do not need estimation because they have cogitation. In this respect Aquinas's position is a fusion of elements from Avicenna and Averroes. See further G. P. Klubertanz, *The Discursive Power: Sources and Doctrine of the Vis Cogitativa according to St. Thomas Aquinas* (Cincinnati, OH: Messenger, 1953).

35. Oelze, *Animal Rationality*, 61–62.

36. See P. Adamson, "Abū Bakr al-Rāzī on Animals," *Archiv für Geschichte der Philosophie* 94 (2012): 249–73.

37. Oelze, *Animal Rationality*, 144–45.

38. Fakhr al-Dīn al-Rāzī, *Sharḥ al-Ishārāt wa-l-tanbīhāt*, 2 vols., ed. ʿA. R. Najafzādeh (Tehran: Anjoman-e Āthār va Mafākher-e Farhangī, 2005), vol. 2, 258. My thanks to Michael Noble for the reference.

39. F. Rahman, *Avicenna's "De Anima"* (London: Oxford University Press, 1959), 185.

40. Lorenzo Valla, *Dialectical Disputations*, 2 vols., ed. and trans. B. P. Copenhaver and L. Nauta (Cambridge, MA: Harvard University Press, 2012), vol. 1, 125.

41. This is discussed in great detail in C. Muratori, *Renaissance Vegetarianism: The Philosophical Afterlives of Porphyry's "On Abstinence"* (Cambridge: Legenda,

2020); with the example of Campanella at 179–81. See also C. Muratori, ed., *The Animal Soul and the Human Mind: Renaissance Debates* (Pisa: F. Serra, 2013).

42. *The Etymologies of Isidore of Seville*, trans. S. A. Barney (Cambridge: Cambridge University Press, 2008), 12.2.31.

43. On this, see J. Toivanen, "Marking the Boundaries: Animals in Medieval Latin Philosophy," in Adamson and Edwards, *Animals*, 121–50, at 138–39.

44. For in-depth discussions of these issues, see, e.g., J. Marenbon, *Pagans and Philosophers: The Problem of Paganism from Augustine to Leibniz* (Princeton, NJ: Princeton University Press, 2015); and J. E. H. Smith, *Nature, Human Nature, and Human Difference* (Princeton, NJ: Princeton University Press, 2015).

45. Reported by Las Casas at *History of the Indies*, 3.4; for his writings in English, see G. Sanderlin, *Bartolomé de las Casas: A Selection of His Writings* (New York: Knopf, 1971); S. Poole, *Bartolomé de las Casas: In Defense of the Indians* (DeKalb: Northern Illinois University Press, 1974).

46. Las Casas, *History of the Indies*, 1.18. See further L. Hanke, *Bartolomé de las Casas: An Interpretation of His Life and Writings* (The Hague: M. Nijhoff, 1951), 50.

47. Cited from Hanke, *Bartolomé de las Casas*, 80.

48. Cited from L. A. Clayton, *Bartolomé de las Casas* (Cambridge: Cambridge University Press, 2012), 51.

49. Cited from Clayton, *Bartolomé de las Casas*, 35.

50. L. Hanke, *All Mankind Is One: A Study of the Disputation between Bartolomé de las Casas and Juan Ginés de Sepúlveda in 1550 on the Intellectual and Religious Capacity of the American Indians* (DeKalb: Northern Illinois University Press, 1994), 85.

51. See G. L. Huxley, "Aristotle, Las Casas and the American Indians," *Proceedings of the Royal Irish Academy* 80C (1980): 57–68, C. Schäfer, "Juan Ginés de Sepúlveda und die politische Aristotelesrezeption im Zeitalter der Conquista," *Vivarium* 40 (2002): 242–71.

52. Cited from D. R. Brunstetter, "Sepúlveda, Las Casas, and the Other: Exploring the Tension between Moral Universalism and Alterity," *Review of Politics* 72 (2010): 409–35, at 418 (my emphasis).

53. This point is made by Schäfer, "Juan Ginés de Sepúlveda," 257.

54. On this, see, e.g., A. Lisska, *Aquinas' Theory of Natural Law: An Analytic Reconstruction* (Oxford: Oxford University Press, 1996), J. Goyette, M. Latvic, and R. S. Myers, eds., *St. Thomas Aquinas and the Natural Law Tradition: Contemporary Perspectives* (Washington DC: Catholic University Press of America, 2004).

55. Bartolomé de las Casas, *A Short Account of the Destruction of the Indies*, trans. N. Griffin (London: Penguin, 1992), 151.

56. *Summa theologiae* II.1, Q. 94, art. 4. D. M. Nelson, *The Priority of Prudence: Virtue and Natural Law in Thomas Aquinas and the Implications for Modern Ethics* (University Park: Pennsylvania State University Press, 1992), 101, argues that it is only the grasp of principles that is "natural" in the sense of being inborn, whereas

the prudence whereby we learn to apply the principles is a non-natural development. This may not involve conscious application of the principles of the law, which are more a source of normativity than a basis for conscious moral reflection (117).

57. *Summa theologiae* II.1, Q. 91, art. 2, reply to obj. 3.

58. Of course, the mind-set is not only medieval: its most famous expression comes in Plato's *Republic* and its parallel between the tripartite soul and the three-class society of the perfect city. On this and related parallels in classical thought, see P. Adamson, "State of Nature: Human and Cosmic Rulership in Ancient Philosophy," in *Menschennatur und politische Ordnung*, ed. B. Kellner and A. Höfele (Paderborn: Wilhelm Fink, 2015), 79–94.

59. J. A. Dinoia, "Implicit Faith, General Revelation and the State of Non-Christians," *The Thomist* 47 (1983): 209–41, at 223. My thanks to John Marenbon for encouraging me to include discussion of this topic.

60. J. Marenbon, "Virtuous Pagans, Hopeless Desire, and Unjust Justice," in *Vertical Readings in Dante's "Comedy,"* vol. 1, ed. G. Corbett and H. Webb (Cambridge: Open Book, 2015), 77–95, at 83, citing Aquinas, *On Truth*, Q. 14, a. 11, ad 5.

61. Cited from M. García-Arenal, "*Mi padre moro, yo moro*: The Inheritance of Belief in Early Modern Iberia," in *Iberia and the Emergence of Modernity*, ed. M. García-Arenal (Leiden: Brill, 2016), 304–35, at 331.

62. See F. de Waal, *Are We Smart Enough to Know How Smart Animals Are?* (New York: Norton, 2016), 225.

63. As B. Suits, "Aristotle on the Function of Man: Fallacies, Heresies, and Other Entertainments," *Canadian Journal of Philosophy* 4 (1974): 23–40, points out (39), only humans wash their socks, but this is not our function. One response to this has been that the term "peculiar (ἴδιος)" does not actually mean "unique" but simply "distinctive" of humans (or more technically: as belonging to the essence), which is compatible with its being distinctive of other beings as well. This is how Aristotle could think that contemplation is part of human happiness despite also being an activity in which the gods engage. See for this, J. Whiting, "Aristotle's Function Argument: A Defense," *Ancient Philosophy* 8 (1986): 33–48, at 37–38. By contrast, R. Kraut, "The Peculiar Function of Human Beings," *Canadian Journal of Philosophy* 9 (1979): 53–62, thinks that Aristotle means only to divide humans from inferior beings and not from the gods (Kraut calls this "relative peculiarity"). For other studies, see, e. g., C. M. Korsgaard, "Aristotle on Function and Virtue," *History of Philosophy Quarterly* (1986): 259–79; A. Gomez-Lobo, "The *Ergon* Inference," *Phronesis* 34 (1989): 170–84; R. Barney, "Aristotle's Argument for a Human Function," *Oxford Studies in Ancient Philosophy* 34 (2008): 293–322.

64. *On the Prostration of the Outermost Sphere* §X.2–3, in P. Adamson and P. E. Pormann, trans., *The Philosophical Works of al-Kindī* (Karachi: Oxford University Press, 2012).

65. Epistles 23 and 34; for the latter, see Brethren of Purity, *Sciences of the Soul and Intellect Part I: An Arabic Critical Edition and English Translation of Epistles 32–36*, ed. and trans. P. E. Walker et al. (Oxford: Oxford University Press, 2015).

66. As studied in M. Klaes, "Zur Schau und Deutung des Kosmos bei Hildegard von Bingen," in *Kosmos und Mensch aus der Sicht Hidegards von Bingen*, ed. A. Führkötter (Mainz: Gesellschaft für Mittelrheinische Kirchengeschichte, 1987), 37–115.

67. Latin and English translation in Pico della Mirandola, *On the Dignity of Man: A New Translation and Commentary*, ed. and trans. F. Borghesi, M. Papio, and M. Riva (Cambridge: Cambridge University Press, 2012).

68. My thanks to Bethany Somma for extensive discussion of the animal theme in *Ḥayy*.

69. *Hayy ben Yaqdhān: Roman philosophique d'Ibn Thofaïl*, ed. and trans. L. Gauthier (Beirut: Imprimerie Catholique, 1936), *Ḥayy* 80.

INDEX

Abelard, 42, 52, 56
absolute time, 83
Abū Bakr al-Rāzī, 81, 83, 121, 123
Abū Ḥātim al-Rāzī, 81, 82, 121
Abū ʿĪsā al-Warrāq, 64, 70
Abū Rāʾiṭa, 72, 76
affective mysticism, 109, 110
Albert the Great, 131
aloga (irrational or non-speaking), 130
analogy, 4
animal cognition, 126, 129, 130, 136
Anna Komnene, 91, 104, 105
Anselm of Canterbury, 69
Antonio de Montesinos, 132
apatheia (extirpation of the passions), 123
ʿaql (rational faculty), 65, 71, 122
Aquinas, Thomas, 51, 125, 129, 134, 135
Arethas, 92
Aristotle, 22, 23, 67, 74, 77, 78, 83, 86, 88, 90, 92, 95, 96, 120, 121, 123
al-Ashʿarī, 7
Ashʿarites, 7, 8, 10, 11, 17
astrology, 41
Augustine, 102
Averroes (Ibn Rushd), 3, 13, 16, 46, 83, 97, 113, 119, 127
Avicenna (Ibn Sīnā), 3, 29, 46, 66, 85, 113, 126, 127

Bar Hebraeus, 74
Barlaam of Calabria, 52
Bartolomé de las Casas, 132, 134
Basil of Caesarea, 63
bāṭin (hidden), 89
Bernard of Clairvaux, 42
Bessarion, 97
bidʿa (innovation), 16
Boccaccio, 111, 117
Bruni, Leonardo, 97
burhān (demonstration), 14, 49, 58, 83, 86
Buridan, 36

Campanella, Tommaso, 130
Catherine of Siena, 109
Cereta, Laura, 112
certainty, 10, 23, 28, 29, 30, 34, 60
  objective vs. subjective, 37, 39
Christine de Pizan, 111, 116, 117

Dante, 111
al-Dawwānī, 9
determinism, 95
Dhuoda, 106
Diotima, 102
divine causation, 90

emanation, 90
empiricism, 22, 23

Enbaqom, 77
epistemology, 21, 22
  epistemic authority, 134
  epistemic dependence, xiii
  epistemic elitism, 71, 124
  epistemic injustice, 113, 114
  epistemic luck, 8, 10, 12, 15, 19, 29, 44, 45, 54, 60, 79, 119
ergon (function), 120
eros (love), 97
eternity of the cosmos, 23, 24
Evagrius, 124

Fakhr al-Dīn al-Rāzī, 34, 38, 84, 94, 129
Falaquera, 49
falsafa (philosophy), 4, 12, 14, 16, 17, 18, 66, 71, 119
al-Fārābī, 3, 13, 14, 15, 27, 28, 29, 83, 87, 90, 119
Fedele, Cassandra, 112, 113
fiṭra (natural disposition), 47
Forms, theory of, 95, 96

Galen, 41, 83, 86, 121
al-Ghazālī, 12, 17, 31, 35, 43, 59, 60, 79, 82, 113, 119
Gregoras, Nikephoras, 93
Gregory Nazianzus, 92
Gregory of Nyssa, 102, 103

happiness, 97, 107, 120, 121
Ḥasdai Crescas, 51
Hildegard of Bingen, 106, 111, 137
ḥujja (proof), 5, 8, 11, 60, 73, 83, 87, 88
humanism, 111, 115

Ibn ʿAdī, Yaḥyā, 66, 68, 71, 124
Ibn al-Nafīs, xiii
Ibn Taymiyya, 42
Ibn Ṭufayl, xi, 138
ʿiffa (monastic chastity), 124
iʿjāz (inimitability of the Qurʾān), 47
ijtihād (effort), xiii, 3, 5, 6, 7, 8, 9, 10, 15, 17, 18, 19, 42, 45, 60, 83
imām, 6, 45, 82, 84, 88
intellect ,25, 26, 27
Isidore of Seville, 131

al-Jāḥiẓ, 74
jahl (ignorance), 6
jawhar (substance), 67, 72
Jean de Meun, 116
Judah Hallevi, 46, 50
Julian of Norwich, 106, 109
al-Juwaynī, 9, 12

kalām (philosophical theology), 7, 12, 17, 66, 71, 119
khabar (report), 66
al-Kindī, 24, 66, 67, 68, 73, 87, 137

linguistic diversity, 61
Llull, Ramon, 57

Macrina, 102, 103
madhhab (legal school), 4, 16
Maimonides, xiv, 25, 51, 131
maʿnā (intention, meaning), 128
Marguerite Porete, 108, 109, 110, 111
Marinella, Lucrezia, 98, 111, 112
Mechthild of Magdeburg, 107, 111
medicine, 41
Meister Eckhart, 109
Metochites, Theodore, 92
metriopatheia (moderation of the passions), 123
microcosm, 137, 138

miracle, 34, 38, 47
Miskawayh, 27, 31, 122, 123
Moderata Fonte, 111
Monica, 102
mushāwara (legal consultation), 11
Mu'tazilites, 7, 11, 25
mysticism, 106, 107, 108, 109, 124, 138. *See also* affective mysticism

Naṣīr al-Dīn al-Ṭūsī, 34
Native Americans, 132
natural causation, 32, 48
naẓar (theoretical contemplation), 7, 16, 70, 81, 83
Nicholas of Autrecourt, 35
Nogarola, Isotta, 112, 113, 115

Palamas, Gregory, 52, 124
particulars, 126
pathe (passion), 124
Petrarch, 111
Plato, 22, 23, 77, 78, 84, 86, 88, 90, 92, 94, 96, 121
Plethon, 93, 94, 95, 96, 97, 98
Plotinus, 85, 90
pluralism, religious, 46
Porphyry, 65, 67, 85, 124
Proclus, 86, 90
prophecy, 8, 43
Psellos, Michael, 104
Ptolemy, 41

al-quwwa al-fikriyya (the cogitative power), 128

ratio particularis (particular reasoning), 128
al-Rāzī. *See* Abū Bakr al-Rāzī; Abū Ḥatim al-Rāzī; Fakhr al-Dīn al-Rāzī
reason, 119, 120, 122, 125, 129

Saadia Gaon, 25, 70
Sabbath, 50
al-Sanūsī, 10
Scholarius, 96
scholasticism, 52
Seneca, 124
sense-perception, 23, 25, 26, 27
Sepúlveda, Juan Gínes de,133
sexism, 98
al-Shāfi'ī, 4, 11
Shī'ī legal tradition, 6, 45
ṣifāt (attributes), 68, 69, 71
Simplicius, 86
skepticism, 21, 22, 25, 30, 33, 35, 79
slavery, 7, 101, 132, 133, 134
soul
  appetitive, 121, 122, 123
  immortality of, 95
  irascible, 122
  rational, 122, 123
  tripartite, 12, 134
  See also world soul
Suhrawardī, 84, 94
Sunnī legal tradition, 6
syllogism, 23, 128
Symeon, 42
Syrianus, 86

taqlīd (imitation), xiii, 3, 5, 6, 7, 8, 9, 10, 11, 12, 15, 18, 19, 29, 42, 49, 54, 78, 81, 88, 135, 137
  justified *taqlid*, 44, 49, 52, 55, 58, 60, 82, 136
Tarabotti, Arcangela, 111
Tertullian, 42
Theodote, 104, 109
Timothy, I 75, 76
Trapezuntius, George, 96
Trinity, 53, 60, 66, 67, 71, 76, 78

universals, 126, 127

Valla, Lorenzo, 130
virtue, 59, 64, 94, 98, 104, 109, 112, 122, 123, 125
  natural vs. theological, 125
voluntarism, 35

wahm (estimative faculty), 126, 129
Walda Heywat, 78, 79
William of Conches, 53
world soul, 53, 138

ẓāhir (manifest), 89
ẓann (opinion), 6, 14, 89
  ẓann mashhūr (commonly accepted opinion), 14, 17
Zera Yacob, 78

PETER ADAMSON is professor of philosophy at Ludwig-Maximilians-Universität München. He is the author and co-author of a number of books, including *A History of Philosophy without Any Gaps: Philosophy in the Islamic World.*

www.ingramcontent.com/pod-product-compliance
Lightning Source LLC
Chambersburg PA
CBHW061447300426
44114CB00014B/1880